THE END OF AN ERA

THE END OF AN ERA

Africa and the Missionary

ELLIOTT KENDALL

LONDON
SPCK

First published 1978
SPCK
Holy Trinity Church
Marylebone Road
London NW1 4DU

Printed and bound in Great Britain at
The Camelot Press Ltd, Southampton

ISBN 0 281 02989 X

Contents

Acknowledgements

Thanks are due to the following for permission to quote from copyright sources:

All Africa Conference of Churches: Report of an Assembly held in Lusaka in 1974

The Church Herald: John Gatu's speech, Milwaukee, 1971

Fuller Theological Seminary: *Church Growth Bulletin*, July 1974

The Revd Father Adrian Hastings and Fordham University Press: *Church and Mission in Modern Africa* by Adrian Hastings

C. Hurst & Co.: *Black Theology: South African Voice*, edited by Basil Moore. (Printed in the USA under the title *The Challenge of Black Theology*, reprinted by permission also of John Knox Press)

Lutterworth Press: 'The Church and Human Rights in Africa' in *Drumbeats from Kampala: The Report of the First Assembly of AACC*

National Council of the Churches of Christ: 'The Mission of the Moratorium' by Canon Burgess Carr, in the NCCC's *Occasional Bulletin*, March/April 1975.

Abbreviations

AACC	All Africa Conference of Churches
BMS	Baptist Missionary Society
CCIA	Churches Commission on International Affairs
CEVAA	Communauté Evangélique d'Action Apostolique
CIIR	Catholic Institute for International Relations
CMS	Church Missionary Society
CWME	Commission on World Mission and Evangelism
DRC	Dutch Reformed Churches
ESP	Ecumenical Sharing of Personnel
EUB	Evangelical United Brethren
IDOC	International Documentation on the Contemporary Church
IMC	International Missionary Council
IRM	International Review of Mission
IRR	Institute of Race Relations
LMS	London Missionary Society
MHB	*Methodist Hymn Book*
NCCC	National Council of the Churches of Christ
PMS	Paris Missionary Society
SPCK	The Society for Promoting Christian Knowledge
SPG	Society for the Propagation of the Gospel
UCZ	United Church of Zambia
UMCA	Universities Mission to Central Africa
WCC	World Council of Churches

Introduction

In an astonishing period of 200 years the position of Christianity in the world has changed out of all recognition. The change began in some strange happenings in Britain in the last few years of the eighteenth century. These 200 years of the modern missionary movement from the western world to other countries have transformed the position of Christianity as a world religion. Recent research has revealed much more about the beginnings of the most remarkable movement in the Church since the time of the apostles.

The world now is a different place. Churches everywhere share the responsibility for Christian mission; the task is primarily their responsibility in each country. Large-scale missionary work from the West is now inadvisable and misguided. Society generally, and most people in the Churches, realize that the old-style missionary movement from the West is a thing of the past. To deny Churches overseas their essential responsibility is to reject the missionary nature of the Church. This has become more clearly understood as a result of the missionary movement itself.

The missionary period in Africa, as elsewhere, has come to an end. A new era in Christian responsibility to the world has begun. In the Third World there is a widespread conviction among church leaders that separate missionary organizations in the western world, as they have existed for 200 years, need dismantling. However, there is a common assumption among many Christians in the West that the old pattern ought to continue. Many missionary societies believe that they ought to go on, much as they are, into the foreseeable future.

Does the process of history indicate that the missionary endeavour, as traditionally conceived, has ended? We need now to make an honest and rigorous approach to the missionary question. Many Christians do not realize that the traditional missionary period is over, and some still want to enlarge it. At the same time, many Christians, especially those who are perplexed about the nature of Christianity in the modern world, have a clear conviction that the old-time sending of western missionaries belongs to an age which has passed.

Is there a new and more comprehensive understanding of Christian mission which can inspire the Churches in the western world? Can it best be achieved by bringing to an end the 'missionary society' period, and making a fresh start in Christian responsibility to the modern world? Are overseas Christians right in saying to us in the West that we ought to readjust the balance and give far more attention to Christian mission in our own societies? If Christendom no longer exists, how do the Churches of the world share in a global task? Did the founders of the missionary movement have a wider and truer concept of Christian mission than the evangelical has today?

An attempt is made here, however inadequately, to examine the missionary involvement in Africa; to look again at the reasons why it began; to consider sympathetically the remarkable record, remembering that we are treading where the saints have trod. The completion of 200 years is an appropriate time to assess the impact and to take stock. Now is the time to think courageously about our responsibility in the world, not blindly following old traditions, but entering into real discussion with fellow Christians in younger countries, to discover what God is saying through the experiences of Churches in many places. A realistic look at these issues in relation to Africa may help to bring into focus the larger questions about the nature of Christian mission in the contemporary world. Our experience, I believe, ought to convince us that the message, the work, and the spiritual energy of Jesus Christ are more widely relevant and compelling for mankind than ever they have been known to be in the past.

In this task I have been greatly indebted to two writers: neither is well known in Britain, but both have established themselves as the finest interpreters of the birth of the missionary movement in this country. The first is Johannes van den Berg, the author of *Constrained by Jesus' Love*, an inquiry into the motives of the missionary movement in Britain in the period between 1698 and 1815. The study was published in 1956 but is now out of print. The second is Stiv Jakobsson, author of *Am I not a Man and a Brother? . . . British Missions and the Abolition of the Slave Trade and Slavery in West Africa and the West Indies 1786–1838*, which was published in 1972. References to both these books will be made in the text, but the authors are deserving of special commendation and gratitude.

The idea of raising the missionary question in relation to Africa, after almost exactly 200 years of involvement by missionary societies from Britain and Europe, was first suggested in an article I wrote for the

International Review of Mission in January 1975 (vol. lxiv, no. 253). The article itself was based on a paper I had written for a seminar under the direction of Professor Richard Gray and Fr Adrian Hastings at the School of Oriental and African Studies in the University of London. The seminar was part of a wide-ranging series of studies on the theme 'Christianity in post-colonial Africa'. The first publication issuing from the studies is *African Christianity*, by Fr Hastings, and is obviously relevant to the subject of this book.

1

Africa and the Missionary

If an intelligent western observer visits the continent of Africa, he will probably receive certain impressions. Politically, the forty-six separate nations are as different as forty-six individuals. Geographically, the continent has a size, mass, climate, and appearance giving it a tone, ethos, 'feel' which together kindle the emotions of the African and forge a binding relationship for most Europeans. Racially, in spite of great ethnic differences among the Africans, and often fierce rivalries, there is a deep sensitivity to the subservient status and victimization of the African in the past in relation to the European. Economically, while visible signs of impressive development are apparent in some urban areas and industries, they are scattered and spasmodic, and everywhere the traditional African rural life predominates.

The aspect of religion which will strike the traveller – and Africa is a highly religious continent – is the presence almost everywhere of the Christian faith, and the large number of expatriate missionaries. The western missionary is ubiquitous in Africa, as indeed he or she is in most parts of the Third World. It is a phenomenon of some size and significance that a great number of people from Europe and North America are there engaged in some aspect of the Christian religion. The total number of Roman Catholic and Protestant missionaries in Africa south of the Sahara may be between 30,000 and 40,000. There are probably now as many, if not more, than there have ever been. Over the whole of this immense continent there are missionaries working with parishes, congregations, and institutions, creating a particular style of Christianity. It is this objective reality which we need to investigate and reflect upon. It is an integral part of the experience of being a Christian in Africa, and a facet of the Church which the citizen and the politician see.

Africa is not unique in having a large missionary population, but it is on such a continental scale, and so separate physically from other areas of the Third World, that it may be looked at in a separate study. In doing so, we are examining one of the most extraordinary events in church history. The African scene is part of the much wider invasion of the non-European world by Christian missionaries, known as the modern missionary movement. In reflecting upon it we are inevitably making comment and judgement on the much larger phenomenon. As far as possible, we ought to clear our minds of preconceptions, and attempt to consider the subject with impartiality. Africa is necessarily different, but it is not fanciful to regard it as a microcosm of the West's missionary engagement with the rest of the world. Africa exemplifies the missionary movement as does no other continent, with the possible exception of China.

This is an appropriate moment in history for a reappraisal, for circumstances have changed drastically both in the West and in Africa. The Churches in western societies are passing through experiences which are different from any they have known in recent generations; their position, and that of religion in general, is demanding readjustment at every point. The concept of Christian mission is undergoing profound re-examination.[1] The continent of Africa is at the end of the long colonial period and, through the policies of independent nations, is fashioning its own mode of life. It is rapidly becoming a different continent. In 1975 the last traces of European Portuguese colonial rule disappeared. What do the new circumstances suggest in regard to Christian mission? It would be surprising indeed if the far-reaching changes which are taking place do not mean new forms of relationships between Christians in the West and Christians in Africa. Now is the time when one may ask large questions about the nature of Christian mission from the West, and try to see the real needs of the Churches in Africa.

If the missionary question needs now to be looked at in terms of an entirely new relationship, this is in no way exceptional. All the relationships between the West and the Third World are undergoing a similar realignment. Political and economic power is shifting from an historical concentration in the West to a wider dispersal of resources and decision-making to other continents. Examples could be taken from the way in which the great China experiment is an increasing factor in world concerns, or from the immense effect on the old industrial nations of decisions by oil-producing nations in Africa and the Middle East. Africans assert that their lives are now being dominated by the big multi-national corporations, which played virtually no part fifty years ago. Traditional relationships are being fundamentally altered.

The well-established mission to the world by Christians from the West has been part of their obedience to what they understood to be the call of God and their service to Jesus Christ. This has been the basis on which generations of men and women have left their homelands to preach the gospel overseas, to found churches, and to engage in a great variety of forms of Christian service. The pattern is well known to us and it has borne fruit to an astonishing degree. Missionary societies have been the agencies for an unparalleled growth in world Christianity, and almost everywhere autonomous churches have come into being. The missionary has been the agent. We need not be diverted by the caricature of 'Christian missionary' work which in its simplified and distorted fashion is usually presented to the public by those who are not very knowledgeable about the whole. The questions we must face now are: What are the demands of Christian obedience in a shrinking world in which most of the relationships are changing? and Is the past, with which we are familiar, the norm for the future?

Christians in the West have grown used to the traditional idea that they were living in a Christendom in which most of the world's Christians were to be found. Sending missionaries was a sharing with less favoured peoples a rich Christian culture and experience. To commission, or to go, was both an obligation and a privilege, near to the heart of the Christian gospel, and worthy of esteem and support. It is now less obvious that there is a Christian West at all. The West is increasingly secular and as far as religion is concerned is developing into pluralistic societies. Moreover, the numerical strength of Christianity is no longer here. It is in the Churches of the Third World that numerical growth is to be seen, particularly in Africa and Latin America. And to some it would appear that the vitality of the Churches, in relation to their national life, is more apparent in the younger nations than in the old.

One aspect of the past has been that the decision-making in relation to Christian mission has taken place predominantly in the West. Churches and mission boards, where policies have mainly been framed, have had their headquarters in the West. There is an engrained tradition, supported by history, that supporting and sending missionary societies make the decisions. In a world of changing relationships this pattern looks less and less supportable. It may be disappearing but by no means universally. If there is a need to re-examine the position of the missionary, and the missionary society, it cannot be undertaken solely in the West. Rather, a new relationship needs to be created as the result of dialogue between Christians from here and from the younger Churches. If an answer is to be found for the future it must come from listening as intently to the voices from traditionally receiving Churches as to those of the historic sending Churches. This is a new habit which is by no means well established.

Are Christians and missionary supporters in the West prepared for the adjustments that are necessary in their thinking, which in all probability will be forced upon them in the next ten years? A profound reappraisal is easily avoided by the ordinary supporter because he does not have to wrestle with questions of policy. There is a deep inertia against adaptation to change, because it disturbs long-held assumptions and leaves the future uncertain. The revolutionary changes which are coming are being carefully avoided. Missionary education, however much it attempts to adjust to changing circumstances, seems to dwell on the past, reinforcing established attitudes. It is inevitably conditioned by the need to maintain the existing organization. One might consider, for example, the surprise expressed by overseas church representatives at the content of much missionary education material in Europe, or the results of research into missionary history undertaken by indigenous students in Africa, the Caribbean, and Asia. If Christian mission is moving into a situation of radical change, as far as the sending of missionaries is concerned, then perhaps we shall discover that one of the neglected tasks of the agencies in western Churches is to bring about changes in the established attitudes of Christians to world mission. Some will affirm that the basic concept of mission, in Christian obedience, has undergone a fundamental transformation.

Traditional Christian mission from the West has been regarded as concerning itself with two things. The first of these is the founding of Churches, equipped with the Bible in their own language. The second is the individual encounter with Jesus Christ and commitment to discipleship. The history of Christian mission, as given for example by Bishop Stephen Neill, is of evangelism and the establishment of church organizations across the world.[2] Modern thinking on mission, especially from the younger Churches, includes dealing with evil not only in people but in social organization, not only the transformation of people but the transformation of the community. Salvation is seen as something more than an individual experience, but as an experience which includes the release from all that dehumanizes and oppresses.

The poor world feels that it is oppressed by the powerful rich world and believes that this is the continuation of a relationship which has existed for a long time in history. If the traditional missionary supporter and executive is thinking primarily in the traditional terms of mission, and the young Christian leader in Africa is thinking of a wider mission, there is necessarily a profound cleavage between the two, on the question of mission from the West on the pattern established for the past 200 years. The evangelistic element, essential as it is, cannot be undertaken in these circumstances by westerners to any large degree.

There is another aspect of Christianity in Africa which raises questions about the missionary enterprise, not in relation to mission but to the life of the Church. The formation of the All Africa Conference of Churches enabled the Churches to look at and talk to each other. The documents, from 1963 onwards, show the growing attention to the selfhood of the Church. As the Church in Africa has contemplated itself, having first found the opportunity through the growth of an ecumenical instrument, it has brought into question the large-scale expatriate presence in its midst.

Take, for example, *Drumbeats from Kampala*, the report of the First Assembly of the All Africa Conference of Churches (1963):

> The lamentable truth is that after centuries of Christianity in Africa, the Church, on the whole, cannot be said to have attained true selfhood. There were recognized three levels, at which this making real the selfhood of the Church in Africa had to be worked at:
>
> (a) The level of the unity of the Church: the symptoms here were the state of anarchy occasioned by 'the multiplicity of the Churches' which was an importation from abroad.
>
> (b) The tragedy of our situation is that in spite of more than 300 years of contact with our continent, in spite of our boast of so many Churches and approximately 60 million Christians on the continent, Christianity is still a foreign religion to us.
>
> (c) The third dimension of the picture is provided by the administrative side:
> 'We submit that missionary activity on this continent has not followed the New Testament pattern where the Apostle, whose weakness in lack of support from some foreign conquering power was really his strength, planted the seed of the Evangel, trained a few indigenous leaders, and left the Church to develop according to local genius, initiative, and intuition. Ours has been a too-prolonged hot-house kind of atmosphere, and the good and well-planned organization for the Christian nurture of the African by

the missionaries and their societies far away, has perhaps been the greatest weakness of Christianity on this continent.'[3]

The sending of missionaries to Africa has become an intrinsic part of life for many Churches in the West. It has been part of their lives for many generations of Christians, answering their need to be involved in mission, and giving expression to deep sentiments of compassion and generosity. Anyone who has been closely associated with it knows of the self-sacrifice and faithfulness which have been its hallmarks. We are contemplating an expression of dedication and selflessness which in recent generations has been near to the heart of western Christianity. For many Christians it has not been an additional or optional extra, but a profound response of Christian love. We cannot join with those who would lightly dismiss it as an escape from the sterner demands of Christian discipleship, or as a mere religious accompaniment for imperial grandeur or commercial expansion. Yet we must try to look objectively at the whole phenomenon of the western missionary engagement with Africa, assessing it impartially with the aid of those who look at it from different perspectives. From a new point of vantage we may then attempt to see what the future holds. First we should look at some of the current attitudes to this large-scale missionary commitment to Africa.

There is a deeply engrained belief in western Christians that the sending of missionaries overseas is essentially right and that it belongs both to the nature of the Christian faith and to the life of the Church. From New Testament times the Church's mission has been expressed in sending men and women to lands other than their own. The Roman Empire provided the arena for the first generation of Christian evangelists. Church history records the expansion into North Africa, Europe, and beyond. Numerically it was much smaller than the modern missionary movement, but it was one of the fundamental aspects of the Church's life. The saints and heroes of the Church's expansion have provided the essential ingredients for the nurture of the Christian's discipleship. And yet there have been long periods in the life of Churches when there was little attempt to engage in mission in the world. The Churches of Britain had little overseas commitment for 500 years up to the latter half of the eighteenth century. Nevertheless it has now become part of our fundamental attitude, that it is essential to send missionaries. We would find it exceedingly difficult to contemplate a form of church life in which we did not have emissaries prepared to go to the ends of the earth. If economic disaster or political catastrophe made it physically impossible, we should be bereft and cut off from what was regarded as our essential being. If this happens in a particular country there is a large sense of curtailment and tragedy in our response. As it has become part of the very life of the Church, it has come to be regarded as intrinsically right. It must be right to send missionaries and therefore any hindrance which prevents their going must be wrong. If a country expels its missionaries it automatically attracts an adverse judgement. The Great Commission (Matt. 28.19–20) was to go into all the world, and therefore those who are sent are fulfilling a divine mandate.[4] Churches in western communist countries which cannot send money and people experience a profound limitation on their corporate life.

Christians have believed, and do believe, that they are called by God to go as missionaries either to particular places or wherever their denomination appoints them. A sense of call is entirely in harmony with both the Old Testament and the New. Perhaps the vocational factor has been stronger in the world of overseas mission than in other areas of Christian service. It is a term used very loosely, embracing the Christian who feels that in following a particular course he is fulfilling the will of God, to the individual with a sense of being singled out to a special task, such as being a medical worker in Central Africa or devoting his life to international evangelistic campaigns.

If the call to missionary service is so real, how can we relate the problem of great numbers of western Christians, believing themselves to be called to work in Africa, with the necessity to examine the advisability of so many expatriates being there at all? Does the African Church have the same sense of the reality of the vocation?

A sense of call is essentially a subjective experience. It may come from the Holy Spirit, or it may arise from a person's psychological needs. A call may come from another individual or from the Church speaking to one of its members. The confirmation of a call should come not so much from an inward experience as from the judgement of others. There are some Christians who regard almost any happening as the Lord's intervention. When a synod in Africa decides not to renew an invitation to an expatriate, because of a judgement on his or her suitability, a call is being made subject to the mind of the Church. There must always be a sense in which human and spiritual elements enter into the decisions of even the most selfless and dedicated body of people. Extraneous and unworthy considerations may exercise some influence on corporate decisions. An element of uncertainty and scepticism is not misplaced when considering the decisions reached by groups of people. Nevertheless it must surely be right to give pre-eminence to the judgements of the Church, in spite of the shortcomings of committees. An individual and personal sense of call is not by itself an adequate basis for missionary activity, if it is not put to the test alongside the judgement of a body of representative and experienced Christians. There may frequently have been too great a sense of confidence in the validity of a personal awareness of a call, and a greater sense of humility might be looked for. The criticism could be made with some justification that there has on the whole been an exaggerated emphasis on the element of call to service in the modern missionary movement, particularly when the judgement of the Church has not been sought.

If the Churches of Africa have one view of the need for western missionaries, and individual Christians in the West find their personal call at variance with it, then it is right that the will of the Churches should prevail. A sense of personal call should rightly be within the context of the life of the whole Church. Perhaps, then, we may rigorously examine the missionary question in Africa without being challenged by the proposition that there is any fundamental inconsistency with the belief that God calls men and women to be his servants and witnesses. It is the need of the Church which must come first.

The Churches which have been established for a long period in Africa are now generally following a policy of gradually reducing the number of missionaries. In the old Protestant missions of the West the reduction is at the rate of 2 per cent to 5 per cent a year. This is in some cases necessitated by economic circumstances, but it is nevertheless a genuine expression of policy. They accept that the peak of missionary personnel is in the past and make no effort to repeat it. They respond both to the request from the Church to which they are related in Africa for a continuation of personnel, and to the fact of fewer missionary candidates from the Churches in the West. If the Churches of Africa were dealing solely with the old mission boards, the problem would not be so acute.

However, the situation needs to be viewed in its wholeness. The Roman Catholic expatriate presence in Africa is higher numerically than it has ever been. The rapid growth of all sectors of the Church means for the Roman Catholic Church that there is a great pressure to maintain the high number of priests, sisters, and lay persons from overseas. Take, for example, the situation revealed in Uganda by the various crises during President Amin's rule. At the time of the Asian exodus there were 1,300 Roman Catholic and non-Roman Catholic missionaries. During the crisis in the middle of 1975 there were said to be over 800 Roman Catholic missionaries and 38 Church Missionary Society missionaries. Fourteen Roman Catholic missionaries were then deported. The Church authorities would gladly have agreed to their withdrawal earlier, but many of them were senior men who could not be found work in Europe in large numbers. The reason that they continue is because work cannot be found elsewhere.

It is not satisfactory to use the category of 'conservative-evangelical' because there are conservatives and radicals in every denomination, but there is no adequate substitute. The conservative-evangelical societies of Europe and North America are sending more missionaries than ever before. The numerical increase has more than compensated for the steady decrease in missionaries from the old societies. This aspect will be discussed in greater detail later, but in essence it signifies that the conservative-evangelical bodies are seeking to maintain the pattern which has existed for almost 200 years. A commonly accepted criterion of success and effectiveness is the number of missionaries who are maintained. It should be noted that the dramatic increase has been sustained from North America, so that while the main missionary invasion of Africa in the nineteenth century was from Europe, it has now been overtaken in Protestant circles by an expanding army from North America. One country in Africa may have as many as 1,000 North American conservative-evangelical missionaries continuously at work. This is true now of Zaire, which has over 1,000 United States missionaries. The traditional pattern of a mission led by expatriates is maintained, with its own separate ethos, and an exercise of leadership, sometimes overt and sometimes more subtle.

Africa is very sensitive to its relations with the outside world, because of its unhappy experience over many centuries. There are many articulate Africans who are resentful of the European presence and activity in Africa, because they feel that the end of colonization has brought not full independence but only a shadow of the reality. They feel that their political life and economic affairs are influenced and in some cases dominated by the Europeans: specialists, technicians, and multi-national corporations. Whenever a major economic undertaking has to be put into operation, such as a railway or an irrigation scheme, it involves the employment of an expatriate contractor. Capital accumulation is so limited that any large-scale development scheme depends on loans and grants from the old colonial powers. Development assistance usually has some political implication. While the colonial sovereignty has been removed, the economic and financial power and influence appear to remain. The expatriate missionary presence, as a continuation from the old colonial system, seems just another aspect of neo-colonialism. This attitude is reinforced in the minds of those who know their history by the reminder that in so many instances the missionary arrival coincided with the arrival of the colonial power, and in many ways the missionary presence seemed indistinguishable from the imperial system.

A conscious effort is needed by the westerner to feel the power of the hostility of the modern African to the colonial period. Africans probably do not realize how neutral and detached the modern European feels from the colonial past. It is not easy for a young European today to identify himself or feel identified with the colonial period of his grandparents. The jingoism of the South African War period is quite alien to the experience of the modern Briton. He is living in a different world and the nineteenth century is almost as remote as the Elizabethan age. Colonialism as an historical experience has power in the African mind today because it stands for the most recent experience of political rule by alien forces, and is regarded as the external power which perpetuated the old unemancipated Africa and delayed its advancement into the modern world. Such a statement may with equal validity be challenged from either side, that it is too bland and tolerant, or that it is too partial and tendentious. The perspective from which the historical event is studied makes all the difference. It is all too easy for the western, modern mind to rid itself of memories of the colonial past, but in the colonial areas and in the colonial experience the past is an aspect of contemporary experience. For our purpose the important fact is that in Africa colonialism is seen from an African perspective, that is, in large and stark outline. The close association of the missionary movement with it is a factor not to be ignored.

There is a growing volume of African writing, both of fiction and of historical research. The writers of today influence the opinions of tomorrow. The missionary movement is given almost unanimously adverse treatment. There is, of course, emphasis on the destruction of African values and African religion. For example, James Ngugi the Kenyan novelist, said when speaking to the Assembly of the Presbyterian Church in East Africa that the overseas relationship of the

Church was 'an alliance with (the) bureaucratic commercial middle-class élite (whose) members act as agents of foreign capitalism'.

The following quotations from *Black Theology – the South African Voice*[5] demonstrate the attitude of some African theologians:

In South Africa the Christian Church has probably been one of the most powerful instruments in making possible the political oppression of the black people. While the white colonialists were busy with the process of robbing the people of their land and their independence, the Churches were busy, however unconsciously, undermining the will of the people to resist.[6]

It has been alleged with truth that the trader and the settler followed the missionary, who was the agent of European imperialism, working hand in hand with the colonial powers for the subjugation of the black people and the territorial extension of the imperialist power. . . . The acceptance of the Christian Church, the triumph of their missionary endeavour, meant the rejection of African customs.[7]

There are two types of missionaries who have landed on our shores: the van der Kempt type, who wanted Christianity to adapt itself to the everyday life of the black community, and the Robert Moffat and Ayliff type, who felt that the whole life-style of the indigenous community had to be altered to suit the so-called 'Christian way of life'. Now the fact that the latter prevailed was no accident at all. . . . But let us return to our own Church here in South Africa. True to the wishes of its white founders, it is essentially the most colonial institution in the country today. Although the membership is 70 per cent black, the power and the decision-making are still safely in the hands of the white minority.[8]

Sabelo Ntwasa was the original editor of the first edition of this book, but he was placed under house arrest while the material was at the printer's, and he is still under banning orders. He writes on the important question of theological training, which tends to be heavily dominated by expatriates in Africa.

We will need to look seriously and critically at what we regard as adequate criteria for the selection of seminary staff. At present our white-dominated Churches tell us that it is an accidental circumstance that most of the seminary staff are white. This is the way it has to be when the criteria of competence set up by these white-dominated institutions are taken from western models. But are these the criteria demanded by our black situation? Surely criteria such as an intimate knowledge of the black history, culture, community, parish, experience, and aspirations are at least equally important. If such criteria were set up and applied, it might become an accidental circumstance that most of the seminary staff would be black![9]

At the Fifth Assembly of the World Council of Churches in Nairobi in 1975, Dr Manas Buthelezi, a black, internationally known, Lutheran theologian from South Africa said: 'There was apartheid and discrimination in the Church long before it was introduced in the rest of society as a deliberate government policy. . . . Can poor people really belong to the same Church with those who have made them poor?'

A similar situation would be encountered in any large gathering of young African students. A typical viewpoint of an African university student would be that missionaries in the past may have accomplished some valuable work but their presence is no longer required. This would be the stance in almost all African universities today, among both the staff and the students. On the whole, Africans are remarkably tolerant and understanding and give credit to the achievements of missionary pioneers and leaders in the past. When political independence has come, often at the end of a prolonged struggle, they have not adopted a policy of expelling expatriate missionaries. Nevertheless, the widespread sentiment in contemporary Africa is that the missionary period, as it has been known, is at an end.

If an inquiry were to be made into the attitude of African politicians and civil servants, a very similar situation would be discovered. Legislation to expel or prevent the missionary has not been initiated, with one or two exceptions, but the numerical presence of the missionary is an irritant. Speeches by Members of Parliament in different countries occasionally give expression to this. As a group the politicians share the attitude of the writer and the student. The expatriate presence in the Churches speaks to the non-Christian of the foreignness of Christianity.

In 1971 the General Secretary of the Presbyterian Church of East Africa, the Revd John Gatu, delivered an address at the Mission Festival in Milwaukee, USA on the missionary dimension of the Church in Africa. It was reproduced in the *Church Herald* and immediately attracted attention. In the speech, which will be examined in detail later, he said: 'Many of the African politicians, as well as heads of state, are known to pay glowing tributes to missionaries publicly, only to condemn them in private.' John Gatu was chairman of the General Committee of the AACC. Unwittingly he had launched the new concept of Moratorium.

A significant aspect of this incident has been the way in which the notion of Moratorium has taken hold of people's thinking in Africa. This development has reflected the deep sense of unease regarding the dependence of the Churches on overseas bodies. Furthermore, it articulated the frustrated desire of Christian leaders to be themselves with confidence, set free from some of the historical associations with missions. Since the speech was made, no Church in Africa has taken the two major steps of ceasing to receive any financial aid from its traditional missionary support, and of depriving itself of the presence of foreign workers. The Moratorium has become an idea increasingly discussed, and it was formally approved at the third Assembly of the AACC at Lusaka in May 1974. These honest and sincere expressions of thought by African churchmen suggest that, for some time at least, maturity can only be achieved by a cessation of overseas missionaries.

The presence of large numbers of European and North American missionaries on the continent of Africa is now causing reactions which would suggest that it is an important problem. This is recognized in Africa, but it is not generally felt in Europe. We are at a decisive historic point in relation to this issue. It is a large and complex question, with deep roots in history, and it appears to be now growing in seriousness. There are three exceedingly important dimensions which could be deeply affected by the way in which it is handled. The first is the experience of being a Christian in Africa; the second is the relation between Christians of Africa and Christians of Europe and North America; the third is the self-knowledge, obedience, and maturity of Christians in the western world.

Should Christian missionaries still be sent to Africa and the Third World? They may still be needed, but is the old method harmful to the Church in Africa and the Church in the West? Is there any justification for the continued existence of missionary societies in the old pattern?

2

1775

The Christian missionary from Europe and North America is commonplace in Africa today. In most places the missionary presence has been a significant element in the community's development. References to missionaries constantly arise in records of local history, not simply because of their presence, but because so many features in local society have grown out of missionary initiatives. In most African countries the Church is an important aspect of the community, and it has developed either directly or indirectly from missionary activities. Without making any claim that the expatriate is responsible for the astonishing numerical growth, nevertheless it can be said that the Christian population of 120 million indicates the immense historic weight of missionary activity. An historical perspective is an essential dimension in trying to arrive at right judgements now. If raising the question of the missionary in Africa is something of a shock in the western world, contemplation of the preternatural events of the last 200 years may establish the equilibrium.

The establishment and expansion of the Christian Church in Africa has wholly taken place within the last 200 years. There has been no other story in church history of quite the same order. It is astonishing to look at the phenomenon as a whole, for two centuries is not a long period in Christian history. When one visualizes the enormous geographical extent, from the dry, almost lifeless expanse of the Kalahari Desert, to the beautiful plateau mountains of Lesotho, the Atlantic-beaten coast of Senegal, and the deep valleys of the Ethiopian countryside, the fact of the planting of the Church everywhere is phenomenal. It can be more clearly demonstrated if we examine in detail the situation 200 years ago.

In 1775 there was not a single missionary in Africa at work among the African people, nor any expatriate seeking to found an African Church. Africa and its peoples were a closed and separate region, as far as the Christian religion was concerned. The British and European slave trade was at its height, and Africa was the primary source of slaves. The Colonial Secretary, Lord Dartmouth, said in 1775: 'We cannot allow the colonies to check or discourage in any degree a traffic so beneficial to the nation.'[1]

The whole coastline of Africa was known, and ships of several nations were constantly calling at the ports. The route around Africa was the main line to Australasia, the Pacific, India, China and the East. There were no maps of the interior of the continent, and little or nothing was known in Europe about the peoples of the interior, their religion, culture, and economies. The whole immense continent was virtually unknown, except as a source of slaves in the west and the east, and northwards through the Nile Valley.

In the extreme south the Dutch had settled at the Cape in the middle of the seventeenth century (1652), but 100 years later they had not made any real attempt to share their religion with the Bushmen, Hottentots, and Bantu. Because the Cape later became a populous colony, it would be wrong to imagine that during the first 100 years the settlers had much to do with the Africans of southern Africa. The Cape was a fuelling station for ships of the Dutch East India Company, and little more. 'It was no part of the Company's job to colonize or evangelize the Cape.'[2]

In 1775 there was no mission work among the indigenous people. The Dutch had been loyal to the Christian religion in their own households, and had in some cases encouraged their slaves to take part in Christian worship. During an earlier period, of seven years, a Moravian missionary George Schmidt had begun a first attempt to evangelize the Hottentots, but by 1744 he had given up and returned to Europe.[3]

It was not until 1777 that pioneer explorers like William Patterson and Robert Gordon left the Cape and began a series of journeys into the interior of South Africa as we know it today. It was a small Dutch colony, with Boer and some English farmers settled on the land, within 100 miles of Table Mountain. Within the community there was Christian teaching and worship, and local people who became part of the community in some humble tasks were absorbed into the Christian environment; but, not surprisingly, there was no conception of using this base for missionary advance in southern Africa. The modern mission as a crusade of teaching and service had not come into existence.

There were elsewhere two isolated and personal attempts to take the Christian gospel to the people of Africa. Thomas Thompson had worked for some years among the negro slaves in North America,

under the auspices of the Society for the Propagation of the Gospel. In
1751 the SPG allowed him to go to the west coast of Africa at his own
request. He worked for four years at Cape Coast and then returned to
England. One of the three Africans he sent to England for education,
Philip Quaque, became the first African Christian to return to Africa as
an evangelist.[4]

The second attempt was one made, characteristically, by the
Moravians, the Church of the United Brethren in Moravia. From 1737
to 1770 missionaries were sent to the coast of what is now Ghana. In the
last two years of the prolonged but spasmodic attempt, nine
missionaries died from disease, and finally the enterprise was
abandoned.

In the eighteenth century while the Evangelical Revival was taking
place in Britain and Europe, and English-speaking communities were
being established in America, the West Indies, and India, Africa was
without co-ordinated attempts at Christian evangelism. The slave trade
was in operation around the continent's coasts, both west and east, and
perhaps, in the western mind, the miasma militated against a rational
attitude towards Africa.

The Portuguese and Catholic orders had been deeply involved with
Africa in the past, but by the end of the eighteenth century all activity
had ceased and few tangible results remained. The first encounter
between Portugal and Africa had begun with King João II, in 1481.
During his reign successive explorers reached farther down the western
coast until they rounded the Cape of Good Hope and began feeling their
way up the east coast. Bartholomew Diaz, Vasco da Gama, and others
gradually came to know the African coastline well, and in 1498 Vasco
da Gama completed the exploration by reaching Mombasa and Malindi
in East Africa. From here it was possible to pick up the winds and sail to
India and the Far East. Some of the Indian Ocean ships continued
this practice, but very infrequently. This momentous Portuguese
achievement was of great historical importance, but for Portugal the
prize was an opportunity for rich commerce with India and the East.
Such a monopolistic access to trade could determine in large measure
the economic life of the whole society of Portugal. The route around
Africa to Malindi and thence the Orient became a primary factor in
Portuguese foreign policy and external trade. Ports and settlements on
Africa's coastline began to develop: Luanda, the Cape, Mozambique,
Kilwa, Mombasa, start to appear in the records of history. It is alleged
that the first chapel was built in southern Africa at Mossel Bay near the

Cape, a small stone chapel dedicated to St Bras.[5] The Portuguese built chapels for their own small and often temporary settlements. In the Congo and Angola during the fifteenth and sixteenth centuries there were, however, serious attempts to establish an indigenous Church. Jesuit missionaries travelled over much of what is today Zaire, and made a determined effort to establish an African Church. A large missionary organization was directed from both Portugal and Rome. Christian mission and armed colonization appear to have been so closely linked that they must have been barely distinguishable to the local inhabitants. In both West and East Africa there was much resistance to the intruders from local communities. During the sixteenth and seventeenth centuries there was a more concentrated Christian endeavour towards the Congo and Angola than to any other part of Africa. Many groups of Christian missionaries were sent, from different Catholic orders, and according to the contemporary records several thousand people were instructed and baptized, and many villages were described as Christian villages. The slave trade was accepted and continued at the same time.

C. P. Groves says of the period:

In this century (17th) the Jesuits were active in Angola; they established a monastery, as did three other orders. The mission in the Congo was the first considerable Christian mission in Africa since the days of the early Church, and the first at any time south of the Sahara with any continuity of history. Yet it has disappeared. It was not overwhelmed by Islam. It seems just to have faded out.[6]

Two centuries later, when travellers visited the areas, they found remnants of the past. Holman Bentley describes what he and others found on arrival in the Congo:

When we reached San Salvador in 1879, it was to all intents and purposes a heathen land. Some of the ruined walls of the cathedral remained . . . a large crucifix was paraded round the town in times of drought . . . the common charm for hunting was a flat wooden cross.[7]

It was the same story in Angola. When David Livingstone reached Luanda in his epic across-Africa journey in 1854, he saw the remains of an old Jesuit college, and oxen feeding within the ancient ruins of a cathedral. He found that the priests had not been altogether forgotten; they were remembered as those who had brought coffee and other fruit trees into the area for the first time; their memory was still held in high regard.

There is uncertainty about the extent of Portuguese missionary expansion in the eastern areas of Central Africa, but some records speak of the founding of churches, and of educational and agricultural work by the Jesuits and Dominicans over much of what has been called southern Rhodesia and the Zambezi valley. From 1500 onwards the Portuguese rapidly developed the East African route to India and the East. As they established themselves in Goa and elsewhere, some of their great Christian missionaries journeyed around Africa to and from the east. Francis Xavier, for example, journeyed up and down the East African coast. The long Catholic involvement with China, with Jesuits in most provinces, used the new routes. Some attention was given to evangelization in the Zambezi valley, and around Portuguese coastal settlements. From what is now Mozambique, missionaries visited the African kingdom of Monomotapa in Zimbabwe. It was reported in 1667 that there were in the Lower Zambezi 'sixteen places of worship, six of which were Jesuit, nine Dominican, and one under a secular priest. Nine of these were in Portuguese territory, five in the kingdom of Monomotapa, and two in Manika'.[8]

Information on the Christian mission period in Zimbabwe and the Zambezi valley during the Portuguese period has been researched and recorded by writers in South Africa.[9]

During the eighteenth century Portuguese trade with East Africa was increasingly concentrated on the slave trade. In 1760 and 1774 the Jesuits and the Dominicans were formally withdrawn from the whole area. Indeed, in 1774, the Jesuit order, which had met increasing criticism in Europe, was formally dissolved by the Pope.

Fr Adrian Hastings comments on an earlier period of Christian mission in North Africa:

Christianity should have done much better, and in other places did much better. In Africa it missed a supreme opportunity, apparently because it had become identified with the unpopular imperial government, and had come to lack unity, adaptive capacity, and missionary dynamism.

Again, he reflects:

God does not guarantee his Church's fruitfulness, or even continued existence in any given area; he works by grace through the movements of history, and the will and intelligence of the Church's members. It is on such things, things involving Christian and human responsibility, that the survival and growth of Christ's body among the nations depend.[10]

The three centuries 1470–1770 covered a period of Portuguese mission work in Africa involving, at different times, hundreds of Portuguese and French missionaries. At the end of the period practically nothing remained. Christianity had been closely identified with the aggressive invader, and it openly shared in and benefited from the slave trade. At one time more than 10,000 slaves were being shipped from the Congo each year to Portugal; and 10,000 slaves were being shipped from East Africa round the Cape, to South America, each year. The mission work of the Church in Africa was being financed partly by proceeds from the slave trade. This long period came to an end around 1770. There was little remaining to be seen; effort, dedication, and sacrifice had produced few tangible results.

The two great periods of Christian involvement with Africa are the three centuries of Portuguese initiative, and the 200 years of the modern missionary movement. The remnants of the first were fast disappearing during the eighteenth century. The second period began during the last few years of that century. It is interesting to compare the different basic motivations and ambitions for these two great movements. The Portuguese involvement with Africa stemmed from Prince Henry the Navigator's outward-looking policy of exploration and conquest. He was in permanent conflict with the Muslim lands of North Africa, and was thus prevented from exploiting trade with continental Africa. He yearned to reach Africa, but could not penetrate the Muslim barrier; consequently explorations took place down the west coast of Africa to outflank the Muslim north. C. P. Groves quotes from a contemporary chronicler, Azurara, showing that there were five elements in Portugal's spectacular African adventure. Prince Henry's interest was, first, scientific; he wanted to know what lay beyond. Second, he hoped for trade, not with Muslim lands, but with as yet undiscovered countries to the south. He was particularly desirous of entering into trade for gold. Third, because he was involved in conflict with the Muslim Moors, he wanted to discover what lay to their rear. Fourth, he wanted allies in the dire military struggle with the Muslims, especially if he could discover Christian countries in Africa. Fifth, he had a missionary intention to bring as many people as possible to salvation, through faith in Jesus Christ.

The Portuguese encounter with Africa, under Prince Henry's leadership, did not fulfil all his aspirations. There was an increased geographical knowledge for the western world. Portugal extended her influence and laid claim to new colonial possessions. The slave trade developed enormously. Catholic orders – the Dominicans, Jesuits, and Franciscans – began an extensive programme of evangelization in West and East Central Africa.

As will be emphasized later, the springs of action for the second great Christian involvement with sub-Sahara Africa were fourfold: to mitigate and remedy the effects of the African slave trade; to share the Christian faith; to bring men and women to a knowledge of Jesus Christ; and to encourage enlightenment and trade, which would be beneficial to the mother country and to the indigenous people.

There were differences also in the style of operation. The first period of missionary invasion was a male episcopal endeavour, which concentrated on building churches, securing allegiance from chieftains, and establishing religious rites. The second was entrusted to a considerable degree to female medical and educational workers, was more broadly based in its appeal, and dealt with the people as well as with the local potentates.

An example of the religious contribution to Africa during the first period may be taken from looking more closely at the Portuguese presence in Mombasa. Vasco da Gama arrived off Mombasa, with three ships of about 100 tons' displacement, in 1498. That was certainly a remarkable achievement; people who could succeed in such an enterprise could surely have made a great contribution to the area. A later expedition under Cabral found Mombasa resistant, and so he attacked and sacked the island community. During the first 100 years of the Portuguese presence in East Africa, Mombasa was subdued and looted at least four times by the invaders. In 1592 they built permanent fortifications at the entrance to part of the harbour, Fort Jesus, and established a garrison.

A chapel was built in the fort, the Chapel of Our Lady of Sorrows, and Augustinian Fathers used it as a base for evangelistic work on the island. In the course of time seven other chapels were erected. Several hundred local people became Christians, as in the neighbouring Malindi and Zanzibar at the same time.

An evangelistic beginning had been made, and for forty years it continued. An Augustinian monastery was built on the seafront, near Fort Jesus. War then came to the area, as Arabs from Arabia attempted to drive the Portuguese out of East Africa. All the Christians on the island of Mombasa were killed; many had taken refuge with the priests in the monastery, and eventually only two priests escaped. Signs of a Christian presence in Fort Jesus and elsewhere have been discovered, but nothing more remained of that early missionary beginning. In the colonial struggle for hegemony between Arabs and Portuguese, Mombasa was attacked or fought over, on average, every twenty years. By 1750 the Portuguese presence was no more, and the memory of a Christian beginning was disappearing, with few tangible results left behind.

It may reasonably be assumed that the direct association of the Christian mission with the slave trade, which grew considerably under Portuguese rule, was one of the primary causes of the failure of the new religion to take root. Some at least of the Catholic workers saw the inconsistency and were ashamed of their association.

It is also clear that the Portuguese period, both in West and Central Africa, witnessed direct colonization as Europeans came, established extensive plantations, and absorbed local Africans as serfs. The powers which brought the settlers to take the land and propagate a religion, should not have been surprised that the religion made a limited impact.

There is an interesting similarity between the extinction of Catholic missions in Africa, in the seventies of the eighteenth century, and the situation in China. Jesuit missionaries had been at work there for many years, both at the emperor's court and in most of the provinces, making a cultural and religious contribution. The dissolution of the Jesuit order by the pope in 1774 brought to an end this Christian work in China; the number of adherents declined, and the Church almost disappeared from Chinese life.

Fr Adrian Hastings summarizes Catholic mission work, as follows:

By the early nineteenth century, it was all over, apart from a few tiny, ill-instructed groups in places like Ouidah, and Elmina, and rather more in Angola and Mozambique. The Jesus of Fort Jesus was not loved by Africans; they had had precious little opportunity to know him. The Portuguese empire had declined. Fort Jesus itself had become, in 1729, a Muslim Arab stronghold. Missionary fervour had faded away in the Europe of the eighteenth century, and finally the whole home Church was shaken to pieces by the storm of the French Revolution. Her second great opportunity in Africa had come and gone and there was almost nothing to show for it; a land still unevangelized, a continent still dark because, effectively, it had never been offered the light. In 1800, as in 1500, the African Church had its ruins, its memories, its canonized saints, but where were its living members?[11]

3

Why Did it Begin?

The more one reflects upon it, the more astonishing the explosion of missionary activity from Britain at the end of the eighteenth century appears to be. Nothing which came before it suggested its probability. It seems to be part of a new vitality and spirit of creativity. At the end of its main thrust, the world was indeed to be a different place. There were some small beginnings during the last quarter of the eighteenth century, but it was in the final decade that challenges were faced and commitment reached such a degree of intensity that the formation of organizations was called for to undertake the immense tasks which were envisaged. The missionary societies came into existence. Within a period of a few years Britain's historic relationship with the rest of the world took a decisive turn.

A parallel social and economic movement, similar in scope and equally astonishing, began in the Severn valley, between England and Wales. There in Shropshire, where sufficient trees provided timber for fuel, pioneering steps were taken, using wrought and cast iron to fashion rough machines, and the whole Industrial Revolution began its irrepressible course. This economic explosion of vitality was already in progress before the new engagement with the human race began. Why did these two movements happen when they did?[1]

The missionary movement undoubtedly grew out of the conditions surrounding the slave trade and the movement of peoples which it brought. Slavery had, of course, existed from time immemorial in most societies. The old vicious system of human exploitation was now taken hold of by some of the enterprising and seafaring European nations, and turned into a vast international trade. More or less benevolent domestic slavery would probably not have disturbed human consciences sufficiently deeply to produce radical social change. The stark inhumanity of the slave ship began to stir the conscience in some individuals. There were other reasons. The exploitation was now being operated on such a scale that the sheer size of the brutal commerce drew attention to itself and stirred the conscience by its gross inhumanity. An international trade with, on average, 130 sailings a year from Britain alone, could not be lightly brushed aside or fail to attract attention. The horror of the trade was captured by one of England's greatest painters, J. M. W. Turner in his picture 'The Slave Ship'.[2] The picture epitomized the revulsion of many ordinary people. A further aspect which caused a conscience in Britain to stir was that whereas in previous centuries countries such as Portugal had been in the lead, and France and Holland had had a share, in the second half of the eighteenth century England had become the leading slave-trading nation in the world. It was an unenviable position and reputation. Britain's commercial capital was being extracted from the profits and her main ports were developing and visibly prospering on slavery.

In the sixteenth century the main slave traders in England operated from the port of London, under the Royal Africa Company, and in the seventeenth century from Bristol and Liverpool. European indentured labourers and black slaves from Africa were needed in large numbers to provide workers for the growing sugar plantations of the Caribbean islands and on the American mainland. African slaves provided free labour for the planters. During the Stuart period the monopoly of the Company received royal patronage, and permission was granted for garrisoned forts to be maintained on the West African coast. In 1750 the monopoly of the Royal Africa Company was terminated and the important trade from the three English ports was supervised by a committee of nine members, The Company of Merchants Trading to Africa.

In 1787 London had 26 ships, Bristol 22 and Liverpool 73, engaged in this trade. They carried a total of 36,000 slaves from Africa, averaging 494 a ship. In the years 1795–1804, London sent out 155 ships to Africa, and carried 46,405 slaves, Bristol's ships sailed from the coast with 10,718 negroes, while Liverpool's 1,009 vessels carried 332,800.[3]

The triangular trade was exceedingly profitable. A ship sailed from an English port with a cargo of British-manufactured goods which were sold on the west coast of Africa. Slaves taken aboard were sold in the West Indies. The ships returned to home port in Britain with a profitable cargo of colonial products for the English market. The growth in the trade is a sign of its high profitability, which also made it almost impregnable. The Atlantic slave trade had first been exploited by the Portuguese. After 1494, following the pope's arbitration, Portugal exercised a monopoly in the supply of African slaves to Brazil and the

Spanish colonies.[4] Britain first broke into the monopoly when Sir John Hawkins began his intrusion. His first slaving voyage was in 1562, when he procured about 300 slaves in Sierra Leone and sold them very profitably in the West Indies. The voyage was regarded as an illegal but profitable gamble. He used small ships of 150 tons, loaded with dried beans from the west of England, to feed the slaves on the voyage. On later voyages he took on board slaves from the Guinea coast, and delivered them to the West Indies. In 1567 he was on his third voyage, his ships loaded not only with Devonshire beans, but with chains and manacles wrought by blacksmiths in Plymouth, to secure the slaves during the voyage. By this time he had secured the formal authority of Queen Elizabeth I. During the next 100 years the British trade became well established. Between 1680 and 1786, over 2 million slaves were imported into the British colonies, not counting those imported into Brazil and other parts of the Americas. The overall total, including the Spanish colonies, was many times greater.

It was eventually the growth in size of the inhuman trade which horrified enough people to cause groups of protesters and dissidents to react and refuse to ignore the evil. Their objective was to abolish the cruel and degrading trade. The aim of destroying the institution of slavery came later; the commercial transactions in human beings, and the transportation of slaves, had to be abolished first. John Wesley had seen the trade during his stay in North America, and had called it 'this execrable villainy'. In 1774 he wrote: 'I deny that villainy is ever necessary' and in the same year he published his *Thoughts on Slavery*.

The foundation for the remarkable movement against the slave trade and slavery was the persistent work of Granville Sharp, who believed that he could convince an English court that slavery was illegal in England. Hitherto it had been accepted both legally and popularly that slavery was lawful. Landowners and business men from America and the West Indies brought their slaves to England. There were usually 10,000 or 20,000 slaves in London alone. Sharp was brought accidentally into contact with a slave in distress, and became involved in caring for him. For seven years he devoted himself to the issue of slavery, and equipped himself to argue the legal case. The decisive moment came when a test case – that of a slave, James Sommersett – could be brought before Chief Justice Mansfield. In 1772 the historic judgement was given by Mansfield that slavery was illegal in England.[5] Sommersett was set free and permitted to remain in England, avoiding the fate of being returned to Jamaica by his owner, Charles Stewart. (He had been recaptured by Stewart after escaping from his control.) Thereafter it was said that anyone who set foot in England became a free man.

The work of Granville Sharp and Thomas Clarkson secured the end of slavery as an accepted system in England. But during the last quarter of the eighteenth century the slave trade from England was flourishing, as indeed was the whole of English commerce. After Mansfield's judgement, the slave trade continued to grow. Among those deeply offended at the continuing trade were Granville Sharp, Thomas Clarkson, William Wilberforce, Hannah More, John Wesley, Zachary Macaulay, Henry Thornton, and certain members of the Society of Friends. Most of those who pledged themselves to end the trade were zealous Christians. It involved them in thirty-five years of vigilance and struggle to move public opinion before they were successful. William Wilberforce was pre-eminent as a national figure and parliamentarian, using his personal friendship with the prime minister, striving tirelessly throughout a lifetime of devoted endeavour to outlaw the trade from British commerce. Thomas Clarkson was a typical contributor, working assiduously in research and agitation, and creating the necessary resolution to maintain public pressure.[6] The group, with others unnamed, began individually and corporately to issue publications, lobby Members of Parliament, and organize public meetings to outlaw the trade.

The ending of slavery in England as an accepted institution, and the growing campaign by a larger group against the trade itself, had two primary consequences. The first immediate consequence was that between 20,000 and 30,000 slaves were set free in London, Liverpool, and Bristol, and they immediately became a social problem. There were many in the trading ports, but the greater number of destitute and unemployed blacks were to be seen in the Paddington area and in the Mile End Road in London.[7] The second consequence was a new attention to the continent of Africa and the suffering of the African people. The long campaign against the trade had produced in many Christians a deep sense of guilt, because of the gross injustice through commerce to the peoples of Africa. Those who later became involved in the first missionary endeavour to Africa had become concerned, implicated, and educated through the long agitation for emancipation in England and the abolition of the trade. As a missionary publication expressed it, 'the British nation is now, and has long been, most deeply criminal. We desire therefore, while we pray and labour for the removal of this evil, to make Western Africa the best remuneration in our power for its manifold wrongs.'[8]

Those Christians who involved themselves in a particular social and human problem found themselves being educated into a deeper Christian involvement. Study, protest, and legislation about the slave trade led them to a concern for the people involved and the place from which they came. Theological understanding was becoming deeper through social protest. The leaders of the anti-slave trade movement became in fact the same people who concerned themselves with Christian mission in Africa. This became noticeable later when at the formation of the Church Missionary Society in 1799, most of the original committee had been leaders in the anti-slavery movement.[9] Commitment to support for Christian mission in Africa was initially called for on the basis that a debt was owed to Africa.

The identification of the anti-slavery movement among evangelicals with the new sense of Christian responsibility towards Africa is seen with remarkable clarity in the group which met at the village of Clapham (as it was then), some distance south of London. There were less than 4,000 inhabitants, spiritually cared for by the rector John Venn, father of Henry Venn, later secretary of the CMS. It was a popular residential area, which would be described as a middle-class suburb today, although many of the parishioners were very poor. The village seems to have had a particular attraction for keen and intelligent Christians, both from the Church of England and from the Nonconformists. Many of the informal meetings of the alert group of men and women, who later became known as the Clapham Sect, were held in Henry Thornton's house on Battersea Rise. Most of the group were laymen, and some were Members of Parliament. Thomas Clarkson and Granville Sharp did not live at Clapham, but most of the leaders of the anti-slavery movement and the new Christian obligation to Africa, were associated with the group. Apart from their strong Christian convictions, there were three obvious elements in their outlook: they were dedicated to abolition; they were persuaded of the obligation to Christian mission in Africa; and they enjoyed easy relationships with the House of Commons. Here were Christians with a lively faith, with causes worth living for, and with a readiness to approach their tasks on a national level.

The link between the unfinished task of ending slavery and the new responsibility of taking the gospel to Africa is strikingly apparent in the first step made towards Africa. During the years following Lord

Mansfield's judgement, the number of destitute blacks increased alarmingly. Their numbers were further increased by many ex-slaves, who had fled to the British side in the War of Independence, and were evacuated to London from 1776 onwards. Lord Mansfield's judgement, and the American war coming within five years, produced a large, black, immigrant problem.

Granville Sharp and some members of the Clapham group, including Henry Thornton and Jonas Hanway, set up a committee for relieving the black poor. The discussions of this committee led to the formulation of plans for repatriating slaves to Africa, and to the creation of a free settlement on the west coast there. Others had similar convictions: in particular Henry Smeatham, who had spent some time in West Africa and who sought to find a means of establishing slaves in free communities in their own continent.

The Clapham group's contacts with Parliament secured the government's approval and support for plans to set up a settlement in Sierra Leone. Plans were drawn up by Sharp and Smeatham and, with government backing, 400 set sail from London in 1787; other groups joined later.

The difficulties and disappointments in the settlement have been fully described elsewhere. The enterprise was established by Act of Parliament, and a charter was granted later on the initiative of Henry Thornton. For our present purpose, the important aspect of this operation was the intention of the directors in London who supported it. Their aims were to resettle slaves, to open schools, to promote local agriculture, to stimulate commerce, and to advance the cause of Christianity. A later report from the Company (1792) spoke clearly of a moral obligation, describing 'those who feel for the wrongs of Africa, and eager to discover some mode of compensating to her for the injuries she has so long been sustaining at our hands'. The attitude of mind of much later Christian mission in Africa is recognizable. The enterprise was a humanitarian action, suggested by religious conviction, intended to benefit others and at the same time contribute to the commercial well-being of the supporter. Other emancipated slaves from the War of American Independence who had not been moved to England but had been settled in Novia Scotia, decided to join the community at Sierra Leone. More than 1,000 arrived in 1792.

The Sierra Leone community was an extension of the work of the Clapham Sect. Henry Thornton, in whose home they met, was chairman of the board of directors in London. Thomas Clarkson's brother John was the first governor in Sierra Leone, and another member, Zachary Macaulay, was at one time governor. Built into the foundations of the settlement was the determination that slavery and the trade should not be tolerated. When Sierra Leone became a Crown colony in 1807, this resolution was written into the documents. After the centuries of dehumanizing slave trade on the continent of Africa, this small and uncertain community was indeed a new beginning. It did not always succeed in living by its original ideals, but its initial status was an important affirmation. In practical terms a free base had been established on the west coast of Africa, while the trade still flourished, to which captured slaves could be taken and released. To see it in its true perspective, one needs to recall that this outpost of abolition and freedom was established while the trade was being carried on all around it. It was a glimmer of light in the darkness.

This was the historic beginning of the modern missionary movement in Africa, although few of the missionary societies which became the power-houses for the movement had yet come into existence in London. Granville Sharp was a person of great generosity of spirit, imaginative ideas, and forceful campaigning. Sierra Leone, he hoped, would become a free and Christian community of Africa – 'a province of freedom'. The first settlement was called Granville Town. A chaplain, Patrick Frazer, was sent with the settlers; chaplains Nathaniel Gilbert and Melville Horne followed. The link between colonialism and the missionary movement can be clearly seen in the fact that the settlers included many white people from Britain, as well as black ex-slaves from London. Two years later there were almost 200 people remaining in the settlement, living in primitive huts, and in some poverty, near the site of what is today Freetown. The slave trade flourished in neighbouring small trading ports, and many of the settlers were tempted away to join in the lucrative business. Nevertheless Sierra Leone itself maintained its strong defiant attitude, and would not allow buying or selling of slaves in or near the new settlement. A clear Christian witness against slavery was being given at the birth of the new missionary movement in Africa, in sharp contrast to the earlier missionary period. The relationship between the missionary movement in Africa and the exploitation of Africa through slavery, was clear. The objects of the colony were to outlaw slavery and the slave trade, and to demonstrate to the world that 'God had made of one blood all nations of men'. The society of the colony reproduced much of the life-style of British evangelical Christianity from which it was derived. It was ridiculed both in London and Sierra Leone for hypocrisy and excessive piety, and perhaps excelled in both; but with all their human frailty Sharp, Thornton, and Macaulay were trying to establish an emancipated settlement in Africa, the heartland of black slavery, and they were endeavouring to get Christianity to take root in Africa. They were necessarily limited by the culture, religion, and society in which they lived. However open to criticism they may have been – and how easy it is to lampoon people of earlier generations – they were engaged in profound concerns which had far-reaching effects, and at considerable cost to themselves. Their presence and exploits are often recalled with some mockery and even hostility. A balanced reckoning is not easy but should at some point be attempted. They were the forerunners of the whole modern missionary movement in Africa, and that at least gives them a special significance. It is fair to laugh at their foibles, but only if their far-reaching contribution is taken seriously.

The existence of the colony of Sierra Leone, and the arrival of the immigrants from North America and Nova Scotia, provided a new opportunity for churches and missionary organizations to establish themselves on the west coast of Africa. The Anglican Church, with official support, was established from the beginning. One of the Anglican chaplains, Melville Horne, published a book within a few years of the founding of the settlement, urging the sending of missionaries. The Baptists and the Methodists from Britain quickly sent missionaries to the new settlement. They moved out of the small township on the coast and started the task of evangelization of the indigenous people of the interior. From the earliest days of the colony, representatives of the Church of England were at work both among local people and among the freed slaves constantly being brought to the colony, particularly after 1807. In that year, the British slave trade was ended by Act of Parliament. Immigrants and freed slaves were formed into village groups and each group was in the charge of a missionary for instruction and religious worship.

Sierra Leone provided a new and important entrance for the modern missionary movement in Africa. After 1787 there was an established community, a doorway to the mainland, with which missionary bodies in Britain could relate. The new sense of responsibility for Africa, the growing Christian commitment to world mission, and the opportunity provided by the establishment of Sierra Leone, together formed the setting in which the missionary spirit could rapidly expand. This was a part of the historic beginning of the modern missionary movement, and it began in relation to Africa. Sierra Leone came first, with its emancipating spirit and its missionary commitment to Africa, and the formation of the missionary societies in London came a few years later.

Sierra Leone had a particular significance in the birth of the missionary movement from Britain, for another reason. The 1,000 black settlers brought from Nova Scotia and North America came from a background of various denominations, each with its own leaders. Consequently there were soon in Sierra Leone communities of Anglicans, Methodists, Baptists, and followers of the Countess of Huntingdon's Connexion. A wide range of Christian organizations in England, therefore, had an immediate relationship with the new Sierra Leone settlement, and before many years had passed they had all responded by sending denominational workers. All the main Protestant missionary bodies in England later became directly related with missionary work in Africa through Sierra Leone, during the first fifteen years of its existence (Baptists 1795; Methodists 1796; Edinburgh Society, Glasgow Society, and London Missionary Society 1797; Church Missionary Society 1800).

The early development of Christian missionary work, both in Freetown and beyond, became disappointing and in some ways corrupted. The start of the modern missionary movement in Africa was like so much that followed, marked as much by human weakness as by divine grace. It is no part of this record to describe either the dismal failures or the outstanding individual achievements.

The phenomenon which is so remarkable is the intensification of missionary interest in Britain during the last twenty years of the eighteenth century, and the creation of most of the missionary societies. Between the War of American Independence and the Napoleonic struggle – less than two decades – the missionary apparatus was set up, working to no established pattern. With the exception of the Moravians and the Danish-Hallensian mission, the entire weight of overseas work was directed to nationals living abroad.

The Society for Promoting Christian Knowledge (SPCK) had been formed in 1698, not least in response to the spiritual and social needs of settlers in the American colonies. Thomas Bray was largely responsible for the start of the SPCK and for the Society for the Propagation of the Gospel, which received its charter from the king in 1701. The charter, however, restricted the society's work to the English colonies. During the eighteenth century there was constant debate in the societies, particularly in the SPG, that too little effort was being given to work among the Indians and negroes. During this period the two societies were immensely important Christian initiatives towards an expanding world, but they were not then missionary societies on the pattern of what was to follow.

When the Society for Missions in Africa and the East (later to be known as the Church Missionary Society) was formed, the minutes described the existing situation as follows:

As it appears from the printed reports of the societies for Propagating the Gospel and for Promoting Christian Knowledge, that those societies confine their labours to the British plantations in America and the West Indies, there still seems to be wanting in the Established Church a society for sending missionaries to the continent of Africa, or the other parts of the heathen world.

It is not suggested that the modern missionary movement came into existence solely in regard to Africa. Both the Roman Catholic Church and the Moravian Church, for example, had demonstrated a strong awareness of duty to the non-Christian peoples of the world. However, in 1775, there was not a great deal to report. The movement was more closely related to Africa than has generally been supposed, and it gained much of its impetus from a widespread reaction to slavery and the slave trade.[10]

It is illuminating and instructive to set out in order the main events related to the outburst of missionary activity in Britain during the last quarter of the eighteenth century. The actual date when a missionary body was formally constituted has less significance than the events in chronological order, for the organizations varied considerably in form.

1772 Chief Justice Mansfield ruled that slavery as an institution was illegal in England. Immediately all slaves were set free or claimed their freedom. There was an outcry of public anxiety. In the three major ports and other towns large numbers of freed slaves came together in overcrowded conditions and with inadequate means of support.

1776 The American colonists issued the Declaration of Independence. This was followed by the beginning of the War of American Independence, which lasted until 1783. Nearly 200,000 slaves went over to the British side. Some were evacuated to Britain and added to the large number of freed but destitute slaves.

1783 Granville Sharp began to talk about plans for repatriating some of the blacks to Africa. Quakers and others discussed similar plans. In the same year Dr Thomas Coke, the Methodist leader, drew up a scheme called 'A Plan of the Society for the Establishment of Missions among the Heathen'. Subscriptions were collected but the plan was not adopted and no society was formed.

1786 A committee was established for 'Relieving the Black Poor'. The members were drawn from the Clapham Sect and certain Quakers. Free food was distributed to the communities of ex-slaves in London. At the same time Henry Smeatham printed and published a scheme for repatriating destitute people to Sierra Leone.

In the same year William Carey in Northampton submitted to a preachers' conference a question for discussion: whether the obligation to preach the gospel to all nations, which originally was attached to the Apostles, was still a duty for Christians. He was given no encouragement to take the matter further.

At the Methodist Conference in Bristol Dr Coke appealed for money and the setting aside of preachers for overseas work. Money was voted and William Warrener was appointed to proceed to Antigua in the West Indies.

1787 400 people set sail from London for West Africa, in two ships provided by the Navy. Most of the passengers were freed slaves and in addition there were some white immigrants going to join the settlement. Granville Sharp was one of the main organizers in Britain. The settlement was founded near Freetown the following year.

1792 In October a committee known as the Baptist Missionary Society was formed in Kettering.

1793 William Carey and his family set sail for Serampore in Bengal.

1795 A group of ministers and laymen from various denominations, meeting at The Castle and Falcon in London, established a missionary society which adopted the full title of London Missionary Society in 1818.

1796 The first missionaries recruited and supported by the London Missionary Society sailed for the Pacific. In the same year, missionary societies were established in Edinburgh and Glasgow.

1797 A party of LMS missionaries sailed for Sierra Leone.

1799 A Church of England group began meeting, also at The Castle and Falcon. The Revd John Venn from Clapham was made chairman. The group adopted the title of Society for Missions in Africa and the East. After 1812 this became the Church Missionary Society.

The missionary groups or societies were not entirely cut off from one another. The common meeting place at The Castle and Falcon is interesting. There were more serious relationships. William Carey, for example, received much spiritual inspiration from Thomas Scott, the first secretary of the CMS. Similarly the initiator of the London Missionary Society group was much influenced by William Carey. There is evidence that news was being exchanged of what other groups were doing.

On the continent the Moravian Church had already pioneered the way and had been engaged in sending missionaries overseas. We have noted the brief sojourn of George Schmidt in South Africa. Other missionaries had been sent to work among the slaves in the West Indies, for example at St Thomas and on Barbados. From the earliest days the Moravian Church had believed that the propagation of the faith in the world was an obligation on the Church.[11] Overseas missionary work by the Moravians did little, however, to stimulate other continental Churches. It was the immense growth in missionary commitment and organization in Britain during the last decade of the eighteenth century which stimulated a continental response. In 1797 the Netherlands Missionary Society was formed. About the same time missionary training centres were established in Berlin and Basle. Britain had access to the oceans but few missionary recruits. In the early years more missionaries were recruited from Basle and Berlin than from the British Churches.

The startling development of missionary-sending centres in Britain and on the Continent, in a comparatively few years, had repercussions in North America. The link with Sierra Leone was very direct; the book *Letters on Missions* published by the chaplain, Melville Horne, calling for missionaries, had an immense effect in America. But it was only in 1810 that the Board of Commissioners for Foreign Missions came into existence, and not until 1835 that the first missionary was sent to Africa.

The ecumenical London Missionary Society, as it was at that time, displayed far greater energy in finding funds and recruits in Britain than did any other body. In the first decade of the whole movement the LMS was by far the most successful and the most imaginative group. Before five years had elapsed after the society's formation, there were nearly forty LMS missionaries in the Pacific and Africa. Its immediate success was due partly to its freedom from ecclesiastical supervision and partly to its formation from an almost equal number of ministers and laymen; the generosity, experience, and enterprise of laymen were released when a creative new missionary beginning was being made. None of the societies could match the growth and success of the early LMS.

From a social and historical point of view there were three primary reasons why the missionary movement started in Britain with such dynamism, during the period 1780–99. The first cause has been identified as a response to the injury done to Africa by slavery and the slave trade, and the stimulus to involvement in mission and service to Africa afforded by the long anti-slavery campaign. The second was the new religious climate in Britain as a consequence of the Evangelical Revival. The third was the extraordinary opening of the oceans to travel, through the outstanding voyages of discovery and the impact of these on the public. It must be remembered, however, that the missionary involvement at this period concerned only a small number of people.

The second of the reasons is well known and documented. There were sections in all the Churches which had been profoundly influenced by the movement initiated by John and Charles Wesley, George Whitfield, and others. The whole religious life of Britain had been quickened by the Revival, just as John Wesley in an early period had been influenced at a personal level by the Moravians from the continent. It is symbolic that at the moment when overseas endeavours were beginning to be dreamed of, Wesley was building his famous preaching place and home base in City Road, London. The City Road Chapel was opened in November 1778. In his long lifetime Wesley had seen the religious climate of Britain change, with the appearance of a new vitality and respect for personal Christian experience and the reformation of human character through religious commitment. It was in the hearts and minds of people with this newly found experience that a revolutionary attitude to the remote races of mankind was taking place. The universal was suddenly seen to be, in a dramatic yet realistic manner, the area of God's redeeming work.[12]

In the *Collection of Hymns* published by John Wesley in October

1779 there were numerous references to a Christian offer of salvation to all people on earth. The Methodists had been singing these sentiments for many years.

O that the world might taste and see
The riches of his grace!
The arms of love that compass me
Would all mankind embrace.   (37)

Display thy salvation, and teach the new song
To every nation, and people and tongue.   (40)

Lord, I believe were sinners more
Than sands upon the ocean shore,
Thou hast for all a ransom paid,
For all a full atonement made.   (190)

Our heathenish land,
Beneath thy command
In mercy receive;
And make us a pattern to all that believe.

Then let it spread,
Thy knowledge and dread,
Till the earth is o'erflowed,
And the universe filled with the glory of God.   (219)

The third basic reason for the emergence of the new missionary concern for the world was the startling accessibility of a larger world now revealed by explorers. In 1774 James Bruce the Scottish explorer who had spent two years in Abyssinia, returned to London; to astonished and incredulous listeners he described the parts of East Africa which he had visited.

Captain James Cook's voyages to the Pacific were more influential than those of any other explorer. In 1774 he was on his second voyage of discovery; when he returned he became the most popular hero in Britain. Joseph Banks, who travelled with him, provided the material for writings and lectures which reached the general public. The minds of many were stirred with imagination of a new world peopled with different races. There was a sudden fascination with the concept of Christian teaching and experience being made available to remote, obscure, and unsophisticated peoples who were just coming into clear view through direct contact with western observers. The unfamiliar world which for two generations people had read about in the writings of Richard Hakluyt now seemed accessible in a new way.

By the last years of the eighteenth century the western missionary engagement with Africa had begun. Certainly this was a great turning-point in Africa's history. Behind lay several centuries of gross exploitation by Europe and Arabia. Ahead were two centuries of modern invasion by colonialism, commerce, and the Christian religion. Looking back over the centuries we can seek to trace the human causes which directed the development, and we remain mystified at the vast process of change. An altogether astonishing transformation has taken place, and the Church has become a primary influence and institution in Africa. The Christianity of the missionary has been replaced by an African Christianity. Most of the colonialism has gone, and attempts are being made to bring the commerce under control. Christianity in post-colonial Africa is now a relevant subject for study. This extraordinary development, which we can examine in greater detail, came about because a few dozen people in London and some small groups in Kettering, Glasgow, Edinburgh, and Bristol took seriously an obligation to Africa, arising from their Christian faith and from a sense of guilt which they shared with their own nation. They were not unique, for individuals in Denmark, Germany, Switzerland, and North America had been imbued with the same spirit. The awakening of thought and spirit made it possible for groups in those European countries to respond quickly and to contribute decisively to the momentum of this remarkable movement.

What were the motives of the men and women in different places of Europe and North America who found themselves at this point in history caught up in the beginning of a great global missionary enterprise? Johannes van den Berg examines them in some detail.[13] He dismisses the *political* motive as being little in evidence; the typical missionary was not prepared to be a tool of the secular powers. There is an element of *cultural* advancement, as the Puritan way of life tended to be reproduced, but the missionaries did not regard themselves as agents of a Christian culture. An *ascetic* attitude is found in individuals but it was never a mark of the early missionary movement. Self-denial was practised by people but the movement as such did not seek to establish ascetic communities. There was clearly a *romantic* element, especially in the response of missionary-minded people to the larger world being revealed through the explorations of James Bruce and Captain Cook. The imagination of men like Dr Thomas Coke was deeply stirred, and without this they would not have undertaken their extraordinary exploits into the unknown. But the movement as a whole was firmly rooted in the real world of the eighteenth century.

The fundamental motive of the missionary awakening was love and compassion, as it had been in the Methodist Revival and the Evangelical Awakening. The great spiritual discovery of the eighteenth century was the love of God in Christ. That love was known as a divine manifestation and gift in Christ. Love was central to the Revival and to the gospel which was felt to be for all mankind. The profound emphasis on love was at the heart of the evangelical experience and the message to be preached.

The moment was caught with genius in the words of Charles Wesley:

> Freely to all ourselves we give,
> Constrained by Jesu's love to live
> The servants of mankind.[14]

These simple words captured the essence of the missionary spirit, expressing the dynamic of the spiritual experience and the mode and posture of the missionary commitment. Nor were they simply a contemporary expression; they adequately describe the missionary attitude for every age. In these words there is suddenly a flash of light, as a recognition of the oneness of the universal element in the Evangelical Revival and the contemporary sense of Christian obligation to the world. It is similar to the more modern expression of commitment to the world:

> The Christian faith challenges us to strive for the worth and dignity of every human being, and to seek to embody justice and love in social structures. We cannot escape a profound concern for *caritas* or love, and for justice.[15]

4

Expansion

It is the fashion of some in our time to write of the missionaries of the past with a mild air of mockery, as if describing some Victorian burlesque. A particular example might be the BBC British Empire broadcasts on 'Light in the Darkness'. Work arising from missionary labours is always regarded as being behind the times, never ahead of its time. The tendency is to be flippant and superficial. The script has popular appeal, perhaps, but judgement is lacking; and the material is without the serious academic evaluation which an historical reckoning calls for. There is no doubt much to laugh about, but only if the serious aspect is remembered as well. For some writers history seems to be a source of material for entertainment. Somewhere there must be a sensible mean between the aura of sacrifice and reverence surrounding the missionary and the attitude of risible ridicule which sometimes passes for history.

Something began in the 1780s which has changed the life of Africa. In its turn Africa may have a decisive effect in coming decades on the life of the international community. It is not fanciful to see the Christian invasion of Africa and the eventual strength of the Christian community as major factors in determining what sort of corporate life the human race is going to reach towards in the future. Statesmen may write down Africa's present military and commercial powers, but its contribution to the human debate is going to be considerable. Africans generally have discovered something which the world has failed to find: how to be happy in the midst of distress. In the long search for human happiness they have much to contribute. Unfortunately the image of Africa is distorted in the western mind by the concentration of the mass media on coups and conflict. There is such an emphasis on reporting conflict and outrage that the whole presentation becomes a lie.

The happenings in Africa in the last 200 years have altered the whole picture of the Christian Church in the world, and particularly its survival in and its relevance to the modern world. Africa is now playing a part in shaping the world Christianity of tomorrow.

The missionary movement to Africa from Europe around 1795 was confined to Sierra Leone on the west coast, and a small beginning at the Cape of Good Hope. The Roman Catholic engagement with Africa had come to an end almost thirty years earlier, and was not to be taken up again until more than thirty years later. Into Sierra Leone had come a variety of denominational workers, white from Europe and black from North America. From Freetown, the capital, some had moved into neighbouring territories. Sierra Leone, among other things, was a base for Christian evangelists to go inland; the first Scottish missionaries to Africa sailed on a slave ship to Freetown and moved up the Sierra Leone river. The colony was also a springboard for parties of missionaries to move north and south along the coast. A great deal of this effort failed and – considering the long West African coastline – was of limited extent; but it was symbolic of the great movement which had been started. The Fula Kingdom, Rio Pongas, and what is now Liberia were the first areas beyond Sierra Leone to be reached. The missionaries were not all from Britain; indeed, most of the CMS missionaries were recruited from Germany. At the turn of the century many of the attempts at expansion had come to nothing. Disease and other difficulties had frustrated the combined efforts at physical extension. Peaceful trade had not flourished along the coast, for it was dominated still by the slave trade. Even after 1807, ships of other countries than Britain continued to pursue the slave trade. A great deal of effort was expended in Sierra Leone on looking after communities of slaves set free as boats were captured. Apart from adults, 1,000 children were set free, requiring care and education, which is a particular revelation of the nature of the trade.

Sierra Leone did, however, eventually become the West African base for two of the major missionary societies. The Church Missionary Society built on its initial commitment there and became increasingly related to West Africa. Similarly the Wesleyan Methodist Church from Britain became involved in missionary work in Africa through Sierra Leone. After many years it was realized by all the Churches that it was not a good beginning. Some later regretted the excessive attention to Sierra Leone, yet it held a pre-eminent position in the minds of many. The dual roles of providing a 'province of freedom' from slavery and a base for continental missionary work became increasingly incompatible. The persistent trade in slaves meant that Sierra Leone used all its resources in ministering to the steady arrival of released slaves from anywhere on the west coast. At the same time an overgrowing population constituted in this way did not make likely a strong cohesive community with qualities of leadership. There were so many disappointments that, later, Sierra Leone came to be neglected and ignored.

The important point to note is that after the initial missionary commitment to Africa (1787), made in relation to Sierra Leone by a wide range of missionary bodies, there was only a limited missionary expansion in Africa from Britain, for another twenty years. The work which had been started there continued, but it was spasmodic and did not lead to much greater expansion.

It is a remarkable fact that we have to jump to the 1830s before there is overwhelming evidence in Africa of the coming missionary invasion. In the meantime further settlements had been made, along the lines of Sierra Leone, as homes for freed slaves – at Monrovia and on the Gambia, providing a base for local missionary work. Overseas missionary work for American Methodism began when Melville Cox was sent to Liberia in 1833.

There was another small beginning, again directly related to the slave trade. Although the use of British vessels was prohibited after 1807, the trade itself expanded on the west coast, as it was growing on the east coast, so that numerically there were far more slaves being handled in 1830 than ever before. These conditions militated against effective missionary work. During this period, between 300 and 400 slave ships of other nations were operating constantly on the west coast.

The Gold Coast, now Ghana, was known along the whole African coastline for the formidable forts guarding the trading stations. Three of them, Christiansborg, Cape Coast, and Elmina were the scene of the next missionary thrust. It was customary to have a chaplain at a fort and a few of these chaplains took more than a passing interest in the local people. Thomas Thompson had worked there for a few years, supported by the SPG. After he left, the society had kept in touch with a local group of Christians.

Christiansborg was a Danish settlement, close to what is now Accra. Elmina, a fort on the water's edge, had belonged at different times to the Portuguese, Dutch, and British. Perhaps no other spot in West Africa can recapture the memory of slave trading more vividly than Elmina. Its dungeons and alleyways seem to hold the atmosphere of brutal and inhuman commercial exploitation.

The Basle Mission and the Bremen Mission, with official support, made a remarkable missionary endeavour based on Christiansborg. Unlike Sierra Leone they were free from the responsibility of running an ex-slave community and were able to concentrate on an evangelistic presentation of the faith. The following incident is a typical example of the many missionary initiatives which were to occur. Four missionaries landed in 1828. Several years later, three more came out to join them. Within seven years all had died, with one exception. The Basle Mission continued its work, meeting similar losses and sending further recruits with the indomitable spirit which took hold of the missionaries in those early decades. They were not flushed with success, for the Christian community was very slow to grow. After the entrance had been made, the concept of sharing the Christian gospel with the people of Africa became uppermost and seemed to be a commitment which could call for almost any sacrificial cost. This example indicates a sudden change from the early missionaries in Sierra Leone who frequently gave up and returned home. Something had happened to the missionary movement between 1790 and 1830. Within a generation the full fire of dedication and determination had become a blaze, and increasing numbers of people in Europe were influenced.

A similar development took place between the Wesleyan Methodist Conference in Britain and local people at Cape Coast. A small school for Africans had been established by the British trading administration, to prepare boys for junior positions as clerks. A Christian teacher introduced religion and a Christian sea-captain made contact with the missionary body in England. Then in 1835 the first missionaries landed at Cape Coast, but within two years they had all died. Thomas Birch Freeman came to take over the slender beginning and with his qualities of mind and character he succeeded in reaching the leaders of the Fanti and Ashanti peoples.[1]

While these developments had been taking place on the west coast, in the extreme south of the African continent a missionary movement towards non-European people had begun on a larger scale. Until the Cape finally passed from the Dutch to the British in 1806, the Churches of Holland had carried the main concern for Christian witness. The Revd Van Lier maintained a Christian missionary approach in this period. The Moravian Brethren in 1792 renewed the Moravian mission of George Schmidt of sixty years earlier, in now working among the local Africans. At Genedendal, the great Moravian centre 120 miles east of Cape Town, the work among Africans began to show the hallmarks of that aggressive and powerful missionary movement towards indigenous people which was to be typical of much of the Christian faith in Africa for the next 150 years. From the mixed Boer and English settlement in South Africa was to come determination and missionary zeal which eventually spread across the whole of southern Africa.

At the turn of the century the London Missionary Society, in association with the Netherlands Missionary Society, began its remarkable involvement with South Africa. After an initial period of hesitation and hostility from local authorities, the mission to the non-European people of South Africa began its advance. Dr Vanderkemp and later the Moffat family, supported by the Directorate in London, pioneered the growth of missionary work which spread northwards and north-eastwards, especially among the people of Namaqualand. Within a few years it had reached almost 1,000 miles northwards to the Tswana people. A particular feature of this development was the outward-going movement of missionaries to dispersed people in a vast under-populated region. Physically the area covered was greatly in excess of the attempts at expansion in Sierra Leone and on the Gold Coast. The LMS work has significance for the growth of the modern missionary movement in Africa, for it provided the first large-scale visible results both geographically and numerically. The missionaries were fortunate to have outstanding leaders such as Vanderkemp, Campbell, Moffat, and John Philip, and a body of clergy and business men behind them in London. By 1824 a mission station had been established at Kuruman; and it was later out of the enterprise, flexibility, and traditions of the LMS mission that David Livingstone was able to launch his extraordinary career.

The first thirty years of the nineteenth century were in strong contrast to the missionary commitment of the Churches towards the Africans in the previous century. While the LMS in South Africa was reaching north across vast stretches of country, new mission organizations began work on the frontier with the Bantu people on the east. As the European frontier pressed constantly eastward, meeting the expanding Zulu and Bantu southward expansion, so the young missions moved into new areas of southern Africa. Scottish missionaries came to begin a great educational centre at Lovedale, which was destined to make an immense contribution to African educational advancement. At the same time the Wesleyan Methodist Church began work in association with and along the same frontier pattern as the LMS. Both these additions were within the eastern expansion of the colony. One aspect is reminiscent of the association of missionary work and colonialism in Sierra Leone. High prices and unemployment in England, following the end of the Napoleonic Wars, meant that something needed to be done to provide a means of livelihood for distressed people. Transportation overseas provided a possible relief. In 1820 a government-financed scheme brought 4,000 English settlers to the eastern border of the South African colony. Again, a chaplain who accompanied them became the agent for a larger local mission. William Shaw and William Shepstone and their wives became the pioneer missionaries in the area beyond the Great Fish river, in what are today Ciskei and Transkei.

During the first two or three decades of the nineteenth century the Anglican Church and the Roman Catholic Church in South Africa maintained a similar attitude to the non-European people as had been adopted by the Dutch Reformed Church in its long period of comparative monopoly at the Cape settlement. The spectacular pioneering missionary invasion of southern Africa during this period came from the LMS, from Scotland, the Methodists, the Rhenish Mission, and the American Board of Commissioners for Foreign Mission. The extensive area and the diversity of peoples made acceptable the idea of encouraging many different mission agencies to join in the endeavour.

In the 200-year period of the modern missionary movement to Africa (1775–1975) it is astonishing to find that in the year 1830, when more than a quarter of the period had elapsed, there were not more than 150 western missionaries working among indigenous people in the whole of Africa south of the Sahara. The assault on Africa had begun in earnest, yet it was still confined to a narrow strip of the west African coast, north and south of Sierra Leone, and to the momentous expansion across the wide spaces of southern Africa. The Church Missionary Society had started in another area by sending a party of five missionaries to Egypt, and was soon to follow with an initiative in Ethiopia. There were in addition Roman Catholic and Protestant chaplains at European trading posts along the coast; and resident pastors at the Cape, many of whom were ministering to mixed congregations or perhaps taking some interest in a local group of Christians.

Nevertheless by 1830 the idea was widespread in Britain and Europe that men and women should sacrifice themselves by journeying to Africa, to India, and to the Pacific, in the wake of the explorers and the naval boats, to universalize the faith. Parents would encourage their sons and daughters to depart, knowing that there was little chance of their return, because an ideal had been established and accepted, and it was clearly gaining strength the more it was honoured. Every heroic missionary endeavour encouraged a larger effort for the future.

By 1830 Britain's missionary involvement with the Caribbean, India, the Pacific, and Africa was a remarkable and historic feature but its numerical strength was not great.

When the missionary societies came into existence around the turn of the century, Africa failed to gain or maintain a pre-eminent attention, in spite of the prevalence of the slave trade. The trade itself and the adverse climate on the west coast were the main reasons. Only limited resources were directed to Africa until after 1830. There were stronger traditional links with the Caribbean and that commitment grew more rapidly. The involvement with India remained on a very small scale. The Pacific attracted most attention because of the fascination of explorers' reports and the imaginative and energetic response of the LMS. Captain Cook's explorations and reports were followed by the voyage of the *Beagle* and the publication of Darwin's classic *Journal* in 1839. In the atmosphere of the period there was a great appetite for knowledge of the globe; the extensive and romantic exploration of the Pacific met the need. Publications by explorers and missionaries were widely read. A missionary with a flair for exploration and writing could become famous in an astonishingly short time.

The Baptist Missionary Society had made the historic and symbolic achievement of securing entrance to Bengal in eastern India. It was not until after 1833, when the charter of the East India Company was renewed, that missionaries secured the right to enter India without the Company's permission.

China had yet to open its doors, although throughout the period there were some Jesuits at work, maintaining unofficially the remarkable work of the Society of Jesus. It was not until after 1836 that the societies began to establish their work on the mainland of China, apart from the quite exceptional efforts of Dr Robert Morrison of the LMS, from 1807 onwards. At this time therefore the Pacific was claiming the chief attention. India was not yet a missionary field, although a beginning had been made. In the Caribbean the older work of the Anglican, Methodist, and Baptist Churches continued. In China one Protestant missionary had begun; the smaller number of Jesuits really belonged to an earlier era.

The impact of Christianity on Africa around 1830 needs to be examined because it is well in advance of the main colonial period, which later complicated the scene by the acquisition of territories and the establishment of foreign rule. What did the missionaries stand for?

What assumptions could Africans make about them, on the basis of the overall experience? It is comparatively easy to investigate the motivation at the European end, but what did it look like at the receiving end? Is it a canard to describe their aim as that of transforming the Africans into Victorian puritans, or is it sober history? Two elements had become apparent during the early period. There was a readiness to meet the demands of great physical danger from disease, and secondly, the movement had gained enormous momentum from explosive sources of vitality in Europe. The birth of the missionary societies and overseas departments of the Churches in the whole of Europe was mutually stimulating; the Churches discovered new confidence and spirit from these developments. The nineteenth-century experience of finding that the unknown world of nations was open to the gospel was as astonishing to the Churches as was the discovery by the early Church that the Gentile world could also respond.

What are the discernible elements in the mission to Africa at this stage? What did the mission look like in 1830?

The missionaries were almost everywhere regarded as the enemies of the slave trade and of slavery itself. Both government officials and white settlers opposed the missionaries because of this aspect of the image they had created. This was true of Africa, the Pacific, and the West Indies.

There is a recognizable element in the thinking of missionaries and their supporters: that they were attempting, as far as Africa and the Caribbean were concerned, to make some recompense for the evils of the European slave trade. The relationship between the new mission and the old slave trade was very strong.

In many places the missionaries were at work redressing the excesses of the slave trade by caring for released slaves and seeking to establish them in free communities. This was apparent both on the West Coast and in South Africa, where the Rhenish Mission and the Paris Missionary Society were thus involved from the beginning.

The growing momentum of the missionary movement in Africa during that time owed something to the long and frustrating battle against the slave trade which persisted after 1807 and continued to grow in spite of all that was being achieved in opposition. The response to the challenge was to give more and to struggle with more determination. If the evil had not been so persistent, the resolution engendered might not have been so strong.

There are certain points connected with the missionaries' personal qualities which must not pass unnoticed. These men and women were the products of their time, and their society, and their religious upbringing, from the thoughts in their heads to the clothes they wore. Yet they developed a remarkable ability to wrench themselves out of one culture and adapt themselves to totally different living conditions, often getting very close to people very different from themselves.

It was not only on the west coast of Africa that the creation of an attitude of mind which prepared men and women to make the final sacrifice of death in the cause which claimed them, was demonstrated. The testimony was given in one continent after another.

People who dealt with the missionaries, whether Hottentots, Fanti or Creole, may indeed have regarded them as intractable, unusual, and formidable, but they recognized qualities of courage, honesty, and humanity. The Matabele, the Xhosa, the Namaqua, and the Ashanti saw some of the qualities which on the whole had seemed to belong to them.

What were the missionaries engaged in? The records, which are extensive even for the early period, make it possible to give a fairly accurate summary. Perhaps no movement in human history has been more covered by publications than the missionary movement. They were declaring a doctrine which was the evangelical message of the eighteenth-century revival. It included a literal interpretation of the Scriptures, the offer of forgiveness and grace, a serious sense of accountability to God, a belief in the love and judgement of God, a puritan ethic, and an emphasis on personal religion. Individual faith in Jesus Christ for personal salvation and a desire to flee from the wrath to come, summarizes the whole. They were prepared to teach a sophisticated dogma based upon the Scriptures and they emphasized the life of the worshipping community. Everywhere the Church, as a constellation of worshipping congregations, was planted. The business of the missionaries was the founding of the Church, according to a variety of traditions in which public worship, with prayer, Bible-reading, and preaching played a pre-eminent part. They were distinct from the trader, who was engaged in commerce, in their concentration on establishing regular and public worship. The life of worship showed clearly that they were where they were to transmit knowledge about God as made known through Jesus Christ. Their convictions about the nature of God were expressed in the reality of Christian worship.

Almost everywhere the initial missionary activity included the setting up of schools. The European invasion for commerce and, later, direct rule, was by people who knew something of education, although general education was in its infancy in the European communities. Like the traders, some of the missionaries were self-taught or had had the benefit of only a few years of elementary education. Nevertheless they shared a profound conviction that education was for the neglected and oppressed people of every community. In every mission station schools were started, even when the work was among the slave communities of the West Indies. Such a novel conception was not everywhere welcome, but it gave evidence of seeking for the well-being of the indigenous and often deprived people. The strength and significance of this aspect were profound. From this first step there began in Africa that commitment to education which marked the whole Christian mission for the next century and a half, in ever-expanding circles, and which refused to be denied until the higher achievements had been reached. From then onwards, wherever the Church took root, it was found to be pioneering new levels of education for African people.

In the period before 1830 it is possible to see a particular attention to the establishment of trade schools, training classes for handicrafts, and what were usually categorized as 'institutions'. In Sierra Leone and in the different missions in South Africa, such as at Genedendal, much time was spent on training for skills to develop both the individual and the community. The Christian Church had come to Africa as an instrument of education.

From the earliest days there was a readiness to provide means for improving local agriculture. Usually the first plough to be known in the rural community was imported by the missionary. Agriculture in most tribal communities was primitive by the standards of the agricultural societies of Europe. The need to develop food production and introduce a wider variety of crops was taken with seriousness by the earlier missionaries and the supporting societies. The 'Bible and the plough' became a watchword in the missionary approach to Africa and the first African bishop, Samuel Crowther, became a keen advocate of agricultural development.

From its inception mission included the provision of medical services, even though they were often of a simple form. The missionary and his wife became amateur medical workers; with the preacher went the doctor. Christian mission became definitely associated with medical care for the whole community. Healing belonged to mission. Here again a pattern was early established, which later led to the setting up of the first hospitals and training schools for nurses; and from the early days special care was given to those suffering from leprosy. A leprosy settlement was one of the first Christian institutions established in South Africa.

It is important to notice that within the first decades of Christian mission the pioneers were often taking the side of the humble and deprived sections of the population. There was a manifest championing of those who were exploited and oppressed. The attitude of the missionary, particularly in South Africa, was different from that of the Boer farmer and the colonial official. It meant that the Christian representatives were recognizing people as persons, with attention to their well-being and dignity. This was a new phenomenon in West and South Africa. A missionary of the Paris Missionary Society gave himself to work solely among the slaves. As much attention was needed to care for the slaves in South Africa as in West Africa. The slaves could often find a place of refuge. In Basutoland the same missionary society came at Moshesh's invitation to be amongst a people who were under great pressure from colonial expansion. The indigenous people, who had suffered constant disabilities from the white intrusion in South Africa and had defended themselves, now found some European representatives who were prepared to stand with them and redress the balance. It is possible to look from the vantage point of our own times and say that the European missionaries accepted the colonial invasion, were its agents, and assisted it to succeed in its work of subjugation. Within the historical processes in which they were caught up and of which they were a part, they were also trying to mitigate the suffering and deprivation which colonial expansion entailed.

Some at least of the missionaries courageously opposed the harshness of the developing imperial system and fought for the oppressed. They may have been similar in outlook to the settlers, but they were palpably different. We have seen how they were known as the enemies of the slave trade, and after the eighteenth century they were clear opponents of slavery itself. In South Africa the missionaries frequently aroused great hostility by opposing the demands for forced labour, and in one famous case they took the matter to the courts. The career of Dr John Philip who in the early years of the last century took every means of defending such few human rights as were available to the African population, is both well-known and adequate testimony to the integral part which the struggle for humanity and justice played in the total mission of the Church. As Dr Philip wrote to the mission in London, 'The question is . . . in what way I can most certainly and effectively secure the emancipation of the poor Natives from their dreadful thraldom.'[2]

In the next generation Bishop John William Colenso in Natal maintained the same tradition. His controversial career was debated within the theological terms of the period, but in essence he was forced to more radical thinking in order to achieve justice for the Zulu people.

There were weaknesses and failures which can also be recognized in those early days. One has to try to be rigorously honest and objective, and to listen to interpretations from both the European side and that of the younger Churches, and to their experience of being at the receiving end of overseas mission. The total experience is different for both sides, and a strong conscious effort is required to reach other than a prejudiced understanding.

The first weakness was that the European missionaries were palpably in association with the overseas administrators, and were part of the whole European invasion of Africa. Often the chaplains at the forts or at the governor's administrative centre were the agents of Christian mission. In many cases the official representatives of government encouraged and enabled the mission to make progress. The missionaries were at times felt to be agents of the government, in establishing conditions in which the overseas administration could prevent opposition and extend its rule. Both in Sierra Leone and in South Africa the power structures were those of the government, and the missionaries appeared to be closely linked with them. The missionary societies often needed the sanction of either the government or the chartered company, and could only operate with the approval of the secular powers. It is therefore possible to say, as some Africans do say in recapturing the past, that the missionary intrusion was part of the colonial subjugation; that as the African became a Christian so he lost his heritage. There was a high degree of compromise, however inevitable, which should be recognized.

Reference has already been made to the view expressed in *Black Theology* that the Christian Church was one of the instruments making possible the political oppression of the black people. It is the view of many today that these two factors were closely related:

This was done in a number of subtle and not so subtle ways. In the first place, the Church made it plain that everything African was heathen and superstitious barbarism. Conversion to Christianity meant rejecting traditional forms of dress, authority, social organization, culture, marriage, medicine, etc. The black people were made to believe not that salvation is in Christ alone, but that salvation is in accepting the new white ways of living. The effect of this was to internalize in the black people a sense of the inferiority which inhered in them as Africans.[3]

Canon Peter Hinchliff has written that

> Victorian missionaries in South Africa inclined to the view that British civilization and Christianity were almost identical. They thought of African culture as heathen, the work of the devil, to be rooted out as soon as possible.[4]

These statements need to be taken seriously, for our understanding of Christian mission in any age must partly rely on an accurate evaluation of Christian mission in the past. Our task is not to defend or justify, but to understand and assess with as great a depth of honesty as possible. Did the mission in Africa 'give a religious and moral authentication to the social situation of masters and servants'? . . . and 'with the whites having no intention of becoming servants, this language served to reinforce and internalize the . . . nobility of black servitude. So the Church helped to colonize the minds of the black people.'[5]

The missionary invasion of Africa was so closely linked with the European secular invasion, both in time and in a common mental response to the situation of Africa, that it is only with difficulty that we can extricate the one from the other. But they *are* different.

Bishop Abel Muzorewa of Rhodesia has written of four major missionary mistakes in the past:

> Missionaries regarded many African customs as evil and forbade their use. Innocent tribal dances, the use of instruments like drums, and time-honoured marriage and funeral customs were banned.
>
> They believed Africans did not know anything about God. Yet our fathers worshipped God who was known to them by different names . . . admittedly, the missionary's main contribution to our religious vocabulary was the name of Jesus Christ.
>
> A devastating and far-reaching blunder was that they tended to make the newly-converted into their own image. One example was having converts at baptism adopt foreign names, as opposed to African names, which have a definite meaning.
>
> The fourth mistake was the practice of paternalism, which was

usually mistaken for racism by many people. I do not believe that missionaries who were brought up in democratic countries were that racialistic, but I believe that they were paternalistic. 'Father knows best' was their problem. Even to this day, the most retarding factor against the growth of the Church is this very attitude.[6]

The early missionaries were charged with failure to understand existing African religion. For example, Robert Moffat failed completely to understand that African religion existed, and regarded most signs of African culture and ritual as evil.[7] Limitations of language and incapacity to penetrate deeply into African experience were obviously there. Not unexpectedly, there is no evidence at this time of an anthropological approach. The missionaries came to bring another faith which was real to them, and largely ignored the experience of God and the religious values of people of a different culture and history. Several generations were to elapse before serious attention was given to this dimension. Nevertheless, in a later generation it was the missionaries who started anthropological research and inquiry. In the earlier period they were certainly bound by their own theological understanding and by the concepts of the social class to which they had belonged. With this limitation it must also be said that they were probably intolerant, unsympathetic, and sometimes arrogant.

The attitude of Christians in the West to other religions has changed considerably since 1830.[8] Because African religion has no written form and no temples, the missionaries regarded it as primitive, heathenish, and idolatrous. They dismissed and opposed it as something which had to be destroyed and replaced by a higher religion. It is only in this century that Christian theologians have begun to take seriously the reality and experience of African religion. Moreover, the standpoint is now different; Christians are ready to enter into dialogue with peoples of other religions and to seek a positive relationship, both in understanding and in service to mankind. Christianity to its overseas ambassadors in the early nineteenth century was a closed circle. There was no conception of respecting deeply the religious experience of others. The prevailing attitudes of Europe made it inevitable that missionaries should have a destructive approach to African religion. We have constantly to remind ourselves that the modern missionary movement, coming into force at the end of the eighteenth century, arose not from the rationalism or scepticism of the age but specifically from the influential evangelical body of Christians who understood

Christianity in terms of the religious experience of the eighteenth-century Evangelical Revival. When people from that background went to Africa, apart from the brutalization of the slave trade, their initial reaction was to be revolted by the many tribal customs which they witnessed. Perhaps they ought to have had the insight of the anthropologist, but they did not. Their interpretation of Africa to the western world was often the dramatization of their own experience, and it was very much culturally conditioned. The highlights of drama became the accepted image.

The missionaries were limited by the particular Christian insights of the religious background from which they came. In our day much of their preaching and teaching may appear to be simplistic and dogmatic, expressed within the religious limitations of their own theological background, but this seems to be true in every age. The phraseology of the reports is often pompous and pietistic, but one must be hesitant in criticism of the forms in which people expressed their religious experience in an earlier age. The experience was real, and that is fundamental to religious life, however much we may question the interpretation. If missionaries took their own style of religion overseas, it could not be otherwise; only thus could they be sincere. At the heart of the Evangelical Revival there was something timeless and profound which was not entirely lost in excessive dogmatism and evangelical simplifications. That core could be expressed in the objective affirmation of Charles Wesley in his immortal hymn, known as 'Wrestling Jacob', and from which all else was derived: 'Thy Nature and Thy Name is Love.'[9]

Among the limitations and failures of the missionaries was one which has repeatedly been described and has without doubt left a deep mark on the sensibility of the Africans. It must be readily acknowledged, articulated, and understood. The missionaries failed to appreciate a culture other than their own and used their position of strength as spiritual leaders to impose a destructive and restrictive attitude towards local communal life and culture. The legacy of the early missionary period is the destruction of African art, which has much later come to be regarded as of the very highest order; and of patterns of communal life – with music, dancing, and handicrafts – which could not be accommodated within the experience of eighteenth- and nineteenth-century evangelicals. So much that was African had to be discarded, as the new European religion thrust its rigid concepts on a people who were at that time at a disadvantage.

It has only slowly been realized that Christianity is inevitably carried in the culture and thought-forms of a particular people and period. The earthen vessel needs to be recognized for what it is. Christians then and Christians now find it extremely difficult to conceive of Christians living and expressing themselves in an entirely different cultural environment. The intention of those missionaries to take 'the gospel and civilization' to other countries suggests that both were to be understood in the context of western Europe at the end of the eighteenth century.

However, the problem must not be over-simplified. African culture in its varied forms had been insulated from other cultures and would inevitably have been greatly influenced by contact with the invasive western civilization, as it had been on the east coast by Arab civilization. African culture was gravely affected by the impact of the West, and the missionaries contributed to the process. They were agents, but by no means the sole agents, who disrupted the ancient African civilization. The process still continues, through the universal technological pattern, but it is not now due to missionary influence.

A further weakness in the missionary attitude can be discerned in the inability to see and trust the depth of wisdom inherent in untutored people. The paternalism which is a constant danger to the individual who goes among people of another race to teach, prevents him or her from seeing the growth and maturity possible in a different people. On the whole the European administrator and missionary took the attitude that he, or his institution, was going to be in Africa for a very long time. Like the colonialist, he was settling down for a long period of leadership. Europeans have been exceedingly slow to plan for their own demise, and in this the Churches have been one with colonial administrators and businessmen. The man or woman who could succeed in the great demands of adaptation tended to develop something like heroic qualities. The pioneer missionary became more than life-size. An unusual development of personality, with sometimes excessive publicity, naturally tended to make people consciously or unconsciously regard themselves as indispensable. Such individuals look upon people of another race as requiring a great deal of tutelage.

The development of leadership and personalities among the missionary community, stimulated by the special circumstances of the mission and the cultural advantage, made it much more difficult for Africans to achieve positions of equal leadership. The whole history of Christian mission in Africa is dominated by the leadership role of the white missionary. Potential African leaders could not easily push through the suffocating layer of senior missionaries. Relics of this situation remain, so that it can be examined and experienced at first-hand today. It can be seen in Rhodesia, Swaziland, and South Africa, and until recently in Portuguese African territories.

The leadership role of the European missionary has tended to cover and suppress the fact that from the beginning the African Christian played a great part in pioneer evangelism, in interpreting the new religion, and in his way of life validating the witness to fellow Africans. Examples could be multiplied, but two may suffice to represent however inadequately the immense share of African missionary labours in the early years. In the year 1875 James Stewart and his colleagues were establishing the great Presbyterian mission in what is now northern Malawi, or Livingstonia. Stewart's co-workers were four young African Christians who had freely accompanied him from Lovedale in South Africa. To a great extent Central Africa has been evangelized by African Christians from the south.[10] In the same year the Revd W. H. During, a Sierra Leone Methodist preacher, was at work on the coast of East Africa. He was taken from the west to the east coast because the casualty rate from disease was so high that it was hoped he might survive longer. He remained for ten years and then returned to Freetown in Sierra Leone.[11]

The final aspect of this list of positive failings by the missionaries in Africa must be the important question of unresolved racial attitudes. In the early years of the eighteenth century the racial attitudes of the British people had not crystallized into the pattern we know today, although there were many examples of racial prejudice in settlements overseas. Racial questions had appeared in literature from Elizabethan times, but they were on the periphery of national life. The basic racial sense of superiority of the Anglo-Saxon developed during the middle years of the nineteenth century, formed out of the Industrial Revolution and influenced by Charles Darwin and his *Origin of Species*, the Indian Mutiny (1857), and the exaggerated myth of the earlier Black Hole of Calcutta; over all was the evolving experience of growing imperial grandeur.

There was something defective in the Europeans' understanding of Man, and particularly in their Christian understanding of relationships with other human beings. They had had limited contact with the remote races of China and Africa and were not convinced that they shared a common humanity. From the arguments in the struggle for the abolition of slavery it is apparent that many ordinary British people regarded the black African slave as another species, lacking in humanity. This understanding was expressed by Prospero to the slave Caliban:

> Abhorred slave;
> Which any print of goodness will not take,
> Being capable of all ill! I pitied thee,
> Took pains to make thee speak, taught thee each hour
> One thing or other: when thou didst not, savage,
> Know thine own meaning, but would'st gabble like
> A thing most brutish, I endow'd thy purposes
> With words that made them known: but thy vile race,
> Though thou didst learn, had that in't which good natures
> Could not abide to be with; therefore wast thou
> Deservedly confin'd into this rock,
> Who hadst deserv'd more than a prison
>
> (The Tempest, I. ii).[12]

The initial approach of the missionary to the African was equivocal, not wholly certain of the brotherhood of man. There was a profound significance in the black slave's retort, 'Am I not a man and a brother?'

The more successful the imperialist, however reluctant, the stronger his inclination towards racial discrimination. Racialism became altogether more engrained in the British citizen after about 1860; Queen Victoria had to struggle to keep it in bounds at Court. Her image was projected as the mother of all her peoples overseas. British people convinced themselves of their special paternal relationship with other races outside Europe. The missionary began the century with a compassionate view of race, and ended it influenced by the insidious growth of racialism and more subject to its prejudices than he would care to recall. Where racial discrimination between blacks and whites has strengthened its hold on a colonial society, the Christian ambassadors have trimmed and compromised, so that the Christian witness of an era has been brought into question. It is a salutary thought, in contemplating the embryonic Christian Church which was being planted in Africa in 1830, that in the ensuing century many Christian congregations would be for 'whites only', and not only in South Africa: that in the year 1975, the issue of whether public worship should be open to people of all races was still an important item on the agendas of certain synods in South Africa. Christian witness on race has been strong at times in Africa, but by no means free from ambiguities; and sometimes guilty of gross and prolonged discrimination.

In recalling the missionary witness in the context of the early eighteenth century, we should take note of a basic ambivalence which belonged to both the missionary movement and the Evangelical Revival which inspired it. The accepted criterion was that 'you have nothing to do but save souls'. Saving the individual through personal evangelism was the beginning and end of the activity. This was one of the pretensions to which the missionaries were prone. In reality the mission, as we have seen, was very different. It had to be different, to be true to its origins and to the human situation in which it was operating. The theological terminology was inadequate for the fullness of the religious and human experience. Mission had to be not simply growth and expansion, but liberation too. Every missionary who set foot in Africa and every supporting society discovered that together they had a great deal more to become involved in and to initiate, in addition to 'saving souls'. Nor was it possible to say that the proclamation of a saving gospel and the planting of a Church came first, chronologically, and that the social and political application of the redemptive message would follow later. The whole resources of the gospel were called upon immediately, for it could not be exported in sections and assembled later. Christian mission in Africa from the beginning included both ends of the spectrum, a deeply personal experience of the spirit and a commitment to transform the communities in which people live.[13]

The missionary invasion of Africa begins a new phase after 1830. From then until about 1880 the Protestant missionary societies of Europe and North America had an almost unlimited field. As we have seen, the work of the earlier Roman Catholic missions had died away. In this new period the Roman Catholic Church made a fresh beginning, but it was restricted chiefly to the work of the Holy Ghost Fathers in Liberia at Cape Palmas. In the major opening-up of the continent by Christian missionaries before 1880 the Roman Catholic Church took little part.

The next area of advance was in East Africa. During the 1830s, C. W. Isenberg, a German missionary, and Ludwig Krapf, a Swiss, were at work in northern Abyssinia, and later in Shoa. These two missionaries, with other colleagues, worked in association with the CMS. Their journals give a remarkable picture of pioneer travel and work in a strange country, with very limited equipment, protection, or support. These men exemplify the particularly religious aspect of the missionary movement in Africa. They were dissociated from trade and colonial ties as in the West, and are more clearly discernible as trained people who had come to teach, to translate, and to proclaim a religion.[14]

In 1842 they were prevented from continuing in Abyssinia. Ludwig Krapf, a very formidable and determined man, therefore decided to attempt to reach the Galla nation of southern Abyssinia by beginning from a new base near the old Fort Jesus at Mombasa. In 1844 as a CMS worker he restarted the Christian invasion of East Africa by establishing a mission on the hills overlooking the ancient port. Krapf and Johannes Rebmann began the task of exploration, translation, education, Church planting, and assault on the slave trade in East Africa. Members of the Hermannsburg Mission, a Lutheran mission from Germany, tried exceedingly hard to join them but were prevented, even after landing on the mainland, by the Sultan of Zanzibar. After 1862 missionaries of the United Methodist Free Churches in Britain joined the endeavour, and together these two societies carried forward the initial struggle until they were joined by others at the end of the century.

In 1833 Britain abolished the slave trade for British shipping, and an attempt was made to enforce legislation by naval power around Africa. A second aspect of the attack on slavery was the establishment of commerce and education in the areas preoccupied with the slave trade. The missionary societies were the instruments for this purpose. The extinction of the slave trade, the modernization of Africa, and the planting of Christianity were interrelated.

The great Niger expedition of 1841 expressed all three objectives, with the backing of the societies and the government, and with the goodwill of the nation. It was defeated by the intransigent reality of West Africa: the heat, malaria, and resistance to the ill-planned European project. It did, however, succeed in stimulating public interest in Africa and its needs, as the long crusade against slavery had done.

The failed expedition had shown how unsuitable West Africa was for European organization, and how ill-equipped the Europeans were for adapting themselves to certain West African conditions. The Church Missionary Society, which had sent representatives on the expedition, had drawn its conclusions and proceeded to put resources into developing training institutions for Africans, particularly in the established base at Sierra Leone. Fourah Bay at Sierra Leone became a new centre for preparing West Coast Africans for leadership. 'The rafters of the roof when completed were made for the most part from the masts of condemned slave ships.'[15]

The college at Fourah Bay was primarily for preparing African Christian leaders. Other Churches had begun a training programme for African men and women, as the new approach to mission in Africa. From Fourah Bay, where training took place in a variety of West African languages, people began to move out as teachers to other territories. Notable above all names is that of Samuel Adjai Crowther, who was born at Osoguni near Ibadan in Nigeria. After initial training he was sent back as an ordained person to Yorubaland. He was to become the first African bishop of the Anglican Church in West Africa.

From Sierra Leone, freed slaves, many of whom had become Christians, found their way back to their old home areas sometimes over 1,000 miles along the coast. After 1833 many thousands of ex-slaves, in ones and twos, tried to find their way back to traditional homes, sometimes relying on only a dim memory of some port of departure.

The Church Missionary Society and the Wesleyan Methodist Missionary Society were the particular instruments for finding a way into new communities, not only along the coast but far inland to Kumasi and Abeokuta. Bishop Samuel Crowther, as he became in 1864, and Thomas Birch Freeman became the outstanding leaders in this task, supported by colleagues such as Henry Townsend, C. A. Gollmer, and W. de Graft. Representatives of two main British societies, with fellow workers from Basle, were together now caught up in a decade of penetration into the inland societies of West Africa. Christianity was finding roots in what is now Ghana, in Nigeria, Benin, and Togo. From Badagry, Lagos, and Abeokuta, African and Western preachers, teachers, and administrators began to reach out into highly populated areas such as Yorubaland in Nigeria.

Another major Niger expedition in 1857, once more with close co-operation between the British government and the CMS, finally made it possible to establish a major missionary field along the line of the Niger river. It is interesting for our purpose to note that the two CMS leaders of the new work were West Africans. Onitsha became a recognized mission post, for future development among the Ibo-speaking people. The CMS sent out three English and two Germans for the new Niger mission, which is symbolic of the whole West African mission; but for various reasons they were posted elsewhere or failed through sickness to take up the task.

By 1860 the west coast had begun to respond, with a declining slave trade, an expanding commerce, and Christian workers getting beyond the ancient coastal forts to the great African cities of the interior. It was a joint endeavour in which Europeans and young Christian leaders from the old slave coast took a part. With the increase in ex-slave settlements, following the pattern of Sierra Leone, experienced black workers from the Caribbean and the American mainland came to participate in the evangelization of Africa. American missionary societies began during this period to play a larger role in new work in the whole area.

In the great kingdom of the Congo, astride the vast river, missionary work had ended about 1773 after the departure of the Jesuits and the Capuchins. After 1865 the Catholic missionary work was resumed by the Holy Ghost Fathers. From the mouth of the Congo river, four stations were opened and the work of evangelization began again.

By 1840 the Protestant missions had established themselves and multiplied in the area of the Cape in South Africa. The LMS, the Moravians, the Church of Scotland, the Wesleyan Methodists, and other missions maintained their expansion. When David Livingstone arrived the following year from Scotland, he immediately felt that it was not for him and that there were probably 'three times too many missionaries' in that area already. His inclination was to be away from crowds, in some isolation and remoteness. Within a year he was living among the Tswana at Molepolole in what is today Botswana. The area had been visited by the German traveller W. H. C. Lichtenstein in 1806. The push to the north into Central Africa which was to be epitomized by Livingstone's personal travels had begun. From 1842 until 1874 Livingstone and others made journeys which called for extraordinary fortitude of mind and physique, revealed the horrors of the flourishing slave trade in the Zambezi valley, and pioneered the beginnings of 'Christianity and commerce' in present-day Zambia, Mozambique, Tanzania, and Malawi. By the time of his death, Livingstone's work of exploration and Christian mission had reached so far north as to necessitate moving the base to Zanzibar, thus making contact with the Christian work already established in East Africa.

The endeavour to establish the Christian religion and to serve the indigenous people by working for them and with them, the hallmark of Livingstone's incomparable career, can be illustrated in a variety of ways. The tradition was maintained by James Stewart in South Africa and elsewhere, and later by Laws in Livingstonia. The Scottish involvement, following in the wake of Livingstone, was to make an unparalleled contribution to Christian mission and African development in South Africa, Malawi, and East Africa.

In this brief survey, covering a continent in a chapter, we may take two examples which illustrate a much larger whole. Every territory could produce a similar story of remarkable tenacity, endurance, and devotion. 'For time would fail me to tell of Gideon, Barak . . . who through faith conquered kingdoms, enforced justice. . . .' (Heb. 11.32).

During the latter half of the nineteenth century an increasing number of missionary societies from the Continent and North America had joined in the missionary invasion of Africa. It is not necessary to mention the additional names, as no attempt is being made here at a comprehensive survey or a description of the evolving nature of the Christian enterprise in Africa. Reference has been made to the Swiss, German, Dutch, and French societies, and to Roman Catholic missionary orders. Special attention could be given to the response of the Scandinavian countries, because it illustrates the way in which every country of Europe, including the smallest, joined in the massive historical Christian evangelization of Africa during this period.

From the middle of the century Lutheran and Reformed societies, with typically Scandinavian quiet modesty, began to take their part in the whole movement. The Norwegians became committed to Madagascar, Zululand, and China. The Finns started an heroic, prolonged, and dramatic relationship with the Ovambo and Namibia. The Swedes became caught up in the life of Ethiopia and the Congo.

At the end of the first 100 years a large international missionary conference was held, appropriately in London. In 1888, 1,600 people came from 139 missionary societies to attend 'the greatest ecumenical conference ever assembled, since the first council in Jerusalem'.

Two examples may be used for the whole mid-century aggressive missionary movement into Africa, both taken from southern and central Africa. The first is François Coillard, and the second is the Universities Mission to Central Africa.

Coillard was engaged in pioneer mission in southern Africa for nearly fifty years. He is chiefly remembered for his work in Basutoland, and in Barotseland in Zambia. Working with the Paris Mission, he was in the midst of the bitter and bloody struggle between white rule and self-determination, involving the Boer, English, and Basuto peoples. Led by the great Moshesh in his kingdom among the Drakensberg Mountains, the indigenous people fought year after year to preserve some vestige of independence. Coillard found himself working and suffering with an oppressed people who were often under severe armed attack from Boer and English invaders. 'Why has God called me into this Africa. . . ? Was it only that I should be a witness to the destruction of these tribes among which I came full of joy and enthusiasm, to offer to God the sacrifice of my life?'[16]

It was not uncommon for people like François and Christina Coillard to travel for 500 miles in the hard iron-wheeled wagons of those days. The quality of their life, marked by intelligence, humility, culture, kindness, and spirituality, among the high mountains east of Bloemfontein, is a genuine picture of one ideal of the European missionary in Africa. They tried to identify themselves with the people among whom they lived. In 1865 the Boers made a final fierce attempt to crush the Basuto, but failed. The Coillards, in an occupied area, were forcibly removed by the Boers and were unable to continue their work. Banished for some years, they served in different parts of South Africa, and in what is now Botswana. With a group of Bantu Christians they tried unsuccessfully to gain access to Lobengula's country in southern Rhodesia.

The particularly dramatic part of their heroic career was the journey by wagon, again with Basuto Christians, to the southern shore of the great Zambezi river, west of the Victoria Falls. For months they had lived in a wagon, crossing the roadless spaces of Bechuanaland, until they waited on the southern side for permission to move north. One of the established crossings was, as today, at Kazungula, and another just west of the Victoria Falls. There are still in the bush some tangible remains of the small settlements which marked the crossing. Even at low water the vast expanse of the river faces one in looking across to the opposite bank: a fearsome crossing of a huge river, in primitive conditions.

Livingstone himself described the manner of this same crossing with an ox-wagon:

After we had remained a few days, some of the herd-men of the Makololo came down from Linyati, with a large party of Barotse to conduct us over the river. This they did in fine style. They took the wagons to pieces and carried them across on a number of canoes lashed together; while they themselves swam and dived among the oxen more like alligators than men. We were now among friends.[17]

Coillard wrote of the crossing: 'It was an epoch in the evangelization

of Africa, when we, with our wagons and families, crossed the Zambezi
– the barrier hitherto unsurmountable to strangers.' They established
themselves at Shesheke and Sefula. The camping spot beside the river is
still remembered. Christian work in Barotseland and north of the
Zambezi had now begun. For years in education, in evangelism and in
relations with the chief's family, they continued this work, and
eventually both died and were buried at Sefula. A presence and a whole
quality of life had been added to the life of the community.

The second example of the missionary penetration and conquest of
Central Africa is that of the Universities Mission to Central Africa. The
events surrounding it, and the vicissitudes of the mission as it tried to
fulfil David Livingstone's call for 'Christianity and commerce' on the
Zambezi and Shiré rivers, are recounted with extraordinary interest and
understanding in *Mackenzie's Grave*.[18] That book does more than any
other to achieve the setting of the missionary period, the hopes and
failures, the idealism, the impracticalities, and the human tragedies.

In 1857 Livingstone preached in the Senate House at Cambridge. He
challenged his hearers, the well-qualified youth of the coming
generation, to carry on the work he was doing in East and Central
Africa. The response of the Church of England to the appeal, and of the
bishops in particular, was very different from that when the CMS was
formed in 1799.

When the UMCA was started in the following year, it was clear that
the ambitions and the purposes of the missionary movement were the
same as originally articulated in 1787. In this instance there was also the
intention to establish a European settlement so that good commerce
could drive out the slave trade.

The object of the UMCA was stated to be 'the establishment of
stations in Central Africa, which may serve as centres of Christianity
and civilization, for the promotion of true religion, agriculture, and
lawful commerce, and the ultimate extinction of the slave trade'.
Accordingly the team which eventually was delivered into the interior at
Magomero on the Shiré river included a bishop, a schoolmaster, a
carpenter, an agriculturalist, a shoemaker, and a printer. The wholeness
and diversity of the mission were well expressed.

The heroic struggle and the utter failure of Bishop Mackenzie and his
companions to establish the Christian faith around Lake Malawi in
1861 are described in *Mackenzie's Grave*. The bishop died, as did
several of his colleagues, and the task was given up. The UMCA
retreated to the commercial headquarters for slavery in East Africa at

Zanzibar, and began a new missionary approach to the mainland.[19]

Experience here had produced the same lesson as in West Africa, that the real work of mission had to be accomplished by Africans. There were limitations to the effectiveness of a European team. However heroically the team lived and worked, in the end it had to retreat from the mainland to the island of Zanzibar. That in turn had become a training centre for African teachers, preachers, and artisans.

The expansion of Christian mission in Africa could be illustrated not simply by Coillard and the UMCA, but by a hundred similar stories of enterprise, dedication, and prolonged periods of service. Each of the new countries of Africa has a remarkable tradition already in its own church history. The extent of the Church's penetration into sub-Sahara Africa is incredible, displaying the same characteristic as the climber and explorer who leaves no peak unscaled or area uncovered. Madagascar, Livingstonia, Uganda, the Congo, the Sudan – the record from 1860 onwards is an extraordinary one of reaching to villages, tribes, and townships with a momentum created from tenacity, resolution, and Christian love. We may criticize its theology, but its fundamental movement of reaching out to others to share a heritage was remarkable. Wherever one chooses in Africa to begin digging into the Christian invasion during the last 100 years, whether in Namibia, the Cameroons, Mozambique, or Tanzania, one comes into contact with one of the most stubborn and immovable phenomena in the whole of Christian history. The 'going out' in Christian mission, against whatever odds, was there supremely.

After the 1860s, the Roman Catholic missionary orders began their new commitment to Africa. They started again on the west coast at Congo, in Gabon and in Benin, and the White Fathers began their memorable work in Uganda and East Africa. One field of special achievement was Senegal. It was not until the first half of our 200-year period was over, that the Roman Catholic Church began to send large numbers of missionaries to Africa. In the 1880s they started to do so at a high rate, and continued for the remainder of the whole of the second half of the period. The Holy Ghost Fathers worked in the west and east, and the Verona Fathers in Sudan and Uganda; the Mill Hill Fathers joined the work in Uganda, and the White Fathers moved down into Central Africa.

This was the period of extreme imperial interest in Africa. Britain, France, Germany, Belgium, and Portugal were competing for privilege, commercial advantage, and territorial control. Sometimes the process was pressed by a government, and sometimes individual pioneers were ahead of the authorities. Missions, Protestant and Catholic, reached a new height of support during the last thirty years of the nineteenth century. The Conference of Berlin (1884–5) achieved some agreed order on the dividing of the territories, after the worst of the scramble was over. Never before in such numbers had missionaries been leaving Europe and going overseas to any continent. The doors were open in Africa, and Catholics and Protestants followed hard on the footsteps of the pioneers.

By the end of the century there may well have been around 8,000 full-time missionary men and women, Catholic and Protestant, at work on the continent. Everywhere the area had been covered by the itinerant preacher; mission stations were established, and the foundations of an educational system were being laid. By the first decade of the next century, 90 per cent of all African education in most of the territories was initiated, supervised, and developed by the churches. The churches were all generally dominated by expatriate clergy, but a start had been made in an African ministry. As far as Christianity in Africa was concerned, the situation was utterly different from what it had been at the beginning of the century. In hundreds of locations across the country there were clusters of buildings, a mission station with flourishing fields and gardens, institutions, and training centres covering the wide range of missionary interests. Missionaries were engaged in and leading a vast movement, supported in both Catholic and Protestant churches by junior workers, African teachers, and African catechists. The evangelism and teaching for the great period of growth which lay ahead were in the hands of first- and second-generation African Christians. Inevitably the existence of a large section of subsidiary African workers meant that the small sector of European missionaries was inordinately elevated. In the next few decades the ever-expanding army of missionaries joined the ranks of those in positions of leadership. The first half of the new century would be the period of a missionary-dominated Church in Africa: 'mission Christianity', as it has been called.

5

The Present Situation

The growth and consolidation of the Roman Catholic and Protestant Churches in Africa from 1900 onwards is beyond the scope of this survey. Nevertheless, it is worth reminding ourselves, in a day when so much of the past is either ignored or taken for granted, that in almost all areas of Africa there is a remarkable record of missionary work undertaken when the foundations of modern societies were being laid. If one turns to any of the modern states – Ghana, Nigeria, Zaire, Rhodesia, Kenya, Uganda – and investigates the early decades of this century, one is faced with an incredible story of Christian vitality, creativity, and commitment. Generally Roman Catholics know little of Protestant history, and vice versa. There was usually intense rivalry, which can now be recalled in more mellow and irenic times. From whatever tradition, men and women have contributed in depth to human relations and development. The nations and Churches are what they are in Africa today because of that period of immense human effort. The much maligned missionary invasion, with all its compromises and limitations, managed to do some exceedingly useful work. In many instances it began when conquest and colonialism had destroyed traditional social systems, but it usually provided the positive and creative element in the new community.

The World Missionary Conference held in London in 1888, a hundred years after the launching of the missionary movement to Africa, produced no statistics. It is only after the conference at Edinburgh in 1910 that it is possible to trace Church growth and missionary participation, for from then onwards there are published returns and missionary atlases. There were no African Christian representatives in London or at Edinburgh among the 1,200 people attending. Africa was represented at Edinburgh by 65 missionary societies: 22 were from Britain, 21 from North America, 19 from Europe, and 3 from within South Africa. A missionary atlas was provided for the conference which gave some indication of church growth, but it covered only non-Roman Catholic churches.[1]

In the atlas Africa was divided into seven divisions; the following summary indicates the missionary complement.

Region	Missionary staff
North East Africa	296
North West Africa (including Mediterranean States)	155
Western Africa	518
South West Africa (from the Cameroons to South West Africa)	664
South Africa (including Swaziland and Basutoland)	1,589
South Central Africa (including the Rhodesias and Nyasaland)	403
East Africa	648

The total Protestant missionary force was 4,273. At this period there were already more Roman Catholic expatriates than Protestant: priests 1,508, lay brothers 1,218, sisters 3,251 – a total of 5,977. The combined missionary force in Africa was therefore 10,250. This is a remarkable figure for the year 1910, when it is remembered that in 1810 there were only a few dozen expatriates giving Christian witness anywhere among the African peoples.

The missionary concern in the West which had brought about this phenomenon had evolved into something different from the precise objectives of the missionary movement of a hundred years earlier. It had now gained a momentum which was derived from more factors than the Evangelical Revival of the eighteenth century and the slave trade. It had been caught up in the political and commercial explosion from the West to other continents. The phenomenon in Africa was of course duplicated in India, Burma, China, and the Pacific. The total of Protestant missionaries to all areas listed at the Edinburgh Conference was 19,280.

This is perhaps a suitable point at which to reconsider the element of guilt for the past which clearly played a part in the original movement towards Africa, especially when the slave trade was at its height. A debt was thought to be owed because of the western exploitation of slavery, although it was known that slavery had been pursued energetically over a long period by other nations, particularly from the Near East. The guilt could of course be shared internationally by many traders and by many middlemen in Africa. A sense of guilt has persisted but has played a more limited part with the passage of time. The wrongs of the colonial period have, however, compounded the original element of guilt in respect of the whole western relationship with Africa. Indeed the colonial movement must first be seen as conquest, before its later consequences are evaluated. There are those who believe that a sense of guilt lies at the heart of the whole western missionary commitment.

The Christian faith deals with guilt through forgiveness. The complex of guilt needs to be brought under the dominance of the forgiveness of love through Jesus Christ. New relationships can be created on the basis of forgiveness, which deals with the evils of the past and extracts the unwholesomeness of old and half-forgotten enormities. One of the messages of the Christian community in Africa and Europe needs to be exoneration of all our societies from the entail of that evil past, so that liberated relationships can develop. All too often bitterness remains and the suffering of the present is too frequently made attributable to the errors of our forefathers. It is of little value to burden posterity with blame for the misguided actions of earlier generations. The sooner we can generally accept a full forgiveness for all our historic entanglements and allow our present relationships to arise out of contemporary circumstances, the better for us all. It is also worth remembering that many of our contemporaries feel no sense of responsibility or guilt whatever for the actions of government and traders in past generations.

The Conference at Edinburgh in 1910 was primarily motivated by the new awakening towards world evangelization, with an altogether larger perspective than the tentative beginnings of a hundred years earlier. The Churches, missionary bodies, universities, and student organizations were enrolled in a rapidly growing movement which now created machinery for co-operation. In 1925 J. H. Oldham looked back after twenty-five years and wrote in the *International Review of Missions* of the significant change which had taken place. The creation of international co-operation was seen as the most vital step. He noted that this occurred nine years before the League of Nations was formed at Geneva. At the same time he saw

the extent to which western thought and society as a whole has become secularized and paganized. The dividing line between Christian and non-Christian countries is tending to disappear and we have to accustom ourselves more and more to thinking of the one universal Christian Church confronting a world which notwithstanding its differences is at one in the repudiation of the authority of the Christian revelation.[2]

From his survey it is also possible to see that in the early years of this century Oldham became aware of a turning-point in world mission, in that the Churches which were born in the old 'mission fields' were now partners in evangelization. 'Indeed, the initiative had passed into their hands and the main responsibility now rested on their shoulders.'

Oldham concludes his survey with a very perceptive observation, certainly relevant to the situation in Africa, that out of the experience of the younger Churches a new understanding of the gospel will come.

It may happen in our time that those who find their way to Christ from a non-Christian upbringing, or it may be from immersion in the new paganism of the western world, will be the means of revealing anew to a largely inert and apathetic Church, dulled and staled by familiarity with the gospel, something of its revolutionary meaning. . . . This ultimate question of human life and destiny is in different ways the primary concern of all the ecumenical Christian movements, and it is important to all of them to discover how through co-operation each movement may make its largest contribution to the common end of strengthening the universal Church in its world-wide conflict with the old and new paganism.

Oldham was writing in the period immediately before the Second World War. Since the Edinburgh Conference of 1910 he and other Church leaders had called constantly for an increase in missionary personnel, to engage in evangelization to all the continents. The attitude to the missionary question of 'as many as possible' expressed the mind of the whole Church up to the outbreak of the Second World War. Christian obedience called for the continuation of the uninterrupted numerical growth of missionaries which had appertained since 1775.

In 1924 Oldham wrote:

The trusteeship of the churches of the West for the great Christian community in Africa which they have brought into being is as binding as that of colonizing western nations for the native races of Africa. . . . To develop this work begun through missionary agencies until the African churches have attained their maturity and can themselves make manifest the redemption of individual and social life through the power of the gospel is one of the most compelling tasks before the churches of the West.[3]

The resolution expressed by Oldham of sending an expanding army of missionaries from the West to Africa is the high-water mark of the modern missionary movement and Africa. It had the sound of validity in the 1920s which it no longer has today. In the meantime indigenous churches and independent nations have been born. Attempts today to recapture that authenticity ignore the changed circumstances and the movement of Christian thought. Oldham continued:

There has also begun in North America and in Europe a new quickening of interest and a stirring of conscience concerning Africa. . . . The preparation of missionaries is being widely influenced by the needs of African fields. . . . The African missionaries of the past have done great preparatory work. . . . The purpose of God for Africa seems ripe for a new fulfilment.[4]

In the report on the Le Zouté Conference (1926) Oldham wrote on the Christian Mission in Africa: 'Christian missions and the forces that are reshaping African life. . . . The New Call is to a fresh advance, a further step forward, an enlargement of our conception of the mission of the Christian Church.'[5]

The following year Oldham produced a memorandum on the 'Relation of the International Missionary Council to Africa'. The first three paragraphs express the missionary thinking of that period towards Africa, in the succinct and forthright style so typical of Oldham.

It is within the lifetime of many of the members of the Council that the greater part of the continent of Africa has for the first time in history been brought into contact with the life of the rest of the world. The problem of the continent is at the same time of immense magnitude and entirely new.

In the early years of the European occupation the main energies of the governments were absorbed in the preliminary tasks of opening up the continent and establishing a framework of law and order. There is now being formed a deliberate and conscious purpose to direct the evolution of the continent along certain lines. This purpose is slowly taking more definite shape and growing in strength. Those who take a Christian view of the relations which should subsist between the different races of the African continent must either take their part in helping to shape this purpose or find themselves, in the end, in a backwater outside the mainstream of the life of the continent.

In the providence of God opportunities greater than might have been expected have presented themselves for missionary participation in the consideration of questions that are of vital importance for the future development of African people.[6]

As a Christian thinker he is looking at the continent as a whole. One of his claims to be listened to is that he saw the crucial significance of the race question, and its relevance to Christian mission, before most other church leaders did.[7] The phrase 'a deliberate and conscious purpose' is interesting but it is not clear whether he is thinking in economic or political terms. It was not obvious at that time that the Churches were going to be in the mainstream of Africa's life. They needed strengthening by concentration on the development of African leadership and by an increase in overseas missionaries. The Church was beginning to grow at a rate which had seldom been seen in India, Burma, or China and which Oldham recognized as of immense importance for the future of the continent.

On the eve of the Second World War, at Tambaram, the International Missionary Council took note of the Church's growth in Africa and of the steady increase in expatriate missionaries since the Edinburgh Conference of 1910. It considered that there were fifty-six Protestant missionaries for every million people in Africa.

The exigencies of the Second World War altered the whole pattern of an expatriate missionary presence in the Church in Africa, through Churches being cut off from the supporting missionary bodies and through recruitment of men and women into the armed services. Travel restrictions made it exceedingly difficult for civilians to move between Africa and Europe, for air travel was undeveloped and most sea transport was commandeered for military purposes. During the war the Conference of British Missionary Societies published a leaflet to stimulate missionary recruitment for Africa after the war.

Africans will expect and in good faith will require that in the Peace Settlement the United Nations will bind themselves to make Africa free, in the shortest possible time, to rule herself. . . . And in those countries where there are large numbers of white settlers, the problems are more intolerable; the danger is not so much that the challenge to face the situation will not be accepted, but that it will be tackled with the philosophy of an age which is dying.

The call then is for young men and women of Britain to serve

Africa after the war. . . . There must be many more men and women
with the highest qualifications sent out by the missionary societies to
serve the Church in Africa. . . . The peace must find the Church
militant and ready to redeem all human life. In so far as missionaries
serve Africa for the love of God and of mankind, and for the building
up of the Church of Christ, so far is the freedom of Africa assured, for
surely many Africans will follow such leadership.

Perhaps the atmosphere of the global military struggle contributed to
the apocalyptic confidence about the future.

When the International Missionary Council met at Willingen in
Germany in 1956 there were 190 delegates and consultants about forty
of whom were 'nationals'; but the latter were not official representatives
of their Churches. This IMC conference really marks the watershed
between the missionary era from 1787 onwards and the new perspective
of world mission by the Churches. The Willingen meeting and Fifth
Assembly of the WCC in 1975 are an age apart. Awareness that the era
was coming to an end was beginning to emerge. 'The Church's mission
is deeper and more far-reaching than can be expressed through the
historic agencies of the foreign missionary movement.'[8]

The meeting at Willingen took place at a time when the world had
been shaken to its foundations by global war. People were not the
same afterwards and neither were conditions. 'The familiar features
of the world in which the foreign missionary movement grew up
have largely disappeared.'[9] Emphasis was given to the view that the
mission of Christ must be seen as the responsibility of the Church and
not of a special agency. The 'younger Churches' were more clearly in
focus but it was obvious that almost everywhere they were directed by
overseas missionaries. The need was clearly expressed for the training
of capable nationals, so that they could become church leaders. Within
five years the first African country was to become independent and set
in motion the rapid process of decolonization. It is astonishing to recall
that this important international meeting, held only twenty-seven years
ago, included special sessions for the selected forty nationals on their
own, so that their statements could be added to the report. It is not
surprising that such a pace of change and progress calls for great
adjustments.

A more objective look was taken at the missionary societies than
had been given before. It was noted that there had been a 'time-lag' in
their participation in the Ecumenical Movement. But there was deeper

questioning: 'Every society should ask itself whether, in the present
state of the Church or churches with which it is linked, the discharge of
the missionary obligation requires it still to be organized as a body in
some sense independent of the Church.'[10] The preponderance of
missionary personnel, particularly in leadership, was perpetuating the
'foreignness', and clearly the churches overseas were slower than
political movements in achieving local leadership. 'So long as a church
bears more evidence of "foreignness" than of relevancy to its local
situation, its redemptive mission is obscure. . . . But the eternal gospel
must be so presented to men and women that its contemporary and
compelling relevance is recognized. It cannot be so recognized as long
as it appears in foreign guise, imitating and reproducing the characteristics of a church in some remote and alien land.'[11]

It is apparent from these extracts and from the report itself that the
IMC at Willingen was moving towards new attitudes which questioned
the role of missionary societies and asked for a reappraisal of the
growth of western missionary personnel. It is therefore mistaken to
suggest, as it often is, that the changed attitude in western Churches
towards world evangelization was a result of the later amalgamation of
the IMC with the WCC to become the Commission on World Mission
and Evangelism. Before the amalgamation in 1961, thinking on the
theology of mission and discussions in IMC meetings had shown that
new attitudes were developing.

In the thirty years since the end of the Second World War the
number of expatriate missionaries in Africa has steadily increased.
Some find this difficult to believe, because overall statistics are not
available. Neither the WCC nor the AACC has missionary statistics
for Africa. Many who write on the subject do so in the context of a
mainline missionary body where numbers have declined, and they
wrongly deduce that this is typical of the whole. At the time of writing
there is no comprehensive evidence that the aggregate of expatriate
missionaries in Africa has ended its 200-year constant increase.

The post-war period has seen a general increase in expatriate
missionaries, both from the Protestant and Roman Catholic Churches.
The background of general statistics may be taken from the fourth
edition of the *Map of the World's Religions*.[12]

Protestant missionaries in the world

1903	1911	1925	1952	1958	1963
15,288	21,307	29,186	35,533	38,606	42,952

The fact that the experience of the few large missionary societies in Britain is atypical of the world situation is underlined by the following figures from the USA:

Protestant missionaries in the world (from the USA)[13]

	1958	1971
American Baptist Convention	407	290
United Presbyterian Church	1,293	810
Presbyterian Church US	504	391
United Methodist Church (including	1,453	1,175
Evangelical United Brethren; later joined with UMC)		
Episcopal Church	395	138
United Church of Christ	496	356
Southern Baptist Convention	1,186	2,494
Evangelical Foreign Mission Association	4,688	7,479
Inter-denominational Foreign Mission Association	5,902	6,164
	16,324	19,297

During this period the numerical strength of the historic missionary societies in the West has declined. In some cases this has been the result of an act of policy by the society. But there are other factors. The climate of religious uncertainty after the war has affected recruiting. Working within autonomous churches, involving new, irritating pressures, is a different experience and challenge. Financial resources have dwindled, with the social changes brought by a world war. The institutional Church has come under particular attack in the post-war years. But these factors do not provide all the explanation. If the major societies, with their vast experience, had felt with absolute certainty that an increasing number of missionaries was necessary they would have surmounted the difficulties. A decrease in number has been acceptable.

A particular example may be taken from one of the older missionary societies. The United Presbyterian Mission from the USA began work in Africa in 1835. One of its main areas of work has been the north-east: in Egypt, Sudan, and Ethiopia. Since the Second World War the United Presbyterian Church has followed a policy of encouraging local initiative and leadership by steadily reducing the numbers of expatriate missionaries, as the following figures indicate:

United Presbyterian Church USA (missionaries in Africa)

1966	1967	1968	1969	1970	1971	1972	1973
209	194	195	174	152	144	114	99

A similar pattern is given by the figures for missionaries from the United Methodist Church USA: 1970: 1,300; 1973: 922; 1975: 885.

The pattern in Britain has been similar. The following table gives numbers for missionaries in Africa from some societies. (If they are married missionaries, only one has been reckoned in the figures.)

Missionaries in Africa

	Baptist Missionary Society	Council for World Mission*	Church of Scotland	Church Missionary Society	Methodist Missionary Society†	United Society for the Propagation of the Gospel‡
1960	94	—	150	443	266	—
1962	79	—	141	412	281	—
1964	78	—	123	406	267	—
1966	68	—	119	373	213	—
1967	69	56	129	384	272	543
1968	69	51	111	360	205	446
1971	72	48	97	—	178	341
1973	72	—	82	244	—	354
1974	59	24	76	199	176	300
1975	57	25	61	215	152	250
1976	58	21	53	189	145	250

* The Council for World Mission was formed in 1971 from an amalgamation of the Presbyterian Missionary Society and the Congregational Council for World Mission. This new body inherited the great tradition of the London Missionary Society.

† Since 1974 the title has been altered to Overseas Division, Methodist Church (Methodist Missionary Society).

‡ The United Society for the Propagation of the Gospel was formed in 1964 from the Society for the Propagation of the Gospel and the Universities Mission to Central Africa. Figures for the separate bodies are not now available.

The coincidence of a decline in the number of missionaries from the historic societies, both in North America and Britain, cannot be without significance. During the period the standard of living of these nations has been increasing, and they have generally been more affluent. Financial difficulty has been an embarrassment only to some of the societies.

A comparison may be made with missionary bodies associated with the German Missionary Council. The reason for the different pattern is the determination of the Churches in West Germany to participate through personnel in world mission, after the war and post-war period when they had been excluded.

German Missionary Council (missionaries in Africa)

1951	1956	1960	1965	1969	1971	1972
147	247	306	353	388	400	367

The number of Roman Catholic expatriate staff is not easy to determine precisely, as often the figures include both overseas and African personnel. The latest figures include 235 expatriate bishops and 11,164 expatriate priests for Africa as a whole.

Some of the individual countries are listed below to indicate the situation and in some cases to show the comparative figures for expatriate and African staff:

	Local bishops	Foreign bishops	Local priests	Foreign priests
Ivory Coast	6	2	108	284
Angola			207	346
Nigeria	16	9	311	530
Rhodesia	1	5	38	332
Burundi			157	277
Tanzania	19	4	494	908
Cameroon			198	523
Uganda	9	3	348	543
Chad			1	160
Ghana	8	1	121	258
Dahomey			69	125
Zambia	4	4	73	384
Botswana	0	1	2	22
Gabon			35	70
Sierre Leone	1	2	4	95
Malagasy Republic	10	6	158	599
Congo (Brazaville)			29	128
Malawi			71	234
Namibia			2	27

The number of missionary priests in the continent almost doubled between 1949 and 1969, rising from 6,420 to 11,400. The number of brothers rose from 2,941 to 5,177 and sisters from 14,078 to 27,555. In the same period the number of African priests rose from 1,080 to 3,623. Numbers are constantly changing; the latest figure (1975) for Roman Catholic expatriate priests is 12,700.

In only eight countries is there a higher ratio than 30 per cent of African priests, namely in Burundi, Cameroon, Tanzania, Togo,

Uganda, Benin-Togo, Equatorial Guinea, Rwanda; but in no country is there a higher percentage than 35 of local-born Catholic clergy.

The Roman Catholic Church in Africa has far and away the greatest 'foreign element' and must be regarded as the least Africanized of the major Churches. No other major institution in Africa has such a non-African image. Its peculiar situation has been created by policies of multiplying expatriate personnel, and redoubling, during the last fifty years. Since the Second World War probably five Roman Catholic workers to every Protestant missionary have gone to Africa. Has the numerical growth of the Church depended on these overseas workers? That is a doubtful proposition. The predicament now is a Church which is so heavily manned by non-Africans that it cannot easily and quickly become a truly African Church. However, there is one hopeful aspect: that the number of those studying for the priesthood, major seminarians, rose from 1,899 in 1962 to 3,463 in 1972.

Zaire is a typical example of the numerical growth of *expatriate personnel* in the Roman Catholic Church in Africa:

1924	1930	1938	1971
1,013	1,552	2,178	2,219

The contemporary situation regarding 'conservative-evangelical' missionary bodies in Britain is surveyed comprehensively in the *UK Protestant Missions Handbook*, published by the Evangelical Missionary Alliance.[14] A list is given of almost 200 missionary societies based in Britain, with 4,600 missionaries overseas, of whom 2,050 are at work in Africa. The handbook includes in its figures the historic missionary societies but is unable to include bodies such as the Brethren, with perhaps 600 overseas missionaries; therefore its numbers are an underestimate. The overall total we may accept as Protestant missionaries working in Africa from Britain is 2,300. An interesting aspect of this figure is that only 900 are working in the smaller and less developed countries of Africa. Where the Church is strong, the attraction for missionaries seems greater. Of the total 1,231 are working in six of the most developed countries where churches are well established: South Africa, Rhodesia, Kenya, Uganda, Nigeria, and Zaire.

What then is the overall picture of the expatriate missionaries to Africa, south of the Sahara, 200 years after the tentative beginning on the west coast? The figures are not exact and they may not be comprehensive, but they give a framework. Political changes sometimes bring a sudden reduction, as in Uganda or Mozambique, but many bodies such as the Seventh Day Adventists and the Brethren are not included, and therefore the figures are probably underestimated.

Expatriate missionaries in Africa in 1974
(to the nearest 100)

Roman Catholic	
Bishops, priests, brothers, sisters	24,200
Non-Roman Catholic	
United Kingdom	2,300
German Missionary Council	400
Scandinavia	1,000
From remainder of Europe	300
USA	9,000
Canada	100
Other countries	100
	37,400

To see this figure in context we should take note of the fact that in this century the figures have been:

1910	1938	1974
10,800	22,000	37,300

The total is as high as it has ever been and in spite of local evidence to the contrary there are as yet no aggregate figures indicating a decrease in the total number. All the assumptions which one might make would suggest a diminution; it may be taking place but evidence has yet to appear. For our purposes we are ignoring the movement within Africa of workers from one country to another; there are West Africans at work in East Africa, Rhodesians in Zambia, Kenyans in Sudan, South Africans in Botswana, and many other variations.

The dilemma which Christian leaders face is whether this large complement is required to sustain the witness and service of the Church, whether a great increase is needed to speed the task of evangelization; or whether the Christian faith, if it is to continue to be within the mainstream of Africa's evolving life, can move forward to a virile African Christianity with this large expatriate element. If Africa is to find the liberation which the Christian gospel promises, and towards which the original mission to Africa pointed, can it discover a relevant Christian understanding and culture with such a heavy non-African presence? It is a reasonable premise that Africa has a specifically African understanding of the gospel, to be increasingly expressed in

African forms and theology. Can that be consummated without a new freedom to be itself? Would the introduction of 10,000 more Christian missionaries from Korea, Australia, the USA, or anywhere else assist the African Church to find its fullness in experience, understanding, and mission?

In contemplating a continent, and thinking in large terms, it is easy to forget that the situation in the world and in the Church is constantly changing. One of the features of Africa today is its changeability; it has for better or worse been caught up in the irrepressible fluctuations of the twentieth-century western world. Another feature is the growth of secularization. Similarly, the Churches cannot be viewed as in the past as if the whole pattern were known; the shape both of congregations and of ecumenical organizations may vary considerably. In these rapidly moving and evolving circumstances will a strong African Church be best able to respond to them, or is an enlarged expatriate missionary presence likely to be beneficial?

It is obvious from the figures already given that the old-established missionary organizations in Britain and North America have positively and steadily declined numerically in missionary staff in Africa. In the decade after the Second World War the societies quickly rebuilt their numbers to as near the pre-war total as possible. The hiatus of the war made possible an adequate number of recruits in the immediate post-war years. From 1960 there has been a widespread and steady decline; there has, however, been a small but constant increase in financial income, therefore the trend has not had a primary financial cause. Missionary thinking and force of circumstances have moved together.

Writing in *Church Growth Bulletin*, Harvey Hoekstra isolates some reasons for the decrease; some of the points he makes are given below, but are not expressed in his words:

the emergence of highly organized churches overseas has absorbed energies, both of missionaries and local personnel, so that the element of expansion is lost;

similarly, the new churches offer an organization rather than a challenge; a new set of relationships between churches and younger churches diminishes the exciting challenge of world evangelization;

church development overseas has seen a heavy growth of institutions, which absorb recruits; serving institutions with all their difficulties does not stimulate missionary service;

the evolution of the old missionary bodies in the West has seen missionary leaders in them become bureaucrats and church politicians, unlike individuals of earlier generations, with a world evangelistic vision;

the post-war period of decline has taken place while established empires have collapsed; the withdrawal from India, Burma, Africa, the French and Belgian colonies, has had an immense psychological effect on the western mind, weakening its sense of involvement and obligation;

perhaps the most traumatic experience during the post-war build-up of missionary personnel was the large-scale evacuation of China, and the virtual disappearance of the Church: the sacrifice and effort seemed to be in vain;

difficulties have been increased by political and military actions, causing missionaries to be expelled and presenting them with a 'closed door', as in India, Sudan, Guinea, Vietnam;

Europe and North America have in the middle years of this century lost confidence in themselves, because of their moral failure, in totalitarianism, extermination camps, racial riots, and yet another recourse to the horrors of war;

after the WCC Uppsala Assembly there was a discernible shift in attitude towards a much greater focus on social and political needs, rather than on the traditional concept of evangelization; the new thrust was to serve rather than proclaim;

in recent decades so much time and thought has been given to church union concerns that the emphasis on a call to evangelize has been weakened, and many have become uninterested in church affairs; churches which have spent so much effort in seeking to come together, and which fail to do so, cannot inspire great commitment.

While this study concentrates on Africa south of the Sahara, it is not inappropriate to make reference to the particular situation of the Church in parts of North Africa, after political independence, in comparison with the remainder of the continent. Political independence has brought the closure of two-thirds of the churches; in Algeria some mission work continues, but in other countries such as Libya and Tunisia expatriates are now excluded.

The statistics indicate a Roman Catholic complement in Africa which is as great as it has ever been and is almost two-thirds of the total missionary presence. The long-established missionary bodies, which all date back to the end of the eighteenth century and the beginning of the nineteenth, have reduced their numbers and continue to do so. The 'conservative-evangelical' bodies in Europe and North America more than make up for the decline, with the result that the overall numbers are maintained and even increase. The difference is not availability of funds and personnel, but of attitude and policy. This is examined in more detail later, but in recording the present situation it is important to distinguish between the 'conservative-evangelical' policy of sending the maximum number of missionaries, primarily identified by an intention to be wholly engaged in individual evangelism, with an authoritarian and literal view of the Bible; and the mainline churches' wider understanding of mission which has grown from theological reflection in the last thirty years and from experience of ecumenical encounter. To the observer the former appears generally to be a closed system, with narrower parameters than the historic missionary movement which is more open, searching, and prepared for conversation and debate. Both seem equally attached to Holy Scripture but in different ways; both seek the power and guidance of the Holy Spirit, but find it in different ways. The criterion can hardly be either the number of missionaries or the resources of finance.

At this point two things may be noted. The first is that the modern evangelical enthusiasm for world evangelism, in some of its present forms, appears to be more restricted than the historic missionary movement and less well equipped theologically and intellectually than it has been during the last two centuries. Compare, for example, the contents of the publication on the Lausanne Congress on World Evangelization (1974) and the mass of reports and studies on world mission issued during the nineteenth century.[15]

The second important issue is the movement of thought on world mission which has taken place in many of the Churches and ecumenical organizations during the last twenty years. The threads in that movement may be summarized briefly as:

a greater commitment to the world and a readiness to respond to its needs; a great awakening to the actual situation and problems of our fellow men, and a strong active responsibility towards the real world;

a new understanding of the Church being in existence for the world;

that church growth for its own ends is not of primary importance, but that a serving and witnessing Church is;

in thinking on mission, the concept of 'the Church' – its foundation, planting, and expansion – retreats from the forefront and gives place to a view of the world as the object of God's love and concern;

a new emphasis on finding a greater experience of God in the world: to find him at work in the world and to co-operate in his purposes;

mission becomes more than the founding of churches – planting churches among non-Christians – and much more than individual evangelism;

the other-worldly aspect of religion receives less emphasis in comparison with the past; there is less attachment to 'religion' and a greater concern for the life of the world.

Today, more than ever before, there are many Christians who have a personal and profound concern for the world and for human beings in their environment. The relevance of the Christian gospel is the subject of most serious debate; people are concerned for peace, relief, justice, and development. The validity of the historic missionary movement is not denied, nor is the reality of religious experience: Christian witness, service, and worship are respected. However, an oversimplified individualistic approach, and an objective of planting more and more congregations, do not by themselves command in many quarters a satisfactory response to our present awareness of the world.

6

Moratorium

The Spirit of Moratorium: a Strategy for Self-reliance

The colonial period has brought four European languages to Africa: English, French, Portuguese, and Spanish. Africans are often divided from one another by their second language and consequently ecumenical consultations have always to be conducted in a European language, with expert and expensive European linguists engaged for the purpose. Churches in Africa are trying to reach out and find one another across the language divide. In 1975 'a unique training scheme was started to train African linguists to serve the ecumenical movement in Africa. The immediate objective is an entirely African team of interpreters and translators at the next assembly of the All Africa Conference of Churches in 1978.' As a participant in the first seminar in Togo put it: 'This is the first practical step towards implementing a moratorium and a real encouragement for the churches in Africa.'[1]

That is the spirit of moratorium. Not retrogression, but a forward movement to handling one's own affairs in the cause of better co-operation towards Christian mission in the whole continent. Many people outside the continent might feel that they could adopt a neutral attitude to such a proposal. What does it matter? To be understood it needs to be considered against the background of Africa's melancholy history, and the contemporary unsatisfied search for release and freedom in a secure identity.

Moratorium is a word in common usage, indicating a temporary or permanent halt to an established practice. The *Shorter Oxford English Dictionary* defines it as 'a legal authorization to a debtor to postpone payment for a certain time'. After the First World War the debts and reparation imposed on Germany by the Allies were eventually ended by an agreed moratorium, as the burden became increasingly intolerable.

A moratorium may be declared by government on the defaulters in payment of council house rents. In a European crisis the members of the European Economic Community might delay or cancel payments to the common budget, by an agreed moratorium.

Prominence was given to the concept, in relation to the missionary question, by the famous address at the Mission Festival at Milwaukee in

1971 by a gifted and experienced Christian leader in East Africa, the Revd John Gatu. Some quotations from his speech will indicate the threads in this notion at its inception.

He began by speaking, as an outstanding evangelist and church executive, of commitment to an unfinished task. He was thinking not only of Africa, but of the Third World: 'The continuation of the present missionary movement is a hindrance to the selfhood of the Church. . . . The time has come for the withdrawal of foreign missionaries from many parts of the Third World.'

He leaves no doubt that his fundamental thinking is that the Church must go forward in Africa, and he is exercised in mind because it cannot do so in its present condition. 'We in the Third World must liberate ourselves from the bondage of western dependency by refusing anything that renders impotent the development of our spiritual resources, which in turn make it impossible for the Church in the Third World to engage in the mission of God in their own areas. . . . The gospel will then have a deeper and a more far-reaching effect than our mission Christianity has provided so far.'

John Gatu acknowledged that his own thinking had been partly influenced by Fr Daniel Berrigan writing on Latin America: 'I suggest we stop sending anyone or anything for three years . . . and face our mistakes.'

There are identifiable elements in his thinking and address which caused him to speak with such challenge, power, and authority at Milwaukee. In his own experience in Kenya he had known, as an African, the rigours of an imperial regime, the struggle for independence, and the indignities of mass imprisonment. In his church he had seen the gross imbalance of wealth and prestige between African and European. An evangelical experience and the East African Revival had brought him from the world of secular nationalist aspiration into the sphere of the established Churches. He felt deeply that the Church was wrongly orientated towards an alien colonial regime instead of towards the people of the land.

In this epoch-making speech there are other elements. Gatu was aware of the close association between the missionary movement from Europe and the commercial penetration of Africa from Europe. It was articulate in the founding of Sierra Leone and given publicity in David Livingstone's famous statement, 'I go back to Africa to try and make an open path for commerce and Christianity.' Livingstone must have been thinking of 'commerce' in an idealistic form. John Gatu and his contemporaries were far more acutely aware of the great, historic commercial involvement between Europe and Africa, namely the slave trade, with the constant reminders by tangible objects and those arising from every historical inquiry.

Another aspect in his mind was the image of Africa created elsewhere, especially in the Churches, by the interpretation of African life given by missionaries, officials, and visiting students. Africa is projected in Europe by Europeans. A distorted view of Africa is given to the Churches of the West by the large body of missionaries who interpret it through their own European experience. At its worst it can be a condemnation of all things African as 'pagan' and 'primitive'; at its best it may be the European self-styled champion of African interests who becomes the spokesman for Africa. 'The African was always defined in terms not of what he was or what he had but in terms of what he was not, according to western values. His destiny was therefore directed by someone other than himself – the outsider; and in many cases missionaries were the African's spokesmen.' Here one touches another facet of European superiority, that they will more readily listen to or read the European's interpretation than attend patiently to the African expressing himself. Many African leaders have returned from visits to Britain and Europe, saying sadly, 'They won't listen!'

John Gatu had also reacted to the common assumption in some places that Christianity cannot survive in Africa without the large-scale presence of western missionaries. After almost 200 years of Christian witness, teaching, and service, such an attitude of mind must either have a low view of the faith or an unappreciative assessment of African capability and response. A section of the speech was given over to a direct challenge to alleged statements by Bishop Stephen Neill that African Christianity is superficial and that a constant flow of foreign missionaries is therefore necessary.

Bishop Neill cannot see an African Church surviving without missionaries from the West. He sees the role of the missionaries as helpers in areas as administrators, treasurers, accountants, theological teachers, etc. The question one likes to ask is, 'What administration, what accountancy, what theological training?' I am sure I can mention churches in Africa that have almost all of these posts taken by Africans. But where it is not yet possible, it is precisely for this reason that we must ask missionaries to leave in order that Africans can take over these jobs, or alternatively, if they do not think they are important enough, formulate some new methods and structures that would suit both their budgetary capacity and personnel.

There is an element of presumption and pretentiousness in the Christian from European societies arriving at the conclusion that Christianity cannot survive in Africa without his help, when its survival in his own community seems at times in jeopardy. The pervasive arrogance of the Anglo-Saxon and the Westerner generally, emerges so often in our attitudes and conversations that it not surprisingly creates a barrier of resentment. The white man's burden and the missionary responsibility of western churches have taken a toll in their effect on the bearers of the liberating message.

I can recall, in a personal reminiscence, Dr Francis Ibiam (a former governor of Eastern Nigeria) and the Revd John Gatu returning to Nairobi at the end of 1966. They had been with others on a courageous and exacting journey to war-torn Sudan, visiting the Government at Khartoum and some of the areas in the south which were slowly being destroyed by a decade of civil strife. The attitude of the Muslim north to the goodwill mission was unknown at the beginning, and whether the attempt would alienate the rebel southerners was unclear. The visit laid the foundation for relationships which made mediation possible five years later.

In their reports they stressed the willingness of the Khartoum Government to allow Christian preachers and teachers from Africa to go to the Sudan, but not in principle to permit the return of European missionaries. John Gatu and his colleagues have found themselves ill equipped to respond to this challenge from a Muslim-African government, while at the same time they are themselves embarrassed by the number and resources of the European and North American missionaries.

John Gatu reported this experience in the Milwaukee address, for it had deepened the seriousness of his thinking about the missionary problem. He felt that the attitude of the Sudan authorities, and the weakness which it revealed, 'characterizes the ferment in many parts of the Third World in relation to the presence of missionaries from foreign countries, especially in Africa'.

His speech revealed a further sensitivity, related to money rather than personnel. It is not simply that the West has a lot more wealth, and that some African countries are among the poorest in the world. The imbalance in the world's wealth, with its historic causes, is a separate consideration. Rather is it that the type of society created in the West has become intensely materialistic and tends to put a monetary value on everything. Income and acquisition have become a measure of position and prestige. John Gatu is alive to the impact on the Church in Africa of this unAfrican sense of values: 'It is certainly not a New Testament idea, but an emanation of the thinking of the industrial society that can see value only in terms of money and statistics. . . . We cannot build the church in Africa on alms given by overseas churches.'

There is the dilemma of churches in Africa moving into a period when society as a whole becomes a wage-economy, when rural Christian communities might engage in their evangelistic tasks more effectively without sophisticated statistics, accounts, and administration. There is too the chronic and unsolved irritant of the foreign worker being housed and maintained at one standard of living, financed from overseas, while African workers are maintained at a different material standard. It is a problem which is usually encompassed by the tolerance and grace of those concerned, but it would be perverse not to realize that it contributes to the tensions inherent in the expatriate presence in Africa. In some cases it has been possible to make practical solutions, but these are exceptional.

John Gatu said:

The need is commitment and a decision to go forward in faith. For Africa has money and personnel, and until we have produced the two loaves and five fishes, our Lord continues to say, 'Give ye them something to eat.' . . . We must liberate ourselves from the bondage of western dependence by refusing anything that renders impotent the development of our spiritual resources, which in turn makes it impossible for the churches in the Third World to engage in the missions of God in their own areas.

The speech seems to suggest that the taking of initiative to actuate a moratorium might come from either the Churches in Africa or from the missionary societies of the West. He says:

We must ask missionaries to leave . . . the withdrawal of missionaries from many parts of the world . . . if all missionaries can be withdrawn. . . . I started by saying that the missionaries should be withdrawn from the Third World for a period of at least five years. I will go further and say that the missionaries should be withdrawn, period. The reason is that we must allow God the Holy Spirit to direct our next move without giving him a timetable.

The final quotation from the speech turns our minds away from the practicalities of western/Third World denominational relationships, to the transcendent vision of a divine purpose.

The Vasco da Gama mentality which went out to explore the world and help the heathen and the poor is still haunting many of the western Churches . . . if we believe that the Vasco da Gama era of the Church must be brought to an end; if we accept the idea that the Church in Africa must find her identity without the tutelage of the West, then we must let the Church be the Church, the Church of the people by the Holy Spirit, through people, for the glory of Christ in people, and their total liberation, and not an extension of our personal, denominational, and historical connections that are being put to question today, and let mission be the mission of God in the world, but not of the West to the Third World.

It could be said that Christian mission to Africa and Asia, originating in the modern missionary movement in the West, has been too distracted and sullied by imperial and commercial relations to produce any other response.

At Bangkok in January 1973 the Conference on 'Salvation Today' and the Assembly of the Commission on World Mission and Evangelism considered both the programme of Ecumenical Sharing of Personnel and the issue of moratorium. Support was given to ESP, but it 'shall not necessarily mean the continuation in a new form of the traditional flow of missionaries, for example in the area of theological education in Africa'.[2]

In the Assembly the moratorium idea was included in the report on the Ecumenical Sharing of Personnel. It gives a clear presentation of the intention of a moratorium.

One of the proposals to develop new patterns of relationship is that there should be a moratorium on the sending of funds and personnel to particular churches for a period of time. The intention is that churches requesting such a moratorium might have an opportunity to work with their own resources to find their own selfhood and identity. Churches no longer able to send money and personnel will be freed from the traditional, institutionalized missionary enterprise to use their resources for new approaches to education for mission amongst their own people. They will also be freed to give financial support to those struggling for freedom from unjust and dehumanizing systems perpetuated by dominant nations and bodies.

How will the sending church express its missionary calling if it is deprived of its traditional avenues of work? One answer is that it may discover neglected missionary opportunities in its own country. As for the financial resources diverted from the former channels, there are many potential uses for these, such as programmes of development, education for mission in the new context, including education for development and justice, neglected areas of mission in the nation, etc.

In the director's report to the Assembly it was pointed out that the USA deploys more than 60 per cent of the Christian missionary force around the world, and the resources that go with it, while western Europe and Australasia account for the remaining 40 per cent of missionary and Christian service involvement.

In the context of Bangkok, moratorium was seen as a radical proposal which would disturb traditional relationships. Nevertheless it was recognized that 'in some situations, however, the moratorium proposal, painful though it may be for both sides, may be the best means of resolving a present dilemma and advancing the mission of Christ'. Consequently it called for the widest possible study and discussion of the call for moratorium as a potential strategy of mission in certain areas.

At the Assembly the Revd John Gatu gave some further insights into his thinking:

In many cases our congregations are left to think that there are certain people who are supposed to do certain things and the idea of each person's stewardship only exists in some very limited circles. Old concepts carried over from early missionaries are still lingering in the churches of the Third World. In a situation like we find in Africa, where it is expected that of a total population of 800 million in the year 2000, there is likely to be a total of 370 million Christians and that the leadership of the Church will be in the hands of lay people, education of the congregations and the preparation of the laity for the mission of the Church has never been more necessary. Mission to Six Continents means that Africa should be sending missionaries out to other continents instead of always receiving them.

The third Assembly of the AACC, meeting at Lusaka in 1974, gave a surprisingly strong impetus to the moratorium. Hitherto, in WCC consultations, much greater attention had been given to ESP than to moratorium. At Lusaka the Assembly unmistakedly chose the moratorium and set aside the notion of ESP, as a possible distraction from the real problem which worried them.

Three aspects of the context in which this discussion took place should be remembered. First, African leaders were aware that the extraordinary numerical growth of the Church in Africa, estimated at over 6 per cent a year, would bring the number of Christians to perhaps 370 million in the next twenty-five years. The spectacular growth has been in effective evangelism by independent churches which have consciously cut themselves off from foreign personnel and money. The African Christian Church is demonstrably able to evangelize, expand, lead, and organize.

The second consideration is the acute awareness by the Assembly, because of its venue at Lusaka, of the struggle in southern Africa between whites and blacks for liberation. Representatives of the liberation movements were present officially as observers and were warmly welcomed. The oppressive white regimes of Rhodesia, Namibia, and the Portuguese territories inevitably have had an influence on the continent's attitude towards the white European in Africa, both as reminiscent of repressive colonial regimes and as a living example of white privilege, exploitation, and superiority. Getting rid of them may be violent and chaotic, but for most Africans that does not detract from their offensive nature.

The third aspect is more specific. Revelations had been made of Portuguese atrocities in Mozambique, particularly at Mucumbura, Wiriyamu, and Inhaminga, with the complicity of the Roman Catholic Church in the maintenance of the Portuguese rule. More recently in Nampula, in northern Mozambique, some of the local Portuguese had demonstrated against and threatened the only Roman Catholic bishop in Mozambique who appeared to sympathize with the African aspiration for emancipation – Bishop Manuel of Nampula. The Assembly took the unprecedented step of giving formal support to the action of the executive secretary of the AACC, in September 1973, in calling for the immediate end of the Concordat and Missionary Agreement between the Vatican and the Government of Portugal. The Assembly spoke directly to the Roman Catholic hierarchy, 'that it publicly denounced not only particular instances of oppression, but

above all, the systems which are their origin. That it denounces the
Concordat and the Missionary Statute, because both gravely deform
the mission of the Church to be the light of the people, and make it
an accomplice of a system which contributes to the cultural genocide.'
The Assembly was addressing itself to one very prominent and
contemporary aspect of the European missionary presence in Africa.

When Canon Burgess Carr, general secretary of the AACC,
addressed the Assembly, he said: 'We must take up the challenge to
regenerate Africa, not by "commerce and Christianity" but by making
a fresh commitment to radically renew the form and content of our
faith, so as to enable it to provide a true spiritual anchor in our
continuing struggle for cultural authenticity and integration, human
development, dignity, justice, and peace.' He paid tribute in the land of
Livingstone to the 'rich inheritance in opportunity, inspiration, and
goodwill' which the famous missionary had left.

Burgess Carr took note of the rapid growth of the Churches in
Africa, but spoke of the rebellion of young people against the violence
done by Christianity to traditional customs. He felt that the crisis of
faith in the minds of the young was not hostility to Christianity, but

> a crisis of anthropology . . . at the very root of the problem is the
> cultural arrogance of the small minority of mankind, located in the
> North Atlantic world, who have imposed upon the world a naive
> hypothesis of cultural progress which places the western man at the
> top of an imaginary scale of evolutionary development. . . . Is
> Christianity still foreign, or has it taken root in Africa? The attitude
> to polygamy illustrates its foreignness: Why should a man be
> required to put away the mothers of his children in utter disregard of
> their human rights, in order to be accepted for Christian Baptism,
> while a blatant racist or a thoroughly corrupt politician is welcomed
> every Sunday morning to the Communion Table?

In the opening address by the general secretary, the issue of
moratorium was clearly presented as an item for consideration.

> The call for a moratorium has essentially to do with enhancing the
> catholicity of the Church through indigenization. . . . On the more
> practical level, the *moratorium* debate is beginning to expose certain
> exploitative aspects of the modern missionary enterprise. The critical
> issue here relates to personnel and finance. We are discovering that a
> considerable proportion of the money allocated for 'missionary

work' by missionary-sending agencies is spent on the salaries and maintenance of their personnel. In one small church in West Africa, the figure was recently shown to be as high as 61 per cent of that church's entire budget. Therefore, the call for a *moratorium* is a demand to transfer the massive expenditure on expatriate personnel in the churches in Africa to program activities manned by Africans themselves.

A preparatory paper for the Assembly ('Evangelism and Selfhood of the Churches', Section 1) suggested that the understanding of salvation, and the contents of the Christian faith in Africa today, can only come from people with an African heritage:

We must accept the challenges of the real meaning of salvation in Africa today in the light of our own religious heritage which sees the whole life as religious without the classical distinction between sacred and secular. We may then see the task of evangelism as the total witness in word and deed to whole persons and communities, leading to liberation and fullness of life. We have therefore to examine critically what we really preach. Do our sermons have any message and concern for the unemployed youth, people facing natural disaster, those fighting wars of liberation, tribalism, and racism, or those in the growing refugee population?

When we talk about the selfhood of the church in Africa we should ask,
What the church is called to be,
How the church in each place can manifest its own
authentic, historical, and cultural identity,
How our churches can contribute to the enrichment
of all the people of God,
To discover our selfhood and sort out our priorities,
it will be necessary, in some instances, to call a
moratorium on financial aid and personnel coming to
our churches.

A paper on cultural renewal ('The Church and Cultural Renewal in Africa', Section 2) referred to the deep need for African Christians to find themselves with confidence in their own cultural background:

We have allowed the 'basic good' in our culture to be smothered by other cultures, by other conceptions of life. As a result many of us are uprooted and alienated. Words like 'primitive', 'fetish', 'pagan', and 'heathen' have been used in the past to describe our cultural and religious heritage.

Our search for identity must be inspired by a sense of dignity in our ancestral past. This does not mean the indiscriminate baptism of everything African into Christian life and thought. But it does mean beginning our research with the conviction that the God who visited the world in human form through Jesus Christ was the same God who revealed Himself to our forefathers. Their perception was limited. And now we have to discover those areas of our heritage which Christ himself came to fulfil.

African traditional religion with its firm belief in both a transcendent and immanent God and the conception of man as having no separate existence from his Creator, from the living dead, or from the community, provides us with the roots on which a firm and permanent Christian faith can survive in Africa.

We too must be prepared to allow the Holy Spirit to lead us to the changes necessary for us to become heirs of the Kingdom of God.

The acceptance of the call to moratorium arises from a background of African Christians thinking about themselves seriously in the light of the gospel. It is not a rejection of what has gone before, or a betrayal of the catholicity of the Church. They are seeking self-discovery, self-expression, self-determination, and self-development. 'The universal Church is always manifested in local churches. . . . African Christians are therefore called upon to discover how the churches in Africa can be both authentically African and at the same time an integral part of the universal Church of Jesus Christ' (Report of Section 1).

It was in the Working Group reports of the Assembly, especially the report on 'Ministry for Social Justice', that the question of overseas personnel and finance was examined in greatest detail, although other reports indicate the pervasive nature of this question. The reports were accepted by the full Assembly, sometimes with amendments. Sitting in the great Mulungushi Hall with 400 people from all over Africa one sensed the historic significance of the occasion as, slowly, positions on crucial questions affecting Africa and the churches began to be adopted.

It is necessary to quote the report in full, as far as it relates to the moratorium:

A Call for a Moratorium
to enable the African Church to achieve the power of becoming a true instrument of liberating and reconciling the African people, as well as

finding solutions to economic and social dependency, our option as a matter of policy has to be a MORATORIUM on external assistance in money and personnel. We recommend this option as the only potent means of becoming truly and authentically ourselves while remaining as a respected and responsible part of the Universal Church.

The call for a Moratorium may undoubtedly affect the structures and programmes of many of our churches today. But a halt to receiving financial and human resources from abroad will necessitate the emergence of structures that would be viably African and programmes and projects of more urgent and immediate priority. A moratorium on funds and personnel from abroad will also enforce the unifying drives of churches in Africa.

The call for a Moratorium will also enable the African Church to perform a service of redeeming God's people in the northern hemisphere whose missionary-sending agencies have in many ways distorted the mission of the Church in Africa.

In an effort to achieve the Moratorium it is vitally important that a strategy of implementation be carefully worked out. We call on the AACC to associate with member churches in evolving a strategy suitable for each situation. Such strategies must involve the development of consciousness and awareness at all levels in the Church.

Two different groups within the larger section produced papers which had important points to make in relation to the moratorium. The following extracts indicate the widespread acceptance of this objective by those attending the Assembly:

The contribution of the African Church cannot be adequately made in our world if the Church is not liberated and becomes truly national. To achieve this liberation the Church will have to bring a halt to the financial and manpower resources – the receiving of money and personnel – from its foreign relationships, be they in the Northern Continents or foreign minority structures within Africa. Only then can the Church firmly assert itself in its mission to Africa and as a part of the ecumenical world.

What does this mean in our relationships with foreign mission boards and to the structure of those bodies and to sending churches? . . . There is no doubt that the Call for a Moratorium will be misinterpreted and opposed in many circles both within and without. But we will recommend this option to the churches of Africa as the only potent means of coming to grips with being ourselves and remaining a respected part of the Catholic Church.

Having declared its mind in favour of the calling of a Moratorium on Finances and Personnel from outside, this sub-group finds it impossible to recommend to the churches of Africa participation in a world-wide Ecumenical Sharing of Personnel and Resources.

Immediately after the Assembly, the AACC set up a working group to give close attention to the question in the future, realizing that caution and prolonged consideration were necessary. An illustrated brochure was sent out from AACC headquarters in Nairobi which said some important things:

What should be the results of Moratorium?
1　To discover an authentic African form of Christianity which can in turn enrich all the Christian Churches of the world.
2　To encourage African churches to leave the dependent attitudes many of us have adopted.
3　To help African churches to establish their own priorities in their work for Christ and to become fully missionary churches themselves.
4　To enable the traditionally missionary-sending churches in other lands to re-examine the nature of their mission and their future partnership with other churches.

Following the Assembly, the Ecumenical Press Service (No. 17/41st year, 20 June 1974) made available some of the documents of the Assembly. Two are worthy of inclusion in this record. The first is a quotation from the Working Group 3 Report adopted by the Assembly:

Another hindrance is the presence of missionaries or expatriate workers which continues to distract from the goal of Africanization. The coming of the missionaries to Africa, with all their past associations, must be seen for what it is even though well-intentioned, viz: an undesirable inhibition, and a counter-action to the prospering and success of African norms, values, and expressions.

One of the memorable occasions of the Assembly was the large outdoor service held in Lusaka Stadium, with Roman Catholic and Protestants taking part, and with many choirs and youth groups from the churches in Zambia present. Remembering the individual journeys of Livingstone, Mackenzie, Stewart, and Coillard as Christian pioneers in this part of Africa 125 years previously, it was indeed a moving scene. Dr Philip Potter, General Secretary of the World Council of Churches, said in his sermon:

> How do these characteristics of injustice show themselves in Africa today? The history of Africa, especially during the past 100 years, has been a systematic display of injustice. Africans were judged by their appearance . . . their race, their dress or lack of it, their failure to have and master the white man's skills, etc. The contacts of white people with them have been superficial, proud, brutal, and deadly. And this is still so in a most inhuman way in southern Africa today and in the dealings of the rich white world with the rest of Africa. Christian missionaries were no exception to this unjust way of life. One of them once admitted to me: 'We have behaved as if we had everything to give and nothing to receive.'

The response of Africa, through the AACC Assembly, to the moratorium proposal presented a special problem to the Ecumenical Sharing of Personnel programme of the WCC, which found itself officially rejected in Africa. A consultation was called by ESP at Le Cénacle in Geneva in January 1975, bringing together representatives from the western Protestant churches and from churches in Latin America, Asia, Africa, and elsewhere – largely from churches which had grown from western missionary enterprise. The impression made by the consultation was that of an experienced and deeply committed international group of Christians, who could see the moratorium discussion in greater depth, and who could hold the debate within the context of a global witness to Jesus Christ.

The difference of opinion between the attitude of western missionary bodies, many of whom want to perpetuate the traditional form, and the churches of Africa and elsewhere which want to discover a wholly new relationship, was likened to the conflict in the New Testament between the Twelve with their mission to the Jews and others with a sense of apostolic mission to the Gentile world. A change in style for the apostolate was sought in the early Church, but sincere Christians on both sides saw the matter very differently. The New Testament reveals the strains between those who were thinking in terms of Jewish Christianity and those who were thinking of a Gentile Christianity. The search for freedom to manifest the faith through different cultural forms is at the basis of both the conflicts in the New Testament and the modern issue of a moratorium.

It was realized that the call to moratorium, if this is the way that God is leading his Church, will be towards a stronger sense of commitment to world mission, and that it will be costly to both sides. For the Churches of Africa it may mean 'self-reliance', without the opportunity to turn to others for funds and workers. This will be so much at variance with long-established habits that it will demand a fearful adjustment. The Churches of the West, adapted to express Christian responsibility through support for younger Churches in the Third World, will have to look anew at their commerical, political, and national relationships with the Third World, and be humbled by ceasing to be benefactors. They have become trapped in too narrow an interpretation of mission and have in part lost a sense of mission in their own societies. They feel also that their national and religious heritage of a record of honourable service to underdeveloped continents has been ignored or falsely represented; they are left with a feeling of hurt and resentment.

The ground of debate and understanding for this, as for most groups of Christian leaders at a WCC consultation, was a deep sense of mission, involvement, and liberation towards the world. 'The modern missionary movement, although closely related in its origin to the awareness of European man's obligation to end the slave trade, became compromised because of its share in colonialist oppression. Thus it largely failed to be a true expression of apostolate which must always be a form of sharing in liberation.'

The world is now very different from that in which the modern missionary movement was born. We can give thanks for the birth of the churches across the world, but the shrinking planetary society which is now emerging needs moulding and liberating through a totally different 'missionary' approach than has existed hitherto. The traditional evangelism through mission from the western world was real, but is now irrelevant to the needs of the modern world. A run-down of the old pattern is seen 'in a manner consistent with the goal of such an operation in order to make possible the emergence of new relationships between churches who are equals insofar as they are liberated to be themselves'. An interesting parallel is found in 2 Corinthians 1.23, where Paul refrains from visiting and imposing himself on the Corinthian Church, so that the church could be itself.

A wider global and historical perspective, with special attention to the growth of the Ecumenical Movement, showed that the issues behind the sharp call to moratorium had been present consistently since the Edinburgh Missionary Conference in 1910. Reports from each continent showed that the call for selfhood and indigenization and 'release from the chains of present missionary relationships' came in different ways from every side. Local churches and regional organizations can often find freedom to evangelize when they are released from the western presence.

A total moratorium for a time is said to be appropriate in some places. In other places, a partial moratorium or a planned process of elimination of foreign control is sought. . . . It is increasingly evident that the moratorium call raises those fundamental questions about selfhood and mission which deeply trouble all churches everywhere. The first step is the placing of the call to moratorium before the receiving churches by their own people. The second is an openness to the possibility of a halt in the present process on the part of traditional 'sending' churches and mission boards and the beginning of a new relationship more in keeping with the maturity and responsibility of the traditionally 'receiving' bodies. All of this is done for the purpose of enabling churches to assume full missionary responsibility in their own communities (Consultation Report, p. 4).

A section of the report (Group 2) is directed to western mission agencies. For Churches in the West to achieve 'selfhood', this must not be at the expense of exploiting the Churches of the Third World to serve their own ends. In some ways this is clearly happening. Many supporters need to be set free from paternalistic and superior attitudes. God entrusts his mission to the Christians in each place in their communities, not to others far away. Do Churches in the West express concern about mission tasks on their own doorsteps, and identify with oppressed and deprived groups in their own nation?

So long as mission agencies in the West exist in their old form they could be advised to move towards certain objectives:

see that new styles of relationship distribute power in a different way from the past;

make block grants of finance, leaving the local church to decide on the manner of expenditure, including whether it wishes to spend any portion on expatriate personnel;

allow self-governing Churches to decide scales of remuneration for local and expatriate workers;

hold periodic consultations within the local church, not just with secretarial visits, but with a small mission board delegation;

aim to alter the nature of the 'sending' institution so that it becomes involved in leadership in mission in its own country and beyond;

allow the institution to become involved in all the relationships with the country in question (investments, political, military);

support organizations which provide for greater manoeuvrability for action than is possible with denominational structures;

help to make the moratorium possible, and seek new relationships in mission which may then be revealed.

Some mission boards have sought to adapt themselves to new understandings of mission, in response to new developing relationships. A notable example has been the Evangelical Community for Apostolic Action (CEVAA) which has broken old relationships by creating a new community of churches. Others have made organizational changes or changes in nomenclature, but with the basic structural situation remaining unchanged.

The moratorium concept has arisen out of African thinking and has been taken up by African churchmen. It was given a wider context at the WCC Bangkok meetings. It is instructive to examine the response and sometimes automatic reaction of mission boards in the West. Reference has already been made to the reappraisal called for and accepted by the Ecumenical Sharing of Personnel at the WCC. The concept was taken seriously at Bangkok, and examined both in reference to the Bible and in an ecumenical and international context. The Commission of World Mission and Evangelism (CWME), meeting in Portugal in 1975 gave it its attention and 'echoed Lusaka's view of a moratorium for mission rather than a moratorium on mission'. It also asked the fifth Assembly of the WCC held in Nairobi in November 1975 to try to take the discussion further, and noted that moratorium was 'one possible way to create mature relationships of churches in mission'.[3]

At the time of writing, the reaction of missionary bodies and their executives in the West to the emergence of the concept of moratorium has been largely negative. On the whole the subject has been treated with indifference. With a few exceptions, the clergy and laity involved in the day-to-day work of societies and their local committees have not entered deeply into study and consultation on the matter. The reactions are usually along one of the following lines.

It is pointed out that no Church in Africa has turned to its overseas supporting agency, with which it is traditionally connected, and has asked for a cessation of funds and personnel from a certain date. It is repeatedly said that no Church has yet decided by resolution for a moratorium.

It is pointed out that the responsible executives of the Churches in Africa, such as bishops and moderators, continue to request funds and to seek to recruit personnel in the West. It is often noted that individual African leaders who take a part in the moratorium discussion are themselves in their denominational relationships actually requesting funds and personnel. All the societies in the West have vacancy lists, to which attention is drawn when the subject of moratorium is brought up.

Another reaction is to draw attention to the fact that moratorium is a general concept, an all-embracing proposal, so wide that it will by its nature stimulate adverse feelings in the West and probably create divisions between different schools of missionary supporters. As a proposal it is felt to be so much against the trend of thinking in the West that it will be counter-productive to give it wider currency.

One opinion sometimes advanced is that the whole missionary enterprise from the West is so entrenched, so backed by reserves and resources, that it will go on doing what it has been doing whatever debate may be raging around it. There is great inertia in the lower echelons which are not desirous of any change, and so many vested interests higher up, that organizations and individuals will continue because sociologically there is no force able to stop them. That is to say that as human institutions they have a life and survival factor which defends them against pressures for fundamental change. Appointed officers are naturally defenders and strengtheners of their institutions, and as they are in office for only a few years they cannot readily entertain proposals for fundamental change. Their deepest instinct is to preserve what they have received and pass it on intact.

There are two responses which are more positive: the first is to accept the principle as worthy of study, to be ready to listen patiently, to seek to understand what is behind the fact of the issue now arising, and to be prepared to share in consultations at any level to pursue the matter further. The second is to advocate a practical rather than a theoretical response, namely that headway will be made with the proposal if it is dealt with unilaterally between the old missionary society and the young church which has grown out of its labours: any ecumenical discussion of the matter is therefore unnecessary.

Some quotations from missionary leaders help illustrate western attitudes. The Revd Paul Hopkins of the United Presbyterian Church writes:

> We have to take Moratorium seriously . . . we need to find out what the Spirit is saying to us. The root problem is the western Church's domination overseas. We, within our structures, are the problem . . . we have to act with integrity, let our sister churches overseas know that we have heard their cry for change. . . . Our integrity is almost gone in Africa and ESP is seen as another guise to keep our same structures. Africans really do not trust us. They know that mission policies related to recruitment, appointment, etc. are made by denominational boards, and impinge on sister churches.[4]

Dr Isaac Bivens of the United Methodist Church USA said at the WCC Geneva Consultation in January 1975:

> There is a vantage point of black Americans. We have read of the generosity of white Americans in foreign aid and mission. But we have wondered why such beneficence is directed to other shores by them, as they denied us justice, liberty, and the ballot.
>
> At Boston in 1970, the Black Methodists for Church Renewal called upon our board of missions to withdraw all of its missionaries from overseas. . . . Indeed, the call for Moratorium is not new. . . . It is a timely call for a new birth. It is not a call to restructure, but to begin again.

The Revd Mervyn M. Temple, for many years a missionary and government employee in Zambia, finally withdrew in 1974 and in withdrawing said:

> I have come to share the view that we have now reached the stage in world mission when priority must be given to the local church to become God's instrument of mission. . . . That statement (that the Holy Spirit can be trusted, and that the local church is ready for mission) is made most effectively at this time and this place in Africa, by the withdrawal of the western missionary from service in the United Church of Zambia.

Dr Colin Morris has said:

> Because I believe in the Holy Catholic Church, I cannot believe in the missionary moratorium. . . . Let us humbly acknowledge that it is our historical infidelities and insensitivities which have been a major

factor in the present demand for a moratorium on missionaries and money. . . . It is of the esse of the Church that it should overleap confessional and geographical boundaries, driven outwards by the gospel, to share its spiritual riches with others, and receive spiritual renewal in return. I fear for the catholicity of the Church if the moratorium concept gains ground. I would plead that the slow but sure consciousness of our interdependence as Christians should not be deadened by the domestication of the Church in whatever place it is set.[5]

The Church of Scotland in the 1975 report *Signs of Hope* declares:

The Overseas Council sympathizes deeply with the longings of John Gatu to help his Church in Kenya to maturity. The working out of the process is not easy. The Churches in Africa speak often with two voices. The Overseas Council must be sensitive to know how to respond. This varies greatly from Church to Church and none has in fact put a moratorium into effect. The list of staff requested from the Church of Scotland is long, its vacancies urgent. All Churches want to be independent; when they ask for help, the need is real.

Early in 1975 Dr Isaac Bivens made a further statement on the subject of the moratorium:

Some are already tired of the debate. Others are frustrated, angered, or frightened by it. The first response that most would consider is the cessation of sending money and missionaries. The initial response reveals more about us than it does about the meaning of the moratorium. Are our funds and our missionaries the *essence* of mission involvement and commitment?

He goes on to suggest that our concern for people and money implies

a preoccupation with aspects of mission which deal with our capabilities, expectations, and fulfilment, to the exclusion of the same concern for the need for self-reliance, self-direction, and the prerogatives of the peoples and churches that we seek to serve.

There have been some responses from the Churches in Africa since the third Assembly of the AACC. In December 1974 the Executive of the Synod of the United Church in Zambia passed a resolution which included the statements:

We shall continue to work together with our missionary colleagues, but we shall see to it that their number is steadily reduced. . . . The UCZ should do everything possible to achieve financial independence, but if sending societies wish to help unconditionally with appeals for capital projects, we shall welcome this with appreciation.

The Ivory Coast Synod of the Methodist Church in 1975 'affirmed the unity and universality of the Church, without wishing to break its ties with any of its African partners'.

Representatives of the Christian Councils in East Africa met together in 1975 to consider this and other common concerns. They preferred not to use the word moratorium and decided to reject some assumptions surrounding the word, choosing rather to concentrate on 'self-reliance' for the Churches.

The Executive Secretary for Development of the Evangelical Churches and Missions of Cameroon, Mr Aaron Tolen, has commented:

> That changes are called for is obvious to everyone. The fact remains that our preaching, our biblical interpretation, our ways of organizing the Church, our decision-making procedures, our specialist staff, our finances, our mandate, our ideas of development, all continue to be dependent, and this is quite unacceptable.[6]

The General Secretary of the AACC, Canon Burgess Carr, has criticized the way in which mission boards in Europe and North America have immediately pressed the Churches in Africa to supply their official reaction to the Lusaka declaration on moratorium. From an African perspective it looked as if fears had been aroused in the northern hemisphere; the responses suggested that a sensitive nerve had been touched.

Canon Carr commented on some of the reactions. He reminded those who affirm that the moratorium is a denial of the catholicity of the Church that the New Testament knows nothing of 'a breed of Christians labelled "missionaries". It is the manifestation of the presence of Jesus through the work of the Holy Spirit which authenticates a Christian community as part and parcel of the One, Holy, Catholic and Apostolic Church.'[7] He goes on to ask whether the absence of foreign missionaries in the Churches of Europe and North America during recent centuries has invalidated their claim to catholicity: Does this condition for catholicity only apply to the churches in Africa?

Furthermore, he asserts that the criticism that the moratorium is asking for the domestication of the Church, or its isolation, is specious:

> Moratorium does not involve a break in fellowship; the Lusaka declaration specifically said so, and clearly sought for a share in the world community of Christians. Isolation is known in the denominational isolationism of the western Churches in, for example, Anglicanism or Methodism. The Churches of Africa have no intention of cutting themselves off from fellow Christians in the world, but they no longer want the link to be the traditional western missionary.
>
> So we would plead for understanding, patience, and enabling support from our fellow Christians, throughout the world, during this critical but crucial period. Leave us alone for a while, so that we may be able to discover ourselves, and you, in Jesus Christ.

This plea was reiterated by the Revd Desmond Tutu, Bishop of Lesotho, and one of the most experienced theologians in southern Africa. 'In the midst of all our difficulties, we are trying to know Jesus Christ, please leave us alone for a while.'

The concept of moratorium has arisen in Africa at this time because the issue of the presence of the western missionary in the Church in Africa is a crucial question for the Church's life. It is not surprising that the question is raised across the continent within a decade of colonies and dependencies' achieving independence. After the immense growth in foreign missionary personnel in the last thirty years it was almost inevitable that the matter would be taken up. Instead of avoiding the question and pushing it politely off the agenda, Christians in the West should respond with alacrity to this new evidence of the Church's increased maturity. The response of the missionary bodies in Britain has said a great deal more about the limitations within which they think and work and the attachment of the Churches to traditional forms of mission, than it has about the needs of the Churches in Africa or about future forms of world mission. It will be of great interest to see what attitudes are articulated at the fourth Assembly of the All Africa Conference of Churches.

7

The Problem in the West

John Gatu said at Milwaukee:

> The imperialistic attitude of the West, that you have something to share with your fellow man, must also be challenged in this context. For we know only too well that behind such good and sentimental sayings there is a cruel sense of the wish to continue the past images and a therapeutic satisfaction for those who do not wish to face the challenge of mission in their own countries and at their own doorsteps.

An African theologian speaking at the Bangkok Conference said: 'We refuse to be merely the raw materials by which other people achieve their own salvation.' Opposition to the idea of moratorium on the grounds that it will lead to the domestication of the Church again suggests a too subjective approach to Christian mission. It is not an activity intended primarily to benefit those who send, or the missionaries themselves.

The missionary problem is indeed one for Africa, with an inherited pattern of dependence and a Church across the continent which is visibly undergirded at every point by Europeans. The situation is a testimony to its dependency rather than its catholicity.

It is in equal degree a problem for the Churches of the North Atlantic. It is not really a long-standing problem, for the real increase in numbers of European missionaries in Africa came after 1880. In the long span of human history, or indeed of church history, this period is very short indeed. For a hundred years there has been a growing commitment to the sending of people to Africa, so that the thousands in the nineteenth century have become the tens of thousands in the twentieth. The attachment of Christians in the West to sending large numbers of people to the Third World as an expression of mission is the real problem. Missionary groups may isolate themselves and operate as in a vacuum, but they are inevitably part of a much larger problem and contribute to it.

To raise questions about the present is not to negate or to invalidate the past. If we look back to one or two moments in Africa's missionary period we can force ourselves to decide whether we judge the workers right or wrong. When Livingstone stood in the Senate House at Cambridge in 1857 he said: 'I beg to direct your attention to Africa. I know that in a few years I shall be cut off in that country . . . do you carry out the work which I have begun.' He was speaking of his own missionary employment in Africa and encouraging others to do the same work. His life and activities, and the work of those who followed him, were evidence of the guidance and power of the Holy Spirit. The missionaries were crossing frontiers, planting the Church and healing the sick, and expressing with unchallengeable clarity the continuing mission of Jesus Christ. We must surely judge that those who supported them and those who volunteered to follow, culturally-conditioned and frail as they were, acted in genuine Christian love and obedience.

A second example may be taken from an earlier period; and because inadequate description has been given of the historic work of Moravian Missions, it is fitting to make amends by referring again to George Schmidt.

At Herrnhut in Germany in 1736 Count Zinzendorf and the community there were alive to the needs of people in the West Indies, Greenland, and Europe. Here was a Christian community involved in the life of the world. A letter was received from two Dutch pastors who in travelling to India had broken their journey at the Cape of Good Hope. The Dutch settlement there was less than a hundred years old. They found the poor Hottentots and Bushmen being treated as animals. 'To hunt them down, like so many jackals, was deemed no crime. To enslave them was akin to conferring a favour. But the slaves were not taught the religion of their masters.'[1]

George Schmidt was a young man of twenty-six living in Herrnhut. In agreement with Count Zinzendorf, within a week he had moved to Holland to learn Dutch. Later he reached the Cape on 9 July 1737 and settled among the Hottentots. He lived at Baviaanskloof, where he gathered together a school of fifty and after six years had a congregation of forty-seven Hottentots, most of them well-trained, being treated as persons, and gaining elementary education. He was sent back to Holland and the authorities refused him permission to return to South Africa.

Such incidents could be reproduced a thousand times from the last two centuries in Africa. Such men and women acted, in their belief, under the compulsion of God's Spirit. We recall their sincerity and deep commitment to others of the human race whom they had come to regard in the light of Christ's teaching. Some may be less than generous in speaking about them, but there are few who would deny the integrity of these individuals and the rightness of their actions. If there is criticism it is in respect of the limitations they had to suffer and the side-effects of their otherwise well-intentioned work. They were right to do what they did, and they have indubitably provided noble examples to succeeding generations. They were not personally to blame that slavery lay behind them and colonialism lay ahead. As Christians they were acting courageously with the support of the Church, and they were surely true to the New Testament commission to the Church to go out into the world to share the knowledge and experience of Jesus Christ. There are but a few who would hold the opinion that they acted wrongly, either morally or religiously.

Those who ask for a profound reappraisal of the present missionary pattern are not betraying the past. They are not dishonouring earlier colleagues, but rather with unstinted esteem for what has happened are ready to concentrate on the future rather than dwell in the past. A moratorium does not mean necessarily that one passes an adverse judgement on those things which are brought to a halt. To stop the sending of European missionaries in a particular period to a limited region does not mean that one is denying the rightness of those who have been thus engaged in the past.

People have difficulty in taking a cool look at the missionary question, because of emotional associations and a natural sadness when old institutions which appeared so good begin to change and perhaps disappear. The pattern must change radically, but we are reluctant to let go what was so exciting and romantic. We Christians in the West need to look at the whole missionary question with objectivity, without the false feeling that we are dishonouring fellow workers in the past. We need to look to our forefathers with immense respect, yet to know firmly that their estimable operations should not be repeated. We must not allow an attachment to the past to prevent us from facing unpalatable issues.

It might perhaps be easier for Protestants to see the situation with greater objectivity if they were to contemplate a Roman Catholic order. Nothing could be more heroic and dramatic than the exploits of the members of the Society of Jesus, the Jesuits, who followed Francis Xavier on that long journey around Africa, across to Goa, and on to Macao. From the second half of the sixteenth century until the order was suppressed by the pope at the end of the eighteenth, they struggled to bring the Christian gospel to the Chinese civilization. They eventually penetrated most of the provinces and established a Christian community of about 200,000 people. The Jesuits were faithful to a particular vow of obedience to the pope, in addition to vows of poverty, chastity, and obedience within the order. Thus they were sent to the Congo, to Abyssinia, and to China. The number of Jesuits is almost the same now as the total expatriate missionary presence in Africa. The order itself has been passing through a period of reappraisal and self-examination. Neither unquestioned obedience to the pope nor an army of shock troops to engage in battle anywhere in the world seems necessarily appropriate to the modern world. To rethink what it means to be a member of the Society of Jesus in the modern world is not to belittle the passion and devotion of Francis Xavier.[2] A reappraisal therefore of the modern missionary movement does not imply that others were wrong in either their missionary service or their support. Even the most radical critic has respect for the extraordinary dedication and service of men and women who under God made Christianity a world religion during the last two centuries.

Those of us who have been involved for decades in the outreach of the Church to distant places know enough about the generosity and kindness of Christian men and women to treat the issue with the utmost respect. We know all too well of the generous lay businessman, the faithful and humble missionary collector, and all the heritage of giving and service. Those who show signs of contempt for the stalwarts of the past, men and women, can surely receive little sympathetic attention.

The 'foreign missionary' concept in western Churches now distorts the fundamental commitment to Christian mission which belongs to the Christian faith: Attention has earlier been drawn to the perspectives of missionary education and propaganda which create a false image and warp the understanding of the hearer. The missionary magazines of the western Churches are usually irrelevant to the actual life of the Churches they depict. Their specialist character betrays the deeper division. Overseas Christians usually find the material sufficiently 'slanted' as to be embarrassing. For example, photographs may show women and children undertaking physical labour which is unthinkable in the societies of the West. A picture of a woman carrying a heavy load of firewood on her back looks quite medieval; but it is taken out of context. Within the rural community from which she comes, with the other members of the family, it may indeed be a rigorous and rustic life but it may not necessarily be the serfdom which the picture suggests.

One feature of most missionary education is the prominence which is given to the activities of the white missionary. The white nurse is caring for black children, the teacher is standing in front of the class or leading a group in an activity. The presentation of the prominent role of the expatriate missionary at work overseas suggests to the Christian here, who reads and observes, that Christian mission is something done by expatriates overseas. It may indeed be so in part, but its pre-eminence in public presentation creates the false impression that world mission is a European operation. It has been for a brief period in the recent past, but it is not now and must not be in the future.

The sending of missionaries overseas has become such a large-scale feature of church life in the West in the last 100 years that it is often out of balance. By its very nature, the sending of missionaries by a Church is something which involves profoundly the person sent out, but the majority of supporters can have only a secondary role. Their missionary commitment becomes expressed through interest in and support for those who have gone out from their midst. Is it not true that the western Church will maintain its interest and support for the overseas Church so long as there are missionaries serving in it, but not if there is no missionary link? The missionary society is often presented with the situation that it must seek to protect the position of the missionary in an overseas Church, for only thus can support be engendered in the home congregation. Most missionary societies know that their *raison d'être* and their support would disappear if they could not demonstrate that they actually supported missionaries overseas. It is not too much to say that the distortion of mission to which the West has become adjusted is that it will participate in world mission if it can send missionaries, but not if it cannot. Generally the societies will not support to any extent the work of ecumenical bodies, either regionally or internationally, because there is no direct link, particularly through a missionary connection. If they can place an expatriate in the organization then they will find financial support. This is, of course, in direct contrast to the mode of operation of aid agencies such as Christian Aid which send resources in finance and practical gifts, but sustain expatriate individuals overseas only if they are recruited and supervised by an overseas Church or ecumenical body. It is clearly possible to maintain a positive relationship with Christian institutions in the Third World, and to achieve a high level of support and commitment here, without any close attachment to people. Few Christian Aid supporters know the names of or have ever met the technicians who are serving for brief periods in the developing countries.

An ordinary member of a congregation in the Churches of the West prays and gives out of a real desire 'to support the missionaries'. This is a concept which has grown up in the last 150 years and has taken particular hold in the Roman Catholic Church. As part of a larger whole, with a wider understanding of mission, this might be commendable. So often it has become the main element in participation in Christ's mission to the world, and by its simplicity inoculates so many from a more vigorous and searching involvement in God's Kingdom in the world. Leaders in Christian education have been responsible for allowing missionary education to operate in isolation from teaching about full participation in mission. Missionary orders and missionary societies have not on the whole moved far from the nineteenth-century ideas of world mission and continue to demonstrate a very limited commitment to concepts of mission other than support for overseas missionaries.

The last 200 years of missionary preaching, teaching, and experience have had their effect on the thinking of many Christians in the West. Any share in evangelism is a commitment to that activity in remote parts of the world and it is participated in vicariously. It has been all too easy to express one's enthusiasm for Christian service by drumming up support for missionary activities. In some Churches children are trained in Christian discipleship by collecting money regularly to maintain a cadre of missionaries overseas. Christian mission, for many, means supporting missionary societies or missionary funds in the Church. On the face of it these activities are of value, but only if they are within the context of a larger and deeper involvement in the Kingdom of God and the life of the world. We have erred in taking many aspects of Christian concern and Christian ethics to excess and pressing them immoderately. An obvious example might be the incredible multiplicity of buildings as places of worship in Britain: these have called for immense resources but they are a tribute to zeal rather than wisdom. The time has come for a profound reappraisal; for example, we should re-examine the tradition of engaging young people in weekly fundraising for overseas missions as a practical and educative programme for the young themselves.

Foreign church visitors to Britain often comment on the lethargy and ennui of the typical Christian congregation in Britain. There is an air of weariness after 200 years of world mission. Church meetings and assemblies lack vigour or inspiration. Local leadership so often appears to be wanting in energy and initiative. Dr Daniel T. Niles used to say that the churches here had all the marks of churches which had been giving but not receiving. From one point of view the mental attitude of Christians seems to be conditioned to the role of being champions of world mission, as if from a rich and abundant experience there were a surplus to give to the churches in the Third World. That position seems to be less and less tenable as time goes by. The continuation of the tradition of giving and sending on the old scale enhances the myth of large resources of wisdom, spirituality, and experience. It is perhaps a disservice to the Church to whip up a sense of vitality by impressing upon the Church that this is a God-given mission, when the pattern so gloriously blessed in the past is perhaps not the divine will in the present. The error is frequently made of identifying God's mission in Christ with the particular organization of missionary bodies at a certain time. If the question were posed to ordinary missionary supporters, so generous and faithful, 'What is the Christian's commitment to the world?', how sure are we that the average answer would approximate to the obligations of a disciple in the twentieth century? One can feel fairly sure that 'the Saints', meeting in Henry Thornton's house on Battersea Rise, were right, but much less sure that we have got it right today. We have no difficulty with Mary Slessor of Calabar or John White of Mashonaland, but what is required of this generation?

Christians in the West have been so conditioned by responding to the challenges of the expanding world in the last 100 years that they have weakened in their total mission to their own societies. It is not necessary here to dwell on the difficulties of the Churches in western cultures, for they are the subject of much study and extensive literature. The Christian faith is having to find itself in the midst of secularization. Nevertheless it is important to draw attention to the irony of the situation. Mission to the world of nations only has integrity if it is coexistent with a similar resolution and application to the society at one's doorstep. The Churches have been declining as institutions in the West yet expanding with great vigour in Africa and Latin America. Church growth by itself is a questionable criterion. It is of more importance that the relevance of church life, and the Faith itself, seems far greater in the young Churches than it does in the sending countries. There it has a strong position, whereas here it seems increasingly to have only a diminishing place, and the future looks more uncertain than it has done for 200 years.

Generalizations can of course be misleading, and there are many exceptions to place alongside the general rule. It can, however, be confidently affirmed that the work and witness of the Christian community, as it is experienced by the majority of Christians, is far more relevant in the societies of Latin America, the Caribbean, and Africa, than it is in the societies of Europe. The mission of the Church has far more of a cutting edge in the former than in the latter. This may be attributable to the Churches' freedom from old traditions, to their present experience of numerical growth, or to their more obvious involvement in the life of the community and the nation. Whatever its cause, it is not surprising that the leaders of the Churches overseas look askance at the apparent priority given to maintenance of the traditional missionary commitment and not to the spiritual and moral needs of the older societies. Mission itself, in its various forms, enjoys more respect in the younger nations than it now does in the nations of the West. In the great modern cities of Africa you are as much in a Christian community as you are in the cities of Europe, even if that is not saying a great deal.

Mission in the western world may be more demanding in the present intellectual climate, and in a technological age. There may be more reason for the Church to lose its nerve, as so often it has appeared to do. But the challenge could be just as stimulating and invigorating as the physical and cultural challenges of other continents. There are some who would say that foreign mission provides an escape from the inherent difficulties of proclaiming, living, and comprehending the faith in the adverse conditions of the old nations. This appears to be so, when large commitments are made to the former while dire human issues here seem to elicit little response.

The critical observer from overseas might point to a number of obvious examples. One of the primary failures of our generation has been the inability of Christians in the West to sustain the movement towards Christian unity. The energy and enthusiasm of countless Christians have been weakened by the fruitless, long-drawn-out attempts to unite at least some of the Churches in common fellowship and Christian mission. It is difficult to commend a faith with such blatant failures. There have been some successful union movements in the younger Churches and in some cases the opportunity for union has been frustrated by the adverse pressure of supporting Churches in the West. Attention was drawn to this at the 1975 Faith and Order meeting of the WCC in Ghana. Some church leaders appear to be under the misapprehension that Christians can be nurtured, or indeed can survive, on a diet of continuous but abortive church union discussions.

We cannot avoid the direct charge made against the Churches in Europe that we are pouring a great deal of energy and resources into traditional overseas work, and far too little into the issues which confront us here. There are many occasions overseas when we are reminded of that place in Europe which has provided more missionaries for Africa than any other area of comparable size. The disruption and conflict in Ireland in recent years, and the inability of Christian people and Churches to make a decisive impact on the barbarism, must rank high in the list of subjects which neutralize the endeavour of Christians in world mission. It is not easy to find a rationale for several thousand Roman Catholic and Protestant workers in Africa at the present time, with chronic conflict and irreconcilable hostility at home. The preponderance of the Churches in Ireland's national life and the exemplary ratio of church attendances do not by themselves warrant a massive involvement in world Christian mission.

A particular example of the apparent inability of Christians in the West to see that overseas mission lacks both credibility and integrity unless it is shown to be supported by a vigorous application of the gospel to domestic society can be seen in the response of the Churches and missionary bodies to exposures of some British commercial practices abroad. A gospel of reconciliation means love, righteousness, and justice. The knowledge that British standards of living and pensions were sustained by exceedingly unfair practices overseas, through less-than-subsistence wages, squalid accommodation, and exploitative and repressive conditions, came as something of a shock to the British people, albeit a temporary one. For five years, until the time of writing, the matter has been examined and written about, and substantiated by many expert inquiries. The response of the Churches and societies has been minimal. The Roman Catholic response has been glaringly ineffectual. An air of comparative indifference pervades Christian assemblies and offices. It does not seem to be unreasonable for an African intellectual to adopt the position that Christian mission connives at unjust commercial exploitation.

A similar point is made by the Christian in the Third World, for so long the recipient of guidance and leadership from Churches in the West, when he contemplates the reception of immigrant minorities in Britain and other European countries. A widespread failure is acknowledged, and it has become increasingly apparent that the experience has revealed not only the existence of deep racial prejudice but also its rapid growth. Human compassionate feelings can be entertained for remote peoples so long as these peoples do not appear in our midst. It has been a traumatic experience for many individuals, and for whole communities. 'You have been sending the Christian gospel to us for so long! We thought that you were Christian societies! Is there not much work for you to do here?'

The engagement of Christians in the West with their own societies has been weakened by a combination of causes. An extraordinary proportion of their encouragement and inspiration seems to come to them from outside their national life. The orientation of Christian response seems to be out of alignment. An engagement in evangelism, in intellectual debate, in an intense struggle for a fair and human social order, in a wrestling for the human rights of others – these elements seem to be inadequately represented in our community. If it is looked at from the perspective of the Caribbean or of Africa, it certainly appears in this light. This point would be recognized, for example, if one made an examination of the programmes and publications of the Church Leaders Conference, 'A Crisis of Faith', which was held at Selly Oak in 1973.

Christian discipleship expects and anticipates a response of obedience, of giving and service. This is frequently abrogated by a sharing in mission overseas, which is not only an indirect involvement but can be a usurping of the challenge of the gospel. Not infrequently one meets the Christian of a younger generation in Europe who has been splendidly fired with an ideal of high Christian service, but it is linked almost entirely with the thought of working in Africa or the forests of Latin America. Young Christians in the Churches of the Third World do not have this opportunity and the Churches gain in virility.

That is not to say that those who are zealous for the spread of the gospel in the world are negligent of their local responsibility. The opposite is often the case. The situations in which it is true to say that the world aspect drives out the particular aspect vary for individuals and for institutions. For many Catholic and Protestant members, mission and giving mean contribution to those representative workers who are at work overseas. Christians have been so conditioned to feeling themselves to be the centre of the Christian world, the base from which ambassadors are sent, that support for that expanding activity is naturally thought to be the essence of mission. Too often the training of young Christians in mission and service means inculcating them with an obligation to people far away, but without any corresponding responsibility in Christ for people near at hand. Christian mission has become foreign mission. Western Christians have often become prone to the old Chinese concept of regarding themselves as 'the Middle Kingdom', surrounded by a world of the partially civilized.

The error, and it is an error of degree, is even more apparent in organizations. When it primarily concerns money, in organizations such as Oxfam and Christian Aid, it is of less importance, because there is essentially an imbalance between the affluent world and the remainder which needs to be redressed. Departments of the Church concerned with overseas mission and the societies demonstrate by their mode of life the comparative weight which is put into mission work overseas, compared with the church bodies dedicated to mission in the home country. In many Churches the missionary bodies have been able to attract the most able individuals and have been supported with immense financial resources. The 'home mission' element has been a Cinderella, both economically and intellectually, to the well-furbished sister 'foreign mission'.

As it is possible to recall the sacrificial work of men and women in the past, and to honour it unstintingly, without at the same time feeling that it needs to be repeated now, so it is possible to respect the generous impulse and the right response of others in earlier generations without feeling that the contemporary need is for a similar allocation of resources. The universal and the particular have to be in a relationship. In those astonishing years of the modern missionary movement, when Europe and the Anglo-Saxon world awoke in the excitement of the dawn to see a new world opening before them, it undoubtedly was right to give and work with open generosity, to act with courage on the basis of a limited experience, yet to give with confidence and proclaim with assurance. The missionaries endured the accusation that they went to the ends of the earth when there was in the sprawling industrial towns of mid-nineteenth-century Britain enough poverty, destitution, and inequality to absorb all their energies. For them, the 'time' had come, and it must be seized. If one now hears the African theologian and church leader's voice aright, he is saying, 'We are grateful to you beyond measure, "for our very souls", but the time has changed; look now to the deteriorating societies about you, partly caused by your over-generosity in the past; you can best serve us by engaging in vigorous mission in the economically and militarily powerful nations in the West. Let us, together, take up as equals a universal responsibility.' This is the exciting, new, and expanding sense of global mission which is being missed in an attachment to the patterns of the past.

The missionary question in our generation is a problem because we have inherited a large institution from the past which is partly in decline, and which does not seem to fit, in its old shape, into the contemporary scene. Problems are created in the younger Churches which have been brought into being in the last century. The real missionary problem is, in large measure, a problem for the western world.

The several hundred missionary bodies in the Atlantic community, including Catholic orders, have had as the core of their being the sending of men and women across the seas to other lands. Institutions have grown up which have enshrined all the heroic effort which went into those activities. The new situation threatens the existence and the traditional activities of those bodies. In the new predicament, with the sense of being threatened, the typical missionary society says after reflection: 'We believe that people will always be needed; we shall go on sending people overseas.' It has the virtues of perseverance, dedication, and fidelity, but fails to look at the size of the problem or to examine the deeper issues of Christian mission. The past is seldom an adequate norm. The reason for defending the pattern becomes, at this point in the argument, less theological. Ronald K. Orchard has written in an unpublished paper, 'A New Centre of Gravity':

Our missionary organizations and their traditional forms of activity are threatened. But there is nothing sacrosanct about them: they are instruments of the mission of Jesus Christ or they are nothing. To assume that they are the only ways God will ever use to continue the mission of Jesus Christ among men is to identify the instrument with the purpose which it serves, which is a form of idolatry. So we are not called to maintain our organizations as such at all costs, but rather to ask what we can learn in present circumstances about the ways in which God wants the mission of Jesus Christ to be carried on tomorrow.

The missionary societies and similar bodies are human institutions, and manifest the characteristics of institutions. They are highly resistant to change. When ideas are put forward which include a threat to the style and hierarchy of the institution, the resistance is automatic.

Organizations usually inherit a structure which may from time to time be restructured, but the organization itself remains basically the same. The aura around the institution is a group of ideas, ideals, and traditions which have grown up during the last 200 years. Those holding responsibility and executive power do so for a few years and naturally seek to maintain and enhance the role in that limited period.

In 1970 Donald Schon delivered the BBC Reith Lectures, analysing the nature of institutions. He said:

> Organizations are dynamically conservative: that is to say that they fight like mad to remain the same. This is such a pervasive characteristic of social systems, that it may be used in effect to define what a social system is; namely, a social entity which has the property of preserving its integrity and boundaries in spite of too many internal and external threats to both. . . . We discover the depths and complexity of organizational resistance to change when we seek to change it. . . . Organizations resist change with an energy that is roughly proportional to the radicalness of the change that is threatened.[3]

It is an irony of church history that the western mission boards and organizations came into existence in large part to follow through the freeing of Africa from slavery. After the incredible accomplishment of the enormous task of bringing the Christian Church into the whole of Africa's life, the western Churches are now imprisoned in missionary organizations. Western Christians have become enslaved to a form of Christian mission, conditioned by two centuries of teaching, so that in reality they need to be set free. The missionary organizations are imprisoned within the natural systems of human institutions, resisting change. The responsible officers feel that their mass of supporters are so linked to old ideas that they are inhibited from fundamental change. In turn the ordinary Christian looks from outside at the institutions and intuitively feels from a well of natural wisdom that the circumstances which called them into being have radically changed; but knowing human nature he does not expect any major alterations.

Unfortunately the structures, as much as theological explanations, affect people's thinking. The organizations remain, and people's thinking remains about the same in spite of educational programmes. Is it possible to affect the attitudes of Christians in the West to their role in the universal mission of Jesus Christ, so long as they have before their consciousness the institutions which have served in the last period? The missionary institutions are not really able to influence greatly the attitudes of western Christians. Until the Second World War, the thousands of missionaries who journeyed across the world usually did so by ship. Passenger liners and cargo ships took them to East Africa and the Caribbean, and anywhere where the Church was at work. Every voyage had a fair percentage of Roman Catholic and Protestant missionaries, usually travelling at reduced fares. The system has changed, and the old pattern has almost entirely gone. The great air networks of the nations enable ecumenical workers, executives, and missionaries to move easily from one continent to another. Is a similarly radical change necessary in the old pattern of western missionary societies and overseas church departments carrying the responsibility for world mission? Organizations in North America and Europe, raising funds and finding people to carry on Christ's mission in the rest of the world, are a replica of a splendid past but a replica which will not hold for tomorrow. Evolutionary changes will be welcomed by the societies, but only insofar as they do not threaten the nature and being of the society itself. The energy which is expended in institutions on restructuring, and in resisting various threats to change, could much better be spent in seeking to discover what the needs of the future are and in finding the instrumentality to meet them. If the example of the very early days of the modern missionary movement is a guide, the response to William Carey's question, to the problem of the destitute blacks, and to the newly discovered responsibility towards Africa, was found not in well-organized institutions but by groups meeting in The Castle and Falcon or in Clapham, and by individuals pursuing their insights with courage and pertinacity. Such a slender beginning reminds us that the weight of responsibility for Christ's mission in the world does not rest on the strength and unchangeability of our institutions. We need to understand God's mission to the world in Christ as his undertaking, in which we and our organizations may or may not be necessary. That mission is so often reduced by our small minds and established institutions to the concept of individuals going from our communities to other countries, usually in the Third World. While this is allowed by our adherence to traditions, we shall not break out into a larger participation in God's great and global redemptive work.

Some Christians and organizations in the Atlantic community limit their interpretation of God's mission to church growth. If the one criterion of Christian mission is the numerical growth of congregations and church members, then almost any form of Christian mission will be acceptable. If people are satisfied so long as the numbers increase, then there need be little discussion about the nature of mission. Is it not necessary to inquire about the quality of life and the nature of its witness as well as the fact that a congregation actually exists? The numerical growth of people who believe in Jesus Christ is obviously important but it is an oversimplification to speak as if this is what Christian mission actually is. This is too narrow an interpretation. *Church growth* can become a rationalization for maintaining the western missionary's predominance in world mission.

An excessive concentration on church growth seems to be out of harmony with the New Testament understanding of Christian mission, which includes a number of elements. There is, for example, the synoptic emphasis on the Kingdom of God, and the mission of the disciples in proclamation and service. There is the aspect of ethical love, for example in Romans 12. There are too the soteriological, sacramental, and ecclesiastical aspects of Christianity. Some forms of Christian mission have found in the New Testament a more human emphasis, as exemplified by the Roman Catholic mission to China in earlier generations. To limit Christian mission to terms of 'gospel-proclaiming, church-multiplying missionaries' is to depart from the fullness of the New Testament, yet this describes a large section of world mission today.

Donald McGavran, Senior Professor of Mission and Church Growth in the Fuller Theological Seminary, California has pressed the claims of a worldwide programme of church growth which places the whole emphasis on planting the Church. Missionaries from many countries are encouraged to go in ever-growing numbers to as many countries as possible, to establish 10,000 new congregations.

> As the divine life flows into ten thousand new cells of Christ's body, especially if good outcomes are consciously sought, all sorts of good outcomes may confidently be expected. Missionaries are sent to establish cells of reborn men and women. . . . The key consideration is not that missionaries work in harmony with existing churches – though that desirable end will often be achieved. The key consideration is that Christ be proclaimed to those who have not known him and that new cells of living Christians be established across all frontiers. As soon as possible there should be a church in each community in all the world. . . . This is the great goal to which missionary effort is directed.[4]

Is 'fast-growing' church growth the clue to world mission? Is it the criterion for Christian mission in the twentieth century? Are the mass-production technique and a pseudo-scientific methodology applicable to Christ's mission? The emphases of 'fast-growing church growth' seem to be so pronounced that the depth of the experience and the quality of the growth appear to receive little attention. Production graphs are all-important and scant effort seems to go into the nature of the message. We may perhaps ask whether a church at the end of every street throughout the world is an adequate interpretation of the ultimate purpose of creation and redemption.

The July *Church Growth Bulletin* of the Institute of Church Growth reported at the International Congress on World Evangelization held at Lausanne in 1974. 3,700 people were present by invitation from 150 countries, 'to seek ways by which the whole world could be confronted with the gospel of Jesus Christ by AD 2000'.

The report has a phrenetic element:

Outstanding characteristics of this Congress emerged as participants worked through ten meeting-packed days. First came commitment to biblically sound solutions to the challenges and problems that face churches in reaching the nearly three billion who are presently without Jesus Christ. From the outset, it was apparent that any proposals offered for world evangelization would be tested against the inspired authoritative Bible – the infallible rule of faith and practice.

A mark of the Congress was the widespread influence of 'church growth thinking' among leaders and participants. . . . In his key-note address Billy Graham sounded many strains familiar to church growth missiologists. Among other things, he commended the School of World Mission at Fuller for its work in compiling the 'unreached peoples survey' and affirmed the 'mosaic of peoples' understanding of the world's population.

A most direct presentation of church growth principles was made by Dr Ralph Winter in his brilliant plenary session paper on the priority of E-3 (cross-cultural) evangelism. He proved that 87 per cent of the 2·7 billion unevangelized can be reached only by E-2 and E-3 evangelism.

Some Latin American speakers made clear their concern over what they considered unwarranted domination by North American wealth and technological methods. They called repeatedly for a greater commitment on the part of evangelical leaders to social justice and 'development'. The Bangkok call for a moratorium on missionaries was rejected. Lausanne called for multiplied sendings of the right kind of missionaries from all churches in six continents . . . an eloquent black minister from the United States wanted evangelicals to send a million missionaries!

Lausanne was a tremendous awakening to global needs. Vast opportunities gripped the imagination. Faith was stirred. . . . The world may well test the significance of this great Congress on Evangelization by the spread of the gospel and the church growth which results from the Lausanne Experience. . . . Dr Harold Snyder of Brazil issued a call to establish hundreds of thousands of Christian cells and churches throughout the world.

Dr Donald McGavran calls for 'missionaries by the hundred thousand', with the aim of establishing in the shortest possible time 2,700,000 new congregations, so that all mankind will hear the gospel (November 1974).

He argues that a new age in missions has begun. The cutting down of western missionaries in the old-established Churches might have been right. However, as the new and ever-expanding wave of missionaries is

continually planting new clusters of congregations in which missionaries have to be the planters and nurturers for some years, tension between national leaders not only exists but will continue.

Today's challenge is to devise new slogans, new priorities, and new principles which excite the Church of Jesus Christ to surge forward on ten thousand fronts sending apostles, sending preachers, sending missionaries across cultural, linguistic, and economic barriers to evangelize any segments of society which the existing churches in any land are not reaching and cannot reach.

In 1965 I was inaugurated as the founding dean of the School of World Mission at Fuller Theological Seminary and called for 100,000 missionaries. I considerably underestimated the need.

The church growth view of world mission, with its exuberance and urgency, is taking increasing hold in North America and by publicity and salesmanship is becoming the nurture of many evangelical Christians elsewhere. In selecting a narrow band on the spectrum, of a limited traditional missionary evangelism with uncertain biblical foundations, there is the obvious danger of repeating and multiplying the weaknesses of the modern missionary movement. There is here the vision of an intensive evangelistic coverage of the world, either by the end of the century, or in order that with the achievement of universal evangelization the Second Coming will be realized. To this main aim an inordinate expansion of tens of thousands of missionaries is called for, travelling in different directions, covering the six continents, and undertaking simple conservative-style evangelism to establish congregation growth.

What is the western world with its high degree of freedom of action going to do to world mission? The 200-year period we know from history, but what is going to follow? The vision of hundreds of thousands of missionaries, perhaps concentrated in the Third World, must fill the sapient person with apprehension. As the wealth lies in the western countries, the possibility of engaging in such a growing enterprise will largely be a privilege of westerners. Is such a dream mission run wild, or is it a logical development from the New Testament? Increasing western wealth could wreak havoc in the world Church.

It can well be argued that church growth and traditional evangelism, interpreted in such narrow ways, is an inadequate approach to the large question of working with God in his mission in the world. The divine pattern of salvation seems to be much more than this. The judgement of history is that over-concentration on individual evangelism does not in fact bring the power of the gospel into the whole of life. Church life based largely on personal evangelism has its limitations, for energy, experience, and commitment are restricted to that facet alone. Such a mission to the world is more retrograde and limited than the previous great missionary periods in the world. Superficial numerical growth as a consequence of high-pressure evangelistic campaigns or church growth techniques must seem to many mature and intelligent Christians an unsatisfactory and fractionary presentation of the biblical message.

The Church is in the world to continue, by the presence of the Holy Spirit, the work of Jesus Christ. It is his Body for his mission. Church growth is an inadequate expression of that mission. Evangelism and the message of salvation cannot be pursued as in a vacuum, unrelated to the local and international environment. The incarnation brings the Word into the life of the world.

There are other aspects which need examination, such as the basic assumption of a particular, literal interpretation of the role of Scripture. There is a paternalistic approach which ignores the importance of the established younger Churches. A strong position is also taken by the commercial element of publicizing certain types of literature. But perhaps the strongest criticism is that the mission of Jesus Christ is one of unity, reconciliation, and love, whereas the methods and aims of the church growth movement are likely to bring less harmony and unity in the Body of Christ.

Once again it is the western response which is creating the missionary problem. A disturbing factor is that the sections in the western Churches which could be described as conservative–evangelical are increasingly drawing their concepts on world mission from the limited world of church growth missiology. The missionary beginning of 200 years ago knew its commitment in greater depth. Third-World Churches need to find, as they are doing, their own understanding of the responsibility of world mission in the light of their new understanding of the gospel. It does not require the wealth and technology of the West to organize and direct the missionary activity of the younger Churches. How can they fulfil their task and grow if they are surrounded by large numbers of unattached western missionaries?

> The School of World Mission at Pasadena is offering courses specially designed to enable founders of new missionary societies [in the Third World] to enter upon their important ministry with the information they need to have.
>
> You are sending missionaries out to propagate the gospel, rather than as fraternal delegates to already established churches, or as men whose primary duty is to champion the oppressed of other lands, or teach them how to grow more food, or to introduce more just political systems (*Church Growth Bulletin*, March 1975).

The Christians of Africa and the Churches of Africa need to have the opportunity to continue their experience of the gospel in their own lives, to find their own responsibilities in mission, and to discover their own resources under the guidance and power of the Holy Spirit. Witness for Christ in Africa will come increasingly from African Christian traditions built up in the experience of being Christians in Africa. The authentication of the gospel in Africa will not come from aggressive power-backed invasion from outside. Western Christians must resist the temptation to organize and direct as if the task were primarily theirs. The propagation of extravagant and frenzied missionary activities in the wealthy and powerful western world, directed not primarily to their own societies but to the less developed parts of the world, is inherently inappropriate. In Africa, as in most of the Third World, the coming of Christianity has been part of an aggressive invasion from the West.

African Christianity needs to be dissociated from its historic past in the colonial period; an expansion of the expatriate missionary enterprise would obstruct this essential development. The Christian faith has the chance, perhaps a slim one, of bringing a unified religion to Africa which is above all what Africa seeks. The divisive consequences of an enlarged foreign missionary encounter could be disastrous.

One could go even further than the application solely to Africa and indeed ask whether, in the perplexing modern world with all its tensions and uncertainties, this is the way to present Christianity to mankind. The Christian religion is not in an unassailable position in the world. With an increasing pace of change the world is moving amid great dangers towards a closely knit global society, sharing increasingly a common form of social life. The full biblical message, in all its range and depth and sensitivity to the age, will be necessary to meet the coming generation.

8

Christian Mission and Africa

One of the fundamental changes which has taken place in the last thirty years has been that whereas it could formerly be said that responsibility for Christian mission in Africa belonged in Europe, it is no longer so. That responsibility could hitherto be pressed upon the consciences of Christians in Europe. It produced generous responses and a sense of strength and resourceful superiority. Responsibility for mission in Africa now does not belong in Britain, Rome, or Pasadena. Christians of Africa are numerous, growing, experienced, and ably led. The major responsibility is theirs. Perhaps it should have been at an earlier date. They must now bear the mission; they must be faithful to it; and they must marshal the resources, both spiritual and material, to the ongoing task.

The need of mankind everywhere is for the religion of Jesus. The varied panaceas of the western world, in its ideologies, agnosticism, and new fashionable religions, have nothing very substantial or convincing to offer modern man. In Africa the resurgence of traditional religion, the imported secularization of the West, or the religions of Asia, have nothing comparable to offer to the religion of Jesus. Its form, content, and theology will be evolved between African people and their experience of Jesus Christ. It will not be the same as medieval or modern Christianity in Europe, the conservative evangelicalism of North America, the varied pattern of British Anglicanism, Nonconformity or Presbyterianism, or any other form of western Christianity. It will not be in isolation from them, for Africa clearly cherishes its relationships with Christians in other continents and consciously draws on their experiences. An example of what African Christianity may mean has been shown in the growth of independent Churches, or of the Kimbanguist Church in Zaire. Nevertheless, these Churches have developed in response to certain socio-political conditions which are changing, and they may manifest a different aspect of church life in the future.

Christian mission in Africa is first and foremost a concern for African Christians. We must be on our guard against those who for a variety of reasons want to circumvent that affirmation. The traditionalists tend to universalize mission with twentieth-century techniques, like a multi-national corporation which will override unwelcome restrictions. The modernists tend to evade the issues by creating new-style international and regional organizations, to find new forms which perpetuate western pre-eminence. The most difficult exercise of all for western Christians with their historic background and cultural ethos is to be humble, retiring, and patiently understanding. In some ways the academic achieves greater success in this aspect of human relations than does the Christian missionary.

It is not our task to indicate the shape of Christian mission in Africa. We may learn from the experience of the last 200 years. We may also find it of immense importance to grapple with the experience of African Christians as we try ourselves to understand the evolving nature and application of Christian mission in the world. If the Holy Spirit is patently at work in African Christians, as evidenced by their developing maturity and the relevance of their life and work, then there may be a great deal for us to learn and to experience. Many young people from Britain and elsewhere have been to work among Christians in Africa and have returned home invigorated by the experience. Many western Christians have lived and worked in African churches and communities and have rediscovered the vitality and pertinence of the faith.

Christian mission sums up the total impact of the life and message of Jesus, and the God-given task of the Church in the world. It therefore cannot be identified with personal evangelism. Neither can it be so inclusive that it encompasses the whole of the Christian religion and humanitarian concerns. There are aspects of Christianity which are not directly related to Christian mission, such as contemplation, study, and care of the Church of God, although they may be indirectly related. Unlike some phrases 'Christian mission' has not become so debased or equivocal that it can no longer be used. It is important to maintain and defend the term so that it continues to signify the whole redemptive and re-creative work of God through Jesus Christ. Thus it expresses the heart of biblical religion and the very core of the faith.

One of the most valuable publications on the subject in recent years has been Johannes Blauw's *The Missionary Nature of the Church*. Dr Blauw begins from the premise that we are at the end of an era; churches have come into existence through missionary enterprise, and now we are faced with the question of what is our task in the light of the Bible. He recognizes that the modern missionary movement began from a variety of motives and says that, looking back, we now sense the need for a clearer biblical foundation or 'a conception of missionary work that is as closely as possible related to what the Bible tells us'.[1]

Blauw first examines the Old Testament, pointing out that there is a great deal about God's creation of the nations and his dealing with them, but far less than has been supposed of direct missionary commitment. The 'universal' element is that which is applicable to the whole world; the 'missionary' is related to actually being sent. In the beginning God deals with the nations, who reject him and are dispersed in disobedience. Then through Abraham the nation of Israel is called into being, so that 'in you all the families of the earth will be blessed' (Gen. 12.3). God's dealings with Israel are for the purpose of new relationships with the nations, to bring them in peace and unity to the Kingdom of God. Israel is not chosen for its quality but to serve a special purpose. The people of God have a universal role (Exod. 19.6).

In the Old Testament God's dealing is primarily with Israel, but the world of other nations who do not know God comes into view. Through Israel these nations can share in the salvation of God. 'God punishes Israel for her infidelity and uses the nations as His instrument' (op. cit., p. 26). The psalm of the nations (Ps. 67) is quite specific: 'May God be gracious to us [Israel] and bless us and make his face to shine upon us, that thy way may be known upon earth, thy saving power among all nations.' The restoration of Israel from exile is that the world may know.

Blauw examines the only two passages in the Old Testament which can be considered as having the missionary concept of 'being sent', that is, Isaiah 40–55 and the Book of Jonah. 'Never in the whole period of the Old Testament was there any deliberate missionary activity' (op. cit., p. 34). In the former passage Israel by its existence is called to be a light to the nations, and to bring them justice. Scholars do not support the interpretation of Jonah as a missionary intention; if there is reference in the Old Testament to a missionary purpose, it is something which belongs to the future. In the present Israel's task is to be what God wants it to be and to be ready to be used by God in his time. Isaiah 42 is perhaps the only passage in the whole of the Old Testament which expresses the idea of mission as 'going out to the nations' (op. cit., p. 39).

Bengt Sundkler has drawn attention to the concept in the Old Testament of Israel and Jerusalem as centres to which the people of the nations would come. Blauw comments that 'the thought of mission in the centripetal sense occurs with great frequency both in the prophets and in the Psalms . . . the coming of the nations as a response to God's acts in Israel' (op. cit., p. 40).

The expectation of a Messiah has clear reference to the nations as well as Israel, but in the Isaiah passages there is no idea of the Messiah going out to the nations. God's salvation will be seen in him, and the nations will be his reward; the Messiah's role is that of suffering rather than proclamation.

In Matthew 23.15 Jesus refers to the zeal of the Jews: 'You traverse sea and land to make a single proselyte.' After the exile, and between the Testaments, the Jews had established a new pattern of missionary activity. In the Roman Mediterranean area there were over 4 million Jews. A large-scale and important missionary pattern had been established before the beginning of Christianity. Diaspora Judaism had greater vitality and spirituality than the legalism of Palestinian Judaism. It was a religion with greater moral depth and substance than the religions with which it came into contact.

The missionary activity of the Jews developed out of political circumstances, namely their sojourn in exile, their experience of living in other nations, and their return to their native land.

The New Testament missionary pattern was a development from the already existing Jewish missionary activity. Nevertheless 'the New Testament brings us something totally new which is quite lacking in the Old Testament: the mission of proclamation to the nations' (op. cit., p. 66). Jesus himself restricted his mission to the Jews (Matt. 10.5—6.24), yet in the parables and in some of his actions he clearly is thinking of light and salvation for the nations. The Kingdom of God is not for Israel, although it is a fulfilment of Old Testament prophecies, but it is for all mankind. Jesus points forward towards a new mission with a universal character. He is the Sower scattering the seed, one who is to suffer and to die, and in due time, after the resurrection and Pentecost, the harvest will begin to appear. 'Unless a grain of wheat falls into the earth and dies, it remains alone; but if it dies, it bears much fruit' (John 12.24). A new age has dawned in which these historic happenings have to be told to the nations. The apostles are not the missionaries but those authorized to bear witness to the facts; after the resurrection they are charged with the responsibility of witness to the nations. On the apostolic foundation is built the Church of Jesus Christ (Eph. 2.20), witnessing and testifying as the people of God to these events and to the power of his resurrection. Blauw writes:

Nowhere in the New Testament is the Church made the equivalent of the Kingdom of God, but neither is the one set in opposition to the other. The Church is the community gathered around Christ. . . . She is not herself the Kingdom, but she is its manifestation and its form . . . a sign of the new future which has broken in for the world . . . an expectation of the Kingdom of God, but only insofar as she receives the eschatological expectation of the fullness of the Kingdom (op. cit., p. 79).

Mission comes into view when this hope for the world takes the form of acts of proclamation on behalf of Christ (op. cit., p. 80).

The new age has begun in which the world may see and experience the salvation of God, and in which the Lordship of Christ is proclaimed among the nations. 'Mission is the summons of the Lordship of Christ' (op. cit., p. 84). Now for the first time is given the commission to go out and make disciples of all nations, with the promise: 'I am with you always.' But the commission is not simply to proclaim and to make disciples but to teach 'all that I have commanded you', and to establish the Lordship of Christ over all life until the final consummation which is the goal of Christ's work.

'The enduring presence of Christ in and through the Holy Spirit is to enable the disciples now in their turn to carry out the commission to preach the gospel to all nations.' The point of departure for world mission is the congregation in Jerusalem, and from it to the world. In Paul and his mission to the Gentiles the young Church experiences the astonishing reality of the new age; the Christian community of Jew and Gentile replaces the old Israel as the instrument of God's salvation of the world. 'The closed world of nations that God has allowed to walk in their own ways is now confronted with the great salvation which calls on all people everywhere to repent' (Acts 14.16; 17.30; op. cit., p. 101).

In the new age which has dawned, mission is involved in the actualization of Christ's dominion of the world. The Church and the concept of the Kingdom of God are not to be identified. The call to mission is both geographical, 'to the ends of the earth', and universal to those near or far who do not know Jesus Christ. The universality of the Christian message is the important feature. There is nothing of special significance about places at 'the ends of the earth', and indeed the phrase has no meaning geographically when we are considering a world Church. It is a subjective viewpoint from the place where you happen to be. The gospel for the whole inhabited earth is the essential notion.

The Church in its essential missionary nature is concerned with the *ecumene*, the whole world of peoples, and not simply with its own locality. As a consequence of what Blauw refers to as the 'Vasco da Gama period . . . during the last three centuries' the name of Christ was declared among the nations, and the vast community of Churches in the world was brought into being. Frontiers have been crossed, but that is not of primary importance, for they can be temporary, political, and insignificant. The essential point is the proclamation of Christ in a universal dimension. This is the work of God and no cause for boasting in the West. The Church throughout the world sees and knows Christ in a new way.

> The proclamation of the gospel must therefore make progress even if the pattern of present-day mission work be completely forgotten. It is gradually becoming clear that the pattern which has been followed up to now (one-way traffic in missions, spiritual and financial dependence of the younger Churches, and the like) is old, obsolete, and thus about to disappear (cf. Whitby, Willingen, Ghana). The sooner we are ready to follow the God of history, the more clearly will He show us the image of future missionary activity of His whole people over the whole earth (op. cit., p. 114).

The missionary nature of the Church has been made abundantly clear. Every congregation must know itself to be part of the universal mission. Christians need to participate in the mission to the world. 'The Church is a missionary Church or it is no Church . . . there is no other Church than the Church sent into the world, and there is no other mission than that of the Church of Christ' (op. cit. pp. 120–21). Missionary societies have fulfilled a vital role in restoring the essential element of universal mission to the sometime static Churches, but in our new understanding that mission belongs essentially to the Church and not to particular groups or missionary societies. The Churches of the world *together* have the task clearly upon them of *together* continuing the mission of Christ.

The root of God's mission to the world, as we understand it, is in the biblical experience. As the community of Jesus Christ, the Church has a nature which is essentially missionary. Men's experience of God differs from age to age. The conditions in each generation vary. What then is the nature of Christian mission at the end of the twentieth century? In the search for understanding we have to be true to the biblical revelation, to the experience of history, and to the insights of our contemporary conscience.

It may be said that there are five irreducible elements in our understanding of Christian mission. They avoid on the one hand the extremism of including the whole of the Christian faith and humanitarianism, and on the other the narrowness of restricting mission to an ecclesiastical framework. Some would limit it to evangelism, but it is much larger than that. Others would stress the danger of too broad an interpretation, in order to make it unduly restrictive.

The five essential aspects, which must be equally included if we are to be true to missionary experience, are:

1 setting forth in word and deed the historical events which manifest to the world in Jesus Christ the presence and the love of God;

2 confidently offering to men and women a new life in the experience of forgiveness and love, through the power of his Holy Spirit;

3 strengthening, invigorating, and caring for the Church of God in its worship and witness;

4 service and healing to all mankind, especially to those who are deprived, impoverished, and oppressed;

5 working with God for righteousness, justice, love, and freedom for all people both individually and corporately.

At the end of St Matthew's Gospel and in the first words of the Acts of the Apostles there are two phrases which we need to remember. The great commission (Matt. 28.19) includes the words 'teaching them to observe all that I have commanded you'; and Luke says (Acts 1.1) 'all that Jesus began to do and teach'. We are referred back to the fullness of Jesus' actions and teaching. Our comprehension of mission must be rooted and grounded in the life and work of Jesus of Nazareth. If the most important events in human history are those surrounding the life, death, and resurrection of Jesus then his witness in the gospels must be the basis for Christian mission. The Jesus whom we follow and in whom we have faith must be one with the Jesus of the synoptic gospels.

The report of the World Conference on Salvation Today (Bangkok 1973) has this to say on the mission of God:

In the power of the Spirit Christ is sent from God, the Father, into this divided world, 'to preach the gospel to the poor, to heal the broken-hearted, to preach deliverance to the captives and recovering of sight to the blind, to set at liberty the oppressed, and to proclaim the year of God's favour' (Luke 4.18). Through Christ men and women are liberated and empowered with all their energies and possibilities to participate in his messianic work. Through his death on the cross and his resurrection from the dead, hope of salvation becomes realistic and reality hopeful. He liberates from the prison of guilt. He takes the inevitability out of history. In him the Kingdom of God and of free people is at hand. Faith in Christ releases in man creative freedom for the salvation of the world. He who separates himself from the mission of God separates himself from salvation (p. 88).

We seek a Church which is the catalyst of God's saving work in the world, a Church which is not merely the refuge of the saved but a community serving the world in the love of Christ (p. 89).

In our contemporary understanding of Christian mission we have behind us 200 years of work and witness in Africa, a microcosm of the world missionary movement. We have also the wider context of the experience of Churches in Europe and the rest of the world. These aspects must rightly be set alongside the basic biblical understanding of God's work in history for the salvation of mankind. There are new perspectives which come into view from the total experience of the Christian community.

Whereas in previous periods it was possible to think of certain areas in the world having a responsibility for mission in other regions, it is no longer so. There is now no geographical area of the world Church which can *give* for another to receive. The churches of the six continents have come together and they can all *give*, both to one another and to the whole mission to the world. No one area can rightly feel that it is in a special position to give. If one geographical group of churches acts as if it has a priority in giving, it is truncating and impoverishing the other parts of the body. To do so is to offend against the nature of the Church. We have to come to terms with the new reality of many churches in other continents and a meeting of them together under ecumenical councils such as the WCC.

If one considers, for example, the churches in Africa south of the Zambezi, they are both numerous and strong and have behind them a long period of evangelism and service. A large-scale deployment of missionaries from North America or Europe in that area is depriving the churches of their responsibility and limiting their mature growth in Christian responsibility. They may, chiefly from established tradition, express the need for many expatriate missionaries, but it would be inimical to the true well-being of the Church. There is no longer a reason for western mission boards to send large numbers of expatriates to southern Africa, although in mutual sharing of the varied tasks there will be adequate reasons for a limited number of workers from other countries to share their mission on a reciprocal basis.[2]

One of the outstanding developments of this century has been the growth of Christian councils on a national basis, and of regional councils of churches. In most countries in Africa there is a council of churches which provides a forum for consultation and a means of joint action in various forms of mission. Not invariably but frequently the council is the initiator of new applications of the gospel to aspects of social and national life. Africa is witnessing the extraordinary growth of great cities hitherto unknown. Understanding the problems of urban life and directing attention to its peculiar needs, setting up programmes of service and witness, have been typical functions for a council of churches. Special resources can often be brought together through the freedom of action which a council enjoys, different from the more rigid and traditional organization of the established Churches. A similar flexibility has enabled the councils to respond in the newly independent states to challenges of nation building. There are immediate needs in agricultural development, community development, and special education for the handicapped which are beyond the resources of a denomination but which can be responded to by an alert council of churches. At the same time, a council can relate to government and its ministries in a more satisfactory way than the several score of missions and denominations can possibly do.

A particular example might be the way in which members of the National Council of Churches in Kenya did the necessary research on the growing problem of unemployed teenagers and produced a carefully thought-out programme of 'village polytechnics'. In co-operation with the Churches the council initiated experiments, provided international funds, and set the Churches moving in a new direction of service. Later it saw the scheme taken up by government departments.

The ecumenical work of councils is not usually supported by missionary societies. Some Churches, especially with a strong overseas orientation, have kept apart from all their co-operative work. It is unfortunate that only in some cases have the Roman Catholic and

Protestant Churches joined wholeheartedly in all the aspects of Christian council work. Nevertheless here is a dimension of Christian witness in which an ecumenical and international team can work together under African leadership in the wholeness of Christian mission. If one of the tasks of the Church is to so demonstrate by word and deed the caring and liberating power of the gospel, in order that men may believe, then here is a very relevant aspect of Christian mission in the life of Africa. So often through fear or traditionalism the Churches have held back from co-operation, often under the leadership of expatriate missionaries. Those Churches which stand aloof, or criticize the councils most strongly, are invariably those which contribute least to their effectiveness.

A larger dimension in which the Church is becoming relevant to the life of Africa, and in which a new understanding of mission is being discovered, is in the growth in this generation of the All Africa Conference of Churches. Starting at Kampala in April 1963 the AACC has developed through its consultations and assemblies so that it has now created a new sense of the identity of Christians in the whole continent. An African Christianity is becoming visible through the meeting of many Christian leaders having a sense of their own ethos and effectiveness in the whole continent. From the phenomenal growth, out of such slender historical beginnings, the experience of a continental assembly is miraculous in its occasions of worship and its confident relevance to the new emerging Africa. It provides an awareness of belonging to a world fellowship of Christian Churches and awakens Christians to the immense tasks lying before them. An AACC assembly, or its committees, can see from a different perspective than its member Churches. It can speak to the contemporary issues of refugees, national conflict, and reconciliation, to the particular problems of race and oppression in Africa. The mission of the Church is not altered but it is enlarged as the Christian community becomes increasingly conscious of the broader issues before it. It does not detract from the mission of the local congregation but deepens it and sets it in a larger context. Inevitably a congregation of peasant farmers or new industrial workers in Botswana cannot now be acutely aware of the existence, influence, and relevance of the AACC, and it is unimaginative to suggest that it is to be expected. It is equally certain that the true growth and maturity of any Christian congregation is towards knowing itself to be part of the people of God in the world and increasingly to share in local and universal mission.

The third Assembly of the All Africa Conference of Churches met at

Lusaka in May 1974. The report of the Assembly, *The Struggle Continues*, gives an indication of the leading concerns and attitudes of the Churches in Africa at this time. The agenda of the Assembly had arisen from discussions within the Churches, and some of its major topics were: Evangelism and Selfhood of the Church in Africa; The Church and Cultural Renewal in Africa; The Prophetic and Serving Church; Church Union or Church Co-operation. The Church is an entity in Africa, seeking to live for Christ and to be engaged in his service. It seeks to be more fully involved in evangelism and service: 'that the whole church should regard evangelization as the total witness, in word and deed, to the whole life of persons and communities, leading to liberation and fullness of life' (p. 34).

One of the fundamental experiences of mission in Africa has been the inseparable nature of evangelism and service. It is misleading to give priority to either. The ministry of Jesus was unequivocally that of speaking about God and doing the work of God as the servant of all. The experience of the Church in Africa has been that, in serving, the Church is setting forth the love of God in Jesus Christ. Phrases such as 'you have nothing to do but save souls', or 'the primary task of the Church is to increase the number of those who believe in Jesus Christ', or 'the missionary work of the Church is to preach the gospel' are unhelpful and misleading. The gospel and the ministry of Jesus are larger than these narrow definitions. Fortunately the Church in Africa has not suffered nearly as much as in the West from a fatal division between speaking about the Good News of what has happened to the world in Jesus Christ, and striving for social righteousness.

The work of Christianity has been authenticated in Africa because on the whole it has maintained the essential unity of preaching and service. Where neither has been subordinated to the other, the wholeness of mission has been sustained and the Church has become strong. Across the continent of Africa the Christian faith has become established as the preaching and worshipping congregation, and a community committed to service to people. The nature of the modern missionary movement in Africa has from the beginning been a transparent commitment to the inseparable aspects of preaching and service. This has become even more marked in this generation than in the earlier period. The growth of the Ecumenical Movement at a period in history when the world has become more productive and affluent has enabled resources of wealth and trained people to be at the disposal of the Churches. It is on a scale which was simply not possible in earlier periods of church history. The

Church in our time is marked by an unparalleled range of involvement in service to the community. The traditional expressions in education and medicine have been added to and in many instances replaced by newer forms of service to the million refugees in Africa, to the handicapped and the deprived, and to the countless groups of people who suffer from the effects of urbanization, industrialization, conflict, and political oppression. The growth of population and the impact of western-style civilization have increased rather than diminished the volume of human need. One of the great facts of our time in Christian mission has been the utilization of world resources by Christian agencies in a service of love to innumerable communities. We have witnessed the Holy Spirit at work in the life of the Christian community.[3]

A particular example may be taken from the work of the Leprosy Mission. The work in Africa supports over forty centres or departments associated with hospitals. Out of approximately £1 million spent annually by the Leprosy Mission in medical and training work, a large proportion enables care and healing to be given to people in Africa who suffer from leprosy. A notable illustration is the All Africa Leprosy and Rehabilitation Training Centre (ALERT) in Addis Ababa. 'The main function of ALERT is to serve as a teaching/training centre for the whole of Africa — a wide range of courses for leprosy workers is operated . . . doctors, nurses, physiotherapists, orthopaedic appliance makers, field and control officers . . . some 250 altogether' (Annual Report, *A Year of Grace*, 1974).

Christian mission in Africa can now only be thought of in terms which include inseparably the witness to the love of God by word and deed. This huge task can only be conceived and undertaken now by the Churches working together, and not by separatist groups who want to work in isolation. Service, not simply to the Christian community but to all people irrespective of their position or creed, is now clearly an inseparable part of the total mission of the Church. Witness in the world to the love of God as made known in Jesus Christ is by the spoken word and by the acts of compassion and service.

Christian mission has often been spoken of in terms of crossing frontiers. The picture is conjured up of people actually going across national boundaries and passing customs and immigration officials. The frontiers that have to be crossed are often those within society, into a new area of Christian involvement. The Church's mission in Africa has brought a new dimension in the struggle for human rights and the liberation of people from oppressive conditions. This is not new, as we have seen from earlier examples of the missionary championing the cause of exploited and oppressed groups of people. It has come to be seen as a much more vital part of the witness of the Church for the whole community. This is one aspect of twentieth-century conditions and insights leading away from a more church-centred mission as understood in the past. The Church finds itself with an inescapable role to play in the defence of human rights and the liberation of people from harsh and oppressive economic and political conditions. In some countries where almost all human rights have been denied, the Church has found itself in the position of being the last defender as other institutions have been suppressed.

The White Fathers in Mozambique did not undertake their mission there with the intention of becoming heavily engaged politically. Their purpose was to build up an African Church in the shortest possible time so that it could be responsible for witness and service in the country. The social and political conditions became so oppressive under Portuguese rule that the order decided in 1971 that its only possible witness to the gospel was to withdraw publicly and thus bear testimony to the rights of people which were denied.

In 1973 Roman Catholic priests, both within and without, courageously drew the world's attention to army atrocities in a number of places in Mozambique, causing political repercussions in the country and in Portugal. The public debate which ensued was in part the cause of a shift in national sentiment which brought about the Portugal upheaval in April 1974 and independence for Mozambique. The White Fathers and the Catholic priests were instrumental, in their obedience to the gospel, in effecting political change. Such change does not automatically produce a guarantee of the establishment of full human rights, but a step is made away from tyranny towards a volatile condition in which the opportunity begins to exist for freedom and human development.

Where human rights are wholly denied by an all-powerful state or a tyrannical leader, it is at times not possible for the Church to do other than suffer, sometimes for a long period; but the suffering is to preserve people's hopes for a day of deliverance. The worship and prayer of congregations may be at times their only expression of hope; one hears on occasion deeper longings expressed movingly in some spontaneous outburst of song. Sometimes courageous individuals alone can give expression to the yearnings for liberation. 'Let my people go' can be the only utterance of faith and love. But where there is the opportunity of giving expression to the people's desire for redress and righteousness, the Church has a role which belongs to its nature as the harbinger of the Kingdom of God. Many Christians in Britain are altogether remote from this experience, and one fears that this is true in southern Africa too.

In the period since 1965 Rhodesia has been living an illegal independence and has experienced a widening gap between the races, emergency conditions of government, and increased racial legislation. The destiny of the nation, both socially and politically, has been in the balance; bitterness, tension, and racial discrimination have increased. The hopes of the people for a real share in their political future have dwindled; and with poignant intensity many individuals have suffered, often at great cost to their families. Inhumanity, discrimination, and oppression have been constant features of the nation's life and have increased with the passage of time. The judgement of most international agencies outside the country would, I think, substantiate this description of a nation's experience over more than a decade which has finally evolved into bitter racial warfare.

Where many people are thus deprived and suffering, the Church in the situation cannot be true to the gospel without making sure that some major part of its organization is constantly bearing the responsibility for witness to righteousness at the national level. To be effective this must be an enunciation of the truth, a courageous witness in action, and a fearless caring for the victims of the oppression, irrespective of race or class.

In those circumstances some Churches and some Christian leaders apparently are able to divorce themselves from the situation and show little or no concern. In the wide fellowship of the Church there are so many responsibilities that there must be differentiation of function. Integrity can, however, only be maintained by Christians and their leaders if they see that some of their number are struggling against inhumanity and if they continue to support them with prayer. The Christian Church will not, one fears, emerge from the colonial period in Rhodesia since 1891 and the aftermath leading to nationhood, with renewed strength, spirit, and vindication. A wide area of its mission has been distressingly weak. Many have apparently found ecclesiastical affairs wholly absorbing.

The Roman Catholic bishops have perforce taken up a task which belonged to the whole Church. An assessment is given by Dieter B.

Scholz S.J. in his essay 'The Catholic Church and the Race Conflict in Rhodesia'.[4] He points out that since 1959 the bishops have commented on political events in more than thirty pastoral letters and statements ('Church and State in Rhodesia 1969–71'). The purpose was to prevent proposed discriminatory legislation or to alter existing laws. By their constant teaching they hoped to influence people's attitudes away from racialism, realizing that suppression had continued hitherto in various forms without public protest. When constitutional proposals were presented in 1969 the bishops said that 'they have clearly been drafted with the deliberate intent of ensuring the permanent domination of one section of the population over the other'. In spite of protests the constitutional proposals were enacted. One of the bishops has died as a result of the conflict and another has been imprisoned and deported.[5]

In 1971 the Commission for Justice and Peace was set up. It has subsequently studied aspects of the national situation; made representations to government; used newspaper publicity; and issued publications the most notable of which has been 'The Man in the Middle', drawing attention to human suffering and pleading for relief. The documentation for the publication includes case studies of the civilian population in the northern part of Rhodesia, pressed on two sides by guerrilla fighters and security forces.

The study concludes that the Roman Catholic Church in Rhodesia has been outstanding in the defence of principles and in making a national stand on political events, but in point of practice the Church is little different from all other Churches in tolerating some social discrimination and racial attitudes which seem to be impervious to change. Nevertheless the Christian contribution in setting up ideals and guidelines, however they may be rejected, is an invaluable service and provides a basis for the nurture of the people's faith and hope. The Commission eventually had to pay a heavy price; the chairman, secretary, and some members were arrested in September 1977.

The experience of the Church in Africa in the twentieth century and the development of attitudes in the Ecumenical Movement, strengthen the understanding that the mission of the Church must include a witness for social and political justice. If we examine again the Gospels and particularly the ministry of John the Baptist and Jesus himself, we read of situations of confrontation and witness with local political leaders – with the Sanhedrin, Herod Antipas, and Pontius Pilate. In his last days our Lord was facing the rulers with their overwhelming power, and his followers in Acts frequently were bearing witness before governors to the truth of God. His love, writes Brian Johanson from South Africa,

> was for the confused broken world, and it was a love which suffered
> in and with and for the world. This love is the basis for the task which
> is given to the Christian community to go with this gospel into all the
> world. The Church will always be ambivalent and indecisive,
> confused and calculating when this fundamental basis in the being of
> God and motivation in the love of God is missing from its
> understanding of its task in the world. Its concern, its passion for
> justice can be sparked only by God's love.[6]

After his initial experience in Africa Bishop Trevor Huddleston wrote: 'If the Church refuses to accept responsibility in the political sphere as well as in the strictly theological sphere, she is guilty of betraying the very foundation of her faith.'[7] The missionary experience of the Church, at this time in Africa, has brought into focus again a fundamental aspect of Christian mission which can apparently be more readily overlooked in the West. Out of the suffering, deprivation, and oppression in Africa has come a renewed understanding of this dimension. This has been reinforced by the experience of the Ecumenical Movement in which representatives from Churches have come together, out of conditions of poverty and exploitation in the Third World, and have shared their understanding of what the love of God must mean.

Dr Philip Potter, in a BBC talk given on the occasion of the twenty-fifth anniversary of the World Council of Churches, said:

> At Bangkok we celebrated personal salvation, and the fact of Christ
> changing our individual lives. We gave equal emphasis to the fact
> which arises from that, namely that Christ demands of us change in
> our social structures, working for the Kingdom of God and his
> justice, working for human dignity, working for social and racial
> justice, and for peace in the world. It is quite inescapable in terms of
> the Christian gospel that we should do this, because this was the
> ministry of Jesus. He never divided his healing and his helping of
> human beings from his proclaiming to them the forgiveness of sins.

A lay theologian, Stephen Travis, has expressed this understanding with authority and clarity. He describes certain expressions of religion to which the gospel is essentially opposed, among them

> . . . religion which is escapist rather than realist. Human religion
> frequently exhibits a strong desire to escape – either to the past, with

its supposed securities, or to the future, with its 'glory for me', or to some inner spiritual experience which cushions men from the harsh world outside. F. D. Maurice suggested: 'We have been dosing our people with religion when what they need is not that but the living God.' Any so-called Christianity which cushions people from the real world rather than enabling them to see it in fresh perspective and serve it with deepened sensitivity is an affront to the gospel. Any religion which purveys 'comfort' to the exclusion of radical discipleship is not the gospel of the Crucified.

. . . religion which divorces spirituality from service. Too much which passes for Christianity is one-sided. Either it is pietistic and inward-looking, or it is so emphatic about social action that it becomes a matter of human effort without a spiritual dimension. Latin American evangelicals such as Padilla and Escobar, and writers like Daniel Berrigan, have argued that prayer and politics, piety and prophecy are essential to each other if the gospel is not to be distorted into religion.[8]

Christian mission in Africa, after its long experience of establishing the Church and making the gospel known, has begun to realize as elsewhere in the world that human rights have their origin in the life and message of Jesus Christ.

A significant event took place in Africa in February 1975 when church leaders met at Khartoum to consider violations of human rights in a continent of newly independent states. The occasion was called under the auspices of the All Africa Conference of Churches and the Commission of the Churches on International Affairs. The representatives became aware, as they shared information, of the many ways in which different peoples were being deprived of fundamental rights. They examined the biblical basis of the Christian faith, beginning with the Old Testament, that God demands that every man and woman must be treated justly, that God hears the groaning of his people in oppression and suffering, and speaks through the prophets in particular historical situations.

The Churches must develop courageous strategies that involve the whole of their individual and corporate lives. It is not enough that only we here and a few others like ourselves should be concerned about the violations of human rights in Africa. It is the whole Church that is called to fulfil Christ's mission of critical, creative, suffering love. It is the whole Church that has been enlisted in God's eschatological fight against the demonic powers of evil and oppression in creation.[9]

There was criticism of the Churches which

emerged from the missionary movement (and) found their *raison d'être* in conversion, and in numerical church growth. We then found ourselves preoccupied with the maintenance of the Church as an institutional entity. We developed an individualistic, pietistic approach to life which contributed to our weakening of the traditional African spirit of community. . . . But the Church must guard against becoming merely a socio-political force in society. . . . God takes sides for righteousness, peace, justice, and love. He stands, therefore, with the poor and oppressed and demands for Christians to be there with Him. He stands against sin, against those who exploit their brothers and sisters. It is our task as Christians, as the Church, therefore, to find our place with God and to serve as He would have us do, those whose rights and human dignity are violated. . . . For the Church in Africa, this implies a return to Jesus Christ, who is the measure of righteousness, and of justice and salvation for the oppressed, those who must suffer the consequences of the sins of others.[10]

As the missionary period in Africa has come to an end, with all its achievements and failures, it is becoming clearer that an African form of Christianity is emerging which will be as valid as an Asian or European form. The western cultural patterns which were inseparable from the missionary invasion are gradually weakening and will be overtaken by the upsurge of African cultures. This can be seen both in the active exploration of African religious roots and in the form of church assemblies and even administration. The emphases which have so far been mentioned indicate the growth of an identifiable African understanding of Christianity. It is also possible to see in the independent Churches a style of Christian life which is at once a rejection of the domination of a western-culture-orientated Christianity and an assertion of a Christianity which is based on African traditions.

If this is a correct analysis there are two important points which follow from it. The first is that it would be inappropriate and inimical to the growth of the Church to thrust a large-scale western missionary presence into the continent at this period of church history. The second is that Christian thinkers in Africa, out of their rich and vital experience, have a contribution to make to the total human experience of God in Jesus Christ. There is no lack of allegiance to the Bible in African Christianity. The immense work of the Bible Societies has made the Bible available in the numerous languages of Africa, so that it is palpably the foundation of the Church's life. Something new out of Africa is coming to the world Church, through the vitality of African life, as Christians with the Bible in their hands experience the power of the gospel in the travail of the continent.

It is in the realm of theology that this will eventually become clear, and it is a point of particular distress that theological training is still to an unacceptable degree in the hands of expatriate missionaries. African theologians need first of all to be trained in Africa and then increasingly to become the trainers. As African theologians are trained they are caught up in church leadership because of the demands for Africanization and the rapid expansion of the Church. Overseas organizations must resist the temptation to send to Africa large numbers of expatriates to train others; rather, they must allow the Church to work through its period of difficulty by increased programmes of preparing African educators.

The emergence of an African Christian experience can be seen more tangibly in the actual situation of Christians in different places. For example, the long agony of Christians under apartheid in South Africa is not something which Christians far removed from the conditions can readily understand. A visitor can perhaps catch a glimpse through sharing in an act of worship, or through entering partially into the experience of an African family, or through the privilege of an intimate conversation. The depth of suffering which lies beneath the Christian experience is greater than one can measure or comprehend.

For many years Mozambique has been comparatively inaccessible to Christians from the West, and African Christians there have been cut off from the fellowship of Churches in the continent. From outside we have dimly understood the perpetual half-light in which Protestants there have lived. In recent days Catholics and Protestants have frequently been harshly treated by governments because of their refusal to co-operate or keep silent. One of the groups which has passed through an experience of profound persecution was the group of thirty-seven Presbyterian preachers and elders who were imprisoned in 1973. The moderator died under ill-treatment and many others were threatened and treated with much inhumanity. That type of experience makes the Church different. To meet and listen to individuals coming out of great tribulation makes one understand the extra dimensions of Christian experience which have influence on the understanding and articulation of the faith. Experience comes first and theology follows. The nature of the total African experience of God, from time immemorial and through the extraordinary events of the last two centuries, is fashioning a distinctive contribution to man's understanding of God's revelation in Jesus Christ. Africa is not making a Christianity of its own but is discovering more clearly areas in the whole revelation in Jesus Christ.

One final aspect of the shape of Christian mission in Africa from its historical experience must briefly be mentioned. The relationship between the Christian faith and other religions is now greatly different from what it was in the main period of the missionary activity. The attitude of many Christians in Britain remains as it was formed by the experience and education of past generations of missionary work. It was an attitude of aggression and hostility against forces which more often than not were described as dark, satanic, and idolatrous. The external world was seen to be in the grip of an undifferentiated world of heathenism. If any note of sympathy or understanding was expressed, the strong claim of the 'uniqueness of Christ' was immediately presented.

An interesting example of the situation has recently arisen in Britain, with the question of people of other faiths using buildings belonging to the Church. Those with overseas missionary experience of living with other religions were generally far more accommodating and liberal than the host Churches in Britain. The former attitude was more positive and the latter more defensive.

It is only in recent decades that Christians have begun to make a concerted effort to give sympathetic understanding to other religions, and with tolerance and respect to be willing to explore together the riches of their experience of God.

Experience of living with the Islamic and other faiths in Africa has created an attitude which is more closely related to the actual conditions of the world yet is entirely true to the gospel. A modern viewpoint has been well expressed by Max Warren in his introduction to J. V. Taylor's *The Primal Vision*:

When we approach the man of another faith than our own it will be in a spirit of expectancy to find how God has been speaking to him and what new understandings of the grace and love of God we may ourselves discover in this encounter. Our first task in approaching another people, another culture, another religion, is to take off our shoes, for the place we are approaching is holy. Else we may find ourselves treading on men's dreams. More serious still, we may forget that God was here before our arrival. We have, then, to ask what is the religious content in the experience of the Muslim, the Hindu, the Buddhist, or whoever he may be. We may, if we have asked humbly and respectfully, still reach the conclusion that our brothers have started from a false premise, and reached a faulty conclusion. But we must not arrive at our judgement from outside their religious situation.[11]

We have, in a word, to be 'present' with them. Here is another area of mission which is awaiting serious attention in the new pluralist societies of Europe. It is perhaps illustrative of our mental condition that we have been for years willing to send grants to Africa and Asia to enable others to thus engage with other religions, but evince little interest in doing the same thing in our society now that other religions have settled in our midst. There are now, however, the first signs that the headquarters of the Churches are beginning to take the new situation seriously. Churches are appointing individuals or committees to undertake this special responsibility, and a full-time appointment for Inter-faith matters has been financed at the British Council of Churches.

The engagement in Africa is being pursued through the Islam in Africa Project, now almost entirely directed by African church leaders. With full-time specialists the Project is trying to know Islam in some depth, to enter increasingly into discussion and common study, and to help all the churches to have one or two members of staff who are taking this subject as their specialization.

In summary, therefore, Christian mission begins in the witness of Jesus Christ, known in the biblical revelation, a testimony to the saving work of God in the world. God has been wonderfully at work in Africa through the lives of people of many nations, and through people and agencies both within and without the organized Churches. The immense experience over many years has deepened the sense of the supreme importance of commitment to Jesus Christ and the healing, saving work of the Christian community in worship and service. It has brought new insights into the relevance and power of the gospel for men's souls and bodies, both individually and corporately. These insights have come particularly in recent years through the experience of African leadership in thought and action. On the one hand there is a deeper awareness of the failures of the past and the present, but on the other hand a greater confidence in the salvation in Jesus Christ, whose mission it is. That mission is a personal relationship with God, but evangelism is only complete if it is within the context of the whole liberating work of God for humanity and the entire creation. The fullest expression of the whole is in the love of God shown in the life, death, and resurrection of Christ. Evangelism is understood, not in the over-exposed individualism of the last century in the West, but in an harmonious relationship with a determined struggle for the Kingdom of God. The Jesus of the Gospels, who speaks about the Kingdom, is the beginning of faith; witness is to the one who described the Spirit of God upon him in very practical terms. Africa fortunately has not on the whole seen the fatal cleavage between those who walk expecting to find the Kingdom and those who describe what God has done in Jesus Christ for man's salvation.

9

Guidelines for the Future

Professor John Mbiti has drawn attention to the feeling which the African Christian has that Christianity is centred in Rome, Athens, Canterbury, Hamburg, and New York.

> The Christian in Africa has still to live with this type of extended allegiance to centres of Christianity which are outside our continent, at precisely the time when he is simultaneously disengaging himself from political distance which has been created by the colonial sense of statehood. In one sense the same Christian has returned to Africa politically, while remaining overseas ecclesiastically. . . . As long as Christians in these mission churches . . . remain tied through this structural link to their counterparts overseas, they will not develop a proper image of themselves and of their part in Christendom.[1]

When Canon Burgess Carr quoted this passage from Professor Mbiti's writing he then went on to make the point that both missionary-sending agencies and many African church leaders are trapped in a cycle of fear. By this he meant, apparently, that the executive officers of a western missionary agency, holding their positions for a few years, can only agree to such modest changes as will leave the institution in a modified form for their successors. They are fearful of radical change during their tenure of office. Similarly, the African church leaders who have taken over leadership of an organization which is locally prestigious from white predecessors are equally resistant to fundamental change. Such threatened changes may come from church union proposals or from ambitious programmes of indigenization; they are fearful that the structure they have inherited may disappear.

The purpose of the church of Jesus Christ is to engage in and continue the mission of Jesus Christ. 'The church in Africa', says John Mbiti, 'has been subjected to so much receiving in mission that it has lost its orientation as a mission-minded body of Christ. We must put this right if we are to carry out the mission of the Church, not only in Africa but also in other parts of the world.'[2]

The end of the missionary period, as it has been understood in the western world, presents us with profound problems of readjustment. There is much to be said for facing these openly, rather than allowing a confused situation to continue, one which does not live up to the past and is uncertain what to do about the future. What is our missionary obligation to the world now and in the future? If, as it has clearly been demonstrated, mission is of the esse of the Church, how can it properly be expressed today by Churches in the Atlantic community? Are we at the end of our participation in world mission, or at the beginning? Missionary societies are slowly retreating from the front of the scene, and national missionary councils in Europe have a diminishing importance. If the nineteenth-century attitude to world mission is not appropriate for the modern Christian, then what attitude is? The past is clearly folding up, but what is to replace it?

Have the Churches of the western world the right to continue the traditional missionary pattern? Is there a divine mandate to warrant sending missionaries to the Third World? Will the Churches in the West suffer irretrievably if they cannot continue to send missionaries across political frontiers – and is that their mission?

The pretension inherent in the view that Western Christians have a God-given vocation to send as many missionaries as possible to the poorer countries and Churches of the world has two aspects.

There is the pretension that the sending Churches can send when they will. The time is chosen by the sender. This period in history is one in which we insist on the right to send. The biblical view is that the time of opportunity is given by God. There is a time to give and a time to withhold. There is no adequate ground for the continuous, uninterrupted sending of many missionaries, without waiting and listening patiently to see what God is saying. It is certainly within our religious experience that the Spirit calls at certain times, and leads through opportunities at certain times and not at others. For the western Christian to say 'we must always send missionaries because it is God's will that missionaries should cross frontiers, as part of the esse of the Church', is to think and act with arrogance, divorced from the biblical pattern.

The second pretension is to assume that Christians must always go out from the Churches to which *we* belong. This means for the Churches of Europe and North America that they can abrogate the right to say that missionaries shall go from them to other nations, notably in the recently decolonized world. The place and direction are surely in the hands of God and are not to be decided by a general principle which we can apply to suit our purposes. Patience, humility, and wise counsel are called for. The voice may have come at Troy to cross into Macedonia and Europe, but the Spirit does not repeat the same thing without variation to all eternity (Acts 16.9). Some people are calling for great numbers of missionaries to travel in all directions; others are insisting on the necessity of sending missionaries for the sake of the gospel and the Church. God's light is shown in different circumstances in a variety of ways. It would seem most appropriate that Christians ought to listen in humility to discover what the next phase of obedience ought to be. It is not wholly clear, and some of the strident claims and fixed positions seem to indicate affirmation and over-confidence rather than patient seeking for the way the Spirit leads. Taking counsel with the Church is one of the obvious paths to follow.

The end of the missionary period might have been expected to occur with the general achievement of political independence, but a great deal more of the earlier-style 'mission work' has continued than was expected twenty-five years ago when political changes began. The achievements of Christianity in Africa have persisted, in a remarkable way, through this drastic change of political independence. Autonomy for Churches has become the point of departure for spectacular growth. The Churches still feel strongly tied to overseas bodies, but they are no longer dominated as in earlier generations. As they are now much freer to examine their own life and problems they have taken issue with the question of the missionary presence by presenting a first reaction in the form of a moratorium discussion.

The first question to which we must now address ourselves, in the light of the extraordinary history of the last 200 years, is that of the expatriate missionary presence in Africa. The second is one intimately connected with it, the issue of the traditional missionary societies in the western world.

It has been shown that the numerical strength of missionaries has increased during the whole missionary period, so that at the time of writing it is probably higher than it has ever been. If there were 10,000 missionaries in Africa at the time of the Edinburgh Conference (1910) there are now three times as many. In the meantime the Church in Africa has come of age and is largely under African leadership. The sense of selfhood is growing, and through its own institutions such as AACC it is wanting to be set free from the vestiges of European tutelage and from the tangible presence of a large number of European and North American missionaries.

The fact that the main missionary period in Africa is over has not reached the minds of most missionary supporters in the western world. There are many who refuse to face it, and far from wanting to adjust their thinking to it, are insisting on the old pattern of sending as many missionaries as possible. If we can think of the Church in Africa as a whole, rather than of the particular pieces to which we may be related, we must also try to think of the missionary question as a whole, and not simply of a particular missionary society. If we believe in the profound importance of the Church and the mission which God has given it, we must think foremost of the well-being of the Church in Africa and not of the interests of our Church in the western world. Are the Churches in the West hindering the real selfhood of the Church in Africa, in its total being and mission, by perpetuating such an extensive missionary presence? Global programmes of evangelization must not be drawn up in isolation from the African Churches with their basic responsibility for mission. If there is to be a regional evangelization programme for the continent of Africa, it should be drawn up by the Churches of Africa and by Christians in Africa.

The initiative and leadership in mission must come first and foremost from the Churches in Africa and from their institutions. Large-scale organizations for sending armies of missionaries from outside Africa should cease. This is now clearly understood in the higher levels of the Churches, but not generally in the body of the Churches or in society.

It should be affirmed unequivocally that the large-scale sending of missionaries to Africa is not in the interest of Christian witness in Africa. The number of missionaries at present is unacceptably high for the true well-being of the Church, for its developing maturity and its effective witness to Christ. We must come to terms with the fact that the historic mission to Africa from the western world, as it has been known, is at an end. It is only as we accept this fact that we can begin to develop mature relationships as Christians in the West with Christians in Africa. To ignore it, and to seek to equivocate and find reasons for maintaining the old pattern, leaves the western Churches in uncertainty and confusion, and increasingly harms our relationships in Christian fellowship. A total of 20,000 or 30,000 expatriate missionaries in Africa is now anomalous and is inimical to the real progress of the gospel. Africa today has roughly the same percentage of Christians (30 per cent) to the rest of its population as in other continents, and is no longer a field for receiving thousands of Christian workers from the Atlantic community who want to engage in world mission. Population growth in

Africa is a challenge to the Churches in Africa and not a reason for the deployment of great numbers of expatriates.

Not unnaturally the past heroism and romanticism which have been so marked in 200 years of missionary history stir thoughtful and zealous Christians to ask themselves if they ought to express Christian missionary obedience by following the established pattern. Our responsibility to the world is a proper question, but we can now only know what that responsibility is if we first of all exorcize the myth of an ongoing western missionary responsibility in the nineteenth-century pattern. Western Christianity will not come to terms with its responsibility in mission to the societies of the West until it has shed the special involvement of leadership in world mission which has characterized the immediate past. Going out in great numerical force to the external world is a novel experience for western Christianity – almost as astonishing and dramatic as the twelfth-century crusades to the Holy Land – but in truth it is only 100 years old. Before 1870 the numbers were much smaller. It has been a remarkable but temporary phenomenon in a mere fraction of time in human history. There may be periods in the future when similar events will occur, according to the purposes of God, but at this juncture the worldwide constellation of dioceses and provinces, and the great organizations of the Church, have the chief responsibility in mission. Christians of the continents are the prime bearers in mission to the continents. Especially for the western world, our social, communal, intellectual, and spiritual needs are so pressing that they must make first claim on our mental and spiritual resources. We can probably best begin by ceasing to use the word 'missionary' and by re-examining the concept.

The cultural element must not be lost sight of, for western Christians are usually thinking of large numbers going to other cultural areas. Would the attitude be different if we were thinking of large numbers of Asian or African Christian missionaries coming to Europe?

As we have seen, the older-established missionary agencies and the Churches have gradually reduced the number of missionaries. It is important that this be accepted and understood and that the process should continue. It should be a cause for satisfaction and indeed of celebration that the resources of the western Churches do not need to be expended in an extensive deployment of evangelists and missionary workers in Africa to establish the Church and to carry the load of *evangelization*. We need to remember that an exceedingly high proportion of expenditure by mission boards is on support for expatriate personnel. It was a calling and privilege which is now almost universally acknowledged in the Churches of Africa and the western world. We can marvel at the faith and devotion which were shown in such abundance and which bore such incredible results. The shortcomings were many, and most of them have been clearly and repeatedly pointed out, but the achievements remain in the life of the Churches, in the spiritual liberation of a host of people, in medicine, in education, and in the very life of young nations. We should take heart and be stirred with gratitude rather than be depressed. The task as it was understood is now over and it is a disservice to the Church of Christ to try to relive and re-establish the continental mission from the western Churches as it once existed. This is now fully understood in many mission bodies in the West and in the minds of most African church leaders. It has yet to be widely accepted in the thinking of great numbers of Christians in the West who have been and still are nurtured with the conception that mission in the world means sending large numbers of missionaries to the Third World. The good has become the enemy of the best.

Canon Douglas Webster quotes an illustration from the life of Florence Allshorn, the famous missionary to Uganda:

> Weeping at the failure of the local missionary community, she was approached by an old African matron who sat at her feet and said: 'I have been on this station for fifteen years and I have seen you come out, all of you saying you have brought to us a Saviour, but I have never seen this situation saved yet.' We need to hear uncomfortable words and warnings such as these, lest we make ourselves ridiculous and bring the gospel into disrepute by speaking of salvation too glibly.[3]

As far as Africa is concerned, the realization exists in many mission boards that there must first of all be *restraint* in the sending of missionaries. There is no virtue in numbers, for they may signify that the Church overseas is living with an excessive expatriate element. They may also mean that the Church is being persuaded by its immediate needs instead of being forced to face up to its own responsibilities. The need for increased staff may be real, but by readily satisfying it the local church is protected from wrestling with its own problem and finding solutions within its spiritual and material resources.

It is not sufficient therefore to report that requests for staff are received from bishops and church leaders. The evidence that mission

boards have long vacancy lists is not by itself an adequate reason for
failing to exercise *restraint*. A comprehensive view must be taken of
responsibility towards the whole Church, and the signs of the times
would suggest that restraint is necessary. The publication of vacancy
lists by missionary societies is not an adequate response to this crucial
question.

It is, I believe, of importance that western agencies should not brush
aside the notion of moratorium which has emerged so forcefully in
Africa. It is being taken seriously by many church leaders and expresses
a deep desire to find a means for the Church to be liberated from its
foreignness and dependence. The spiritual integrity of African church
leaders is involved, for they need to know that their obedience to the
gospel is real and not superficial. If we try to understand the situation
from their perspective, we can easily see that they may feel under
threat if from outside there are powerful and wealthy organizations
pressing their claims to undertake the evangelization of Africa,
irrespective of the experience and the aspirations of the African
Churches. We need to use imagination to enter into the feelings of
African church leaders, as they have the common experience of seeing
American and European church groups and campaigns thrust their
way into African society, often with an ethos which is alien to African
life.

Large numbers of expatriates of a different culture can be
embarrassing and harmful to church leaders in another neighbouring
Church. If a Church can contemplate a moratorium on either personnel
or finance, it can be a sign of its spiritual vitality. It should be welcomed
wholeheartedly, as its request for autonomy may have been, and not
treated as being an affront to the catholicity of the Church. The
Churches of Africa can find their own real catholicity, as they share in
new and different ways with other Christians in the continent and
outside. Why have mission agencies in the West not welcomed a
moratorium if it means a reduction of demands for staff and money?
The most common reason advanced is the need of the home
Church.

In the first year since moratorium was given official backing and
publicity at Lusaka there has been widespread attention in church
assemblies in Africa and the beginning of a growing debate. Of all the
resolutions from the AACC's third Assembly, this has been the one
most widely discussed. Perhaps more than anything else it signifies a
turning-point in the history of the Church in Africa, in that now they are

articulate in their awareness that the missionary period to which they have also become conditioned has come to an end.

The secretaries of the Christian councils in Kenya, Tanzania, Zambia, Malawi, Sudan, and Mozambique met for consultation in June 1974 and appealed to the Churches to put more energy into the struggle for self-sufficiency in finance and manpower. They felt that 'self-reliance' was a better term than the strange word 'moratorium'.

Many synods and church courts have the subject on their agenda. It is too early to say what the outcome will be, but if some Churches accept a policy of a form of moratorium the atmosphere is such that it could quickly develop. It should also be noted that in an ecclesiastical situation in which this subject is a matter of prime debate it would be inappropriate to start a large increase in the expatriate missionary presence. The wider issue of the selfhood of the Church in Africa is one which is constantly under discussion (see the Report on the Selfhood of the Church, Ibadan 1973). Canon Burgess Carr has commented on this current debate in the Churches that 'the Church in Africa can never be itself so long as it depends primarily on money and personnel from outside. The real measure of our capacity to contribute significantly to the humanization of the world is directly dependent upon a rediscovery and a redefining of our identity as African Christians.'[4]

The particular situation of the Roman Catholic Church in Africa is complicated and difficult. Since the Second World War the number of expatriates has grown enormously. Within the total figure of over 20,000 there are 235 expatriate bishops and over 11,000 expatriate priests. These figures betoken a Church which is indeed numerous but heavily under non-African administration and leadership. How can a Church be other than a foreign institution in such conditions? The problem is exacerbated by the fact that the Church is growing so rapidly that it is difficult to give the minimum of religious instruction to adherents and catechumens. The number of African priests and sisters in training is growing rapidly and the number of African bishops shows a constant increase.

In some countries where political events have reduced the expatriate staff, the number of 'vocations' has increased dramatically. An example may be taken from the eastern area of Nigeria, where several hundred expatriate priests were refused permission to return after the civil war. Under Ibo bishops, the number of African seminarians has grown in an unprecedented way.

Roman Catholic bishops with large pastoral and training problems are constantly calling for more expatriate staff, yet in the laity and among the African clergy there is evidence of a strong desire to see more rapid progress towards Africanization. Some of the expatriate leadership, as in Mozambique, has come under heavy and embarrassing criticism. There is clearly no solution within a short time. Nevertheless two things must be obvious: that rapid progress must be made in Africanization if the Church is to lose its foreignness and that the time is past when huge numbers of expatriate priests, brothers, and sisters can be sent, as in the recent past, from the western world. The overall objective and policy must be to achieve in the shortest possible time a Church which is more clearly African. The indications are that the decline in the number of 'vocations' in western countries will in any case hasten the process.

It is clear from statistics given earlier (see chapter 5) that for the non-Roman Churches the increase in expatriate personnel has chiefly been caused by the so-called 'conservative-evangelical' Churches. This increase has primarily come from the United States and from Britain. How far is this a resolute policy and how far is it open to alteration through a recognition that times are changing and that conscious limitation may be the right policy in the circumstances? Evidence suggests that the primary concern is to continue the old pattern and greatly increase the number of missionaries.

Attention has already been given to the 'church growth' school of thought which envisages an ever-expanding army of missionaries, of all nationalities, moving from one continent to another. The World Evangelization International Congress at Lausanne in July 1974 gave indication of some prevailing attitudes and policies. There were 370 people present from Africa, but only a proportion of those were African Christians. All participants were attending by invitation as 'evangelicals': a selective process which is not described in the report.

An undoubted emphasis of the report is that a great numerical increase in missionaries is called for ('missionaries' meaning people who leave one country and go to another); but an equal emphasis is laid on the need for missionaries and missionary societies from all countries and not simply from the West. However, 'it is worth noting that the number of missionaries affiliated with North American evangelical societies has increased by 60 per cent in recent years'.[5]

Our attention here is simply on the issue of the extensive use of expatriate personnel as a method of evangelization. The theme of evangelization is shared by all Christian Churches, although the content which is given to the word will vary in different contexts. The WCC Nairobi Assembly theme of 'Jesus Christ Frees and Unites' could be described as a call for world evangelization. The WCC Commission on World Mission and Evangelism (CWME) has as its objective 'the proclamation of the gospel of Jesus Christ, by word and deed, to the whole world, to the end that all may believe in him and be saved'. One of the differences of emphasis is on whether this task is primarily the responsibility of the local congregation and the Church, or whether it is chiefly to be undertaken by large numbers of full-time 'evangelists' who travel to other countries for this purpose. The first emphasis puts attention on the need for the gospel to be closely related to the culture and conditions of the locality, and the second emphasis raises difficulties, made clearer in the history of the missionary movement, of an extraneous culture being destructive of local culture and creating a Church with a strongly foreign element.

At the Lausanne Congress the main proponent of an increase in missionary numbers was Dr Donald McGavran, who was selected to present policy statements on world mission. He represents the conservative-evangelical position, as commonly understood, that Christians are called to cross all manner of frontiers to evangelize and that urgency calls for maximum numbers.

> World evangelism stressing co-operating strategies towards reaching all men for Christ, presents Christ Jesus to these teeming multitudes. World evangelism, also, is the duty and privilege of all Christians from every land, every language, and every culture, and prepares the way for our Lord's triumphant return. . . . Since two billion, rapidly becoming three billion, do not know Jesus Christ, world evangelism must continue.[6]

We must be on our guard against an hysterical approach to the setting forth of God's acts in Jesus Christ before the world. Emotional passion in support of broad objectives can lead us into unwise strategies. This mood of haste and excitement seems different from the atmosphere of the gospels. Extravagant use of vast numbers, in billions – beyond human comprehension – does not greatly help us to know what to do in our particular situation. A world of 'teeming multitudes' to whom we have to go is evocative of ill-considered actions. Careful thought needs to be given to background and conditions, and to the ways in which people can be brought to hear the Good News.

Generalizations concerning billions of people avoid precise examination of where they live: perhaps a quarter of the world's population is in China; large sections are in Russia or are deeply committed to the other great religions of the world, in India and in the Near and Middle East. Calls for large numbers of missionaries in practice means more expatriates from the West for the evangelized fields such as Africa, Asia, and Latin America. Loose evangelical statements such as that quoted may stir the imagination, but they have only an exiguous element of thought or careful planning.

McGavran anticipates with enthusiasm that Japan and Korea may between them send 3,000 missionaries overseas and hopefully suggests that nations in Europe suffering from 'the strange sickness which has afflicted world evangelism' will follow the same pattern. He says that 'evangelization is the greatest benefit possible to confer on any culture'.[7] The word evangelization is used with different connotations. The impression given by these extracts from the Geneva report is of a limited understanding of evangelism, taking the place of the wholeness of 'mission'. Probably the word evangelization is now so restricted to concepts of evangelism of the individual, as understood and expressed by 'evangelicals', that it has lost its usefulness as a translation of a biblical idea to the modern world.

The concept of an enormous increase in missionaries, as advocated by McGavran and publicized by many evangelical missionary societies, looks for a great surge forward in coming years by sending tens of thousands of missionaries from the six continents, in every direction, as men hurrying with food to feed the hungry. Multiply the number of missionaries who will bring together groups of Christians and then move on, and when every community in the world has thus responded, the triumphant return of our Lord will be prepared.

It is possible to participate in world evangelism without sending huge numbers of people from one country to another. Churches can be supported in their tasks, and can only truly become Churches as they participate in mission to their neighbours and to strangers beyond their borders. International movement on this scale, under a sense of acute urgency, riding rough-shod over the existing congregations and Churches, speaks more of a phrenetic state of mind produced by the modern western world than it does of the New Testament. One would view with foreboding the implementation of such a vision. It ought not to be used to stimulate artificially the ill-informed thinking of many ordinary Christians. It will be a tragedy if the evangelization of the world by the Christian faith should become identified with such a combination of concepts. An organization based in the United States and associated with the evangelistic campaigns of Dr Billy Graham cannot really form the basis for the presentation of the Christian faith in the modern world. This is an attempt to recapture the mood of a previous generation at the end of the nineteenth century, whereas our need is to go forward from the present.

Insofar as our concern here is with Africa and its missionary past, the judgement of Africa and western church leaders would surely be that any invasion of Africa by tens of thousands of new missionaries from outside would be harmful to Christian witness, injurious to the Church of Christ, and a misinterpretation of the intention of the New Testament. The authority of the Bible does not warrant ill-considered intrusion. Christians must not be beguiled by this anxious state of excited haste which fixes a future date, unbiblically, for the achievement of a particular target of world evangelization. Within the whole Christian community there are many variations of interpretation, ethos, and experience; mutual respect and humility warn us to follow our own group insights in a temperate and not an obsessive manner.

Africa is a limited area of the world in which we are able to see the immediate experience of Christian mission in a brief historical period; where we can sense a distinct understanding of Christian mission today; and in relation to which we can fashion our understanding of our missionary obligation to the world in response to the precise challenges of an actual continent. We believe and the Church in Africa believes that mission is the very nature of the Church; Christianity is without meaning if it does not have a dynamic mission to the whole inhabited earth. The word and work of salvation through God's eternal love is of vital contemporary and ultimate importance. Yet the Spirit who gives vision and strength also gives wisdom to the Church. Our task is not only to fire one another with enthusiasm but to reach by common counsel, under the guidance of the Spirit, the will of God for this generation. Some of the heavily financed evangelistic enterprises (largely financed from America), which threaten some of the communities in Africa, fill one with profound anxiety about the future of Christian mission in the world. While other institutions are being increasingly reasonable and are adapting themselves to the new situation, the irrational thrust of so-called evangelism could put in jeopardy so much of what has been achieved. 'Evangelism' and 'missionary' are not headings and programmes under which anything can be condoned and tolerated. The international imbalance of wealth provides the momentum for the threat.

The great asembly at Nairobi in 1975 provided an opportunity for Christians from many countries to consider together their task. Part of the discussion revolved around the tension between those who think primarily of the conversion of the individual and those who see the gospel in terms of its relevance in the whole of experience. 'Confessing Christ Today' is a theme for all Christians. The first section report under that title said:

> Confessing Christ and being converted to his discipleship belong inseparably together. Those who confess Jesus Christ, deny themselves, their selfishness and slavery to the godless 'principalities and powers', take up their crosses and follow him. Without clear confession of Christ our discipleship cannot be recognized; without costly discipleship people will hesitate to believe our confession. The costs of discipleship . . . e.g. becoming a stranger among one's own people, being despised because of the gospel, persecuted because of resistance to oppressive powers and imprisoned because of love for the poor and lost people . . . are bearable in face of the costly love of God, revealed in the passion of Jesus.
>
> We regret that some reduce liberation from sin and evil to social and political dimensions, just as we regret that others limit liberation to the private and eternal dimension. . . .[8]

Kenneth Slack comments in his summary of the Nairobi Assembly:

> It seemed, too, that for all the challenge that came from a speaker like John Stott, and the widely expressed anxiety lest liberation in the political, social, and economic sense replace salvation from sin at the heart of the redeeming gospel, the central conviction of the assembly was that there was more danger in undue stress on an evangelism of individuals than on the other way. Many who were at first uncomfortable as the problems of the world were rehearsed before them in speech after speech seemed to become clearly convinced that for the Christian to do other than try to relate his faith and action to them would be rank disobedience.
>
> There it was seen that any Christian mission which did not liberate man from crushing poverty, vile working conditions, and evil tyranny, and from his own oppressive tyranny of the world of nature, was largely irrelevant to today's world. Not totally, only largely.[9]

How will Christians and Churches in different countries see their responsibilities to mankind? There must be some variation in the understanding and response by the Churches, for this is the given situation in the world. The response of the Churches in East Germany is different from that in West Germany. The Churches in a country which is a great power in the world might entertain different considerations from those in a very small country. So much of the modern missionary movement began from Britain that it is not inapposite that here we should look at this question from the particular context of Britain.

It is not now the task of the Churches in Britain to send large numbers of missionaries to Africa. Christians must be helped to see that in fact as well as in theory the great missionary period is over. Africa has been evangelized in the sense that the Good News has been proclaimed throughout the continent and virile Churches have been called into being. There are many communities which have yet to hear and more which have yet to understand. The answer to this challenge rests first of all with the Christians of Africa and not with the Christians of Europe, Asia, or North America. The Christian leaders in Africa who want to see a great expansion of expatriate missionaries there are indeed low in number; they would voice only a minority opinion among assembled African church leaders. It is not that they are without a compelling sense of mission: that is untrue of the Church in Africa. The numerical growth of Christians in Africa in the last twenty-five years has been an average of 1 million each year and still continues. If present expansion continues there will be over 300 million Christians south of the Sahara by the year 2000.[10] The advocacy of a moratorium is not to end mission but to develop it more fully within an African setting. We must remember that no one group of Christians has a monopoly of commitment to mission. Whether there is a larger interchange of personnel between the Churches of Africa and the Churches of Asia in the cause of mission is for the Churches of those two continents to decide. We must take the Churches seriously and not divorce mission agencies from them. Evangelism cannot be cut off from the life of the Churches and be entrusted to independent organizations, or the world mission of Christ will suffer.

What then is the missionary need? The relationships between Churches in Africa and those in Britain with which they have traditionally been associated have not been so damaged that Christians want to sever them. The relationship in catholicity can be maintained by a few exchanges of personnel as by many. The signs are that there exist, and will continue to exist, mutual needs which can best be met by a comparatively small exchange of personnel. People of particular qualifications and experience can clearly be of benefit to both sides of the equation. Churches in Britain can only really enter into the experience of Christians in Africa by having some of them sharing in mission in Britain. Similarly there are and apparently will continue to be ways in which Christians from Britain will be privileged to share in the ongoing work of evangelism and service within the Churches of Africa. If for shorter or longer periods the Churches at either side believe that their life and witness can best be served by not having expatriate personnel, then this judgement should immediately be respected. There is a time to act and a time to forbear. The strength of the Churches in mission should be the criterion and they must arrive at that at their own judgement. An extraneous and overwhelming development of other agencies in mission, over against the Church, will indeed be harmful.

It should now be axiomatic that missionaries from another continent come and remain at the invitation of the Churches or ecumenical church bodies. If there is such an exchange, whether it is large or small it is one means of expressing the universal nature of the mission of the Church. There may well be special needs which can be met by drawing on the personnel resources of Churches in another continent. One thinks, for example, of the value of international teams at work in areas of primal mission, or in urban areas, or in international ports. It must be obvious that in specialized education, medicine, or leprosy work, there are needs which cannot easily be met from the resources of a local church, just as in the pluralism of contemporary Britain we can gain enormously from the experience and work of Christians from a different cultural background. Asians, Africans, and experienced Christians from the Caribbean are already making a very significant contribution to mission in Britain.

The Churches in Britain can follow their New Testament calling by responding to the call from the Churches of Macedonia to 'come over and help us', but in such a way that they do not overwhelm or suffocate the Church which calls. A brash insistence on this right to send is out of keeping with the circumstances and the spirit of mission today. The history of Britain's missionary involvement in Africa does not give support now to such an attitude. But neither does it warrant a unilateral withdrawal of missionaries that has not been arrived at by careful understanding and mutual consultation. If the catholicity of the Church is real, it means a very high degree of mutuality.

This attitude must similarly apply to the financial element, recognizing that resources are provided by the people of God for the whole mission of God. It is quite appropriate that funds should be provided even though personnel is required only to a limited degree or not at all. Funds can also be an expression of catholicity, as exemplified by the collection by Paul for the assistance of Christians in Jerusalem. It is disturbing to encounter with some frequency the attitude of unwillingness to provide financial resources unless it is also possible to send personnel. There is a similar reluctance to send funds to support the ecumenical work of the Churches in Africa, because this is less directly associated with church work in which missionaries are involved. The view seems to be taken that if a missionary is involved in ecumenical mission there may be financial support, but not otherwise.

There is a very real sense in which the Churches in the West need to be more deeply involved in mission in their own societies if their commitment to universal mission is to achieve credibility. Overseas mission can never be an escape from commitment to mission in one's own territory. There is substance in the comment from overseas Christians that the universal mission apparently detracts the energies of Christians from attention to the challenges of their own society. The existence of separate missionary societies tends to support this attitude. This is perhaps the aftermath of the extraordinary outpouring of resources in the last 200 years of missionary commitment.

Christian mission in partnership with the Churches of Africa necessitates special attention to the implications of our national life for the contemporary life of Africa. If our government is failing in a particular responsibility towards African countries, it must be of direct concern to the Christian community in Britain. This has clearly been relevant during the colonial period, and when constitutional questions have arisen such as over the Central African Federation or the future of Rhodesia. Social and political questions involving justice come within the ambit of the totality of mission. Race relations in Britain are of direct relevance to a participation in mission by the Churches of Britain and the Churches of Africa and the Caribbean. The mode of operation of British firms and their associates in the continent of Africa belongs quite properly within the concern for mission in Britain and in Africa. Greater than any of these issues is the stark fact of the richer world in the north getting richer, and the underdeveloped world south of the equator getting comparatively poorer and in some cases getting poorer in real terms. Christian mission can only be meaningful if it seeks to grapple with and is within the context of the larger problems of human development and justice.

In the British scene, as we have noted, missionary societies grew as organizations out of their awareness of the world which developed in the last years of the eighteenth century, and the new ability to respond to it. With the exception of the SPG, this was true of all the societies. Some more than others were associated with a particular Church. The Evangelical Missionary Alliance grew out of the Evangelical Alliance which was formed in London in 1846 from a strongly Protestant background. During the last century the Evangelical Alliance attracted much attention. The church leaders who supported it were often deeply attached to Protestantism and entertained some hostility towards Roman Catholicism. It was the first attempt by 'evangelicals' to form an organization. It inherited an aura of the eighteenth-century revival and continued to make a great contribution to increased interest in world mission.

If indeed we have reached the end of an era which was typified by sending an ever-increasing number of missionaries, then the role of the missionary society today is necessarily a concomitant question. The *society* was essentially of a group of individuals either in membership of one Church or in membership cutting across church boundaries. Its *raison d'être* was to conduct Christian mission in areas of the world, or among communities, where Churches did not exist. The range of elements in the *societies'* motivation has already been referred to. Young congregations and new churches which were brought into being received from the *society* overseas whatever help could be given, and were guided in their policies by the parent body.

Mission boards are usually regarded as official boards set up by a Church or sometimes by the general membership of a society, to fulfil certain functions on behalf of the Church. A *department* of a Church with overseas responsibilities is an integral part of the Church's constitution.

The missionary societies of the western world have had a disproportionate part in world mission because of their particular calling during a certain historical period. They have played a greater role because of the explosion of missionary concern from the end of the eighteenth century onwards. The specialization of their involvement and their remarkable historic role do tend to create a distance between them and the Church in the home country, and also provide a certain independence which they cherish. The cost of that independence is a degree of separation from the Church and its congregations. They tend to operate in a world of their own and are thus free to take their own initiatives.

The history of the missionary societies, with their leadership role, necessitates their not being the instruments of mission for the Churches in this generation. All the old associations are too strong. The missionary movement in its totality was too compromised, too divergent from the gospel, too closely associated with the western colonial movement to serve as the model for future world involvement. We must no longer envisage the future of world evangelization being the prerogative of 'missionary societies', either concentrated in one continent or scattered across the continents. The world is a different place from the rudimentary conditions of earlier centuries. The modern technical world, with its resources and its dangers, presents a different challenge to faith from anything previously experienced. The old instrumentality will not do. The presuppositions of earlier generations no longer hold.

The missionary societies may indeed be slowly evolving; they may make adjustments and alter their appearance, but so long as they remain 'missionary societies' they will be relics of a particular historic period. It is time to wind up missionary societies as such, with reasonable speed, and attend to the challenges of world mission.

The obvious alternative is to develop 'external departments' of church organizations, so that all the outside relations of the Church can be handled by a specially experienced and appointed group. Should the external responsibilities be carried by a department of the Church? There is a strong movement today away from entrusting work to actual Churches, the preference being to see organized Christian work undertaken by voluntary groups of individuals. There is a contemporary debate between those who favour 'voluntary agencies' over against the monolithic institutional Church. Some would like to see a thousand flowers bloom in the form of voluntary agencies. Clearly the traditional missionary societies fit that particular vision. The contemporary mood partly forms a defensive line for the old missionary society.

The missionary societies and the missionary orders are largely creations of the western world. The twin factors of western expansion in the last 100 years and the contemporary disparity between the rich world and the poor militate strongly against the suitability and acceptability of a continued, large-scale, western missionary society approach to the Third World.

The direction of development in recent decades has been for some missionary societies to alter their constitution and to become official departments of the Church. This is true on the Continent and in Britain. Some missionary societies of the Netherlands have become an integral part of the Reformed Church of the Netherlands. Missionary work of the Church of Scotland is now an Overseas Council of the Church. The Methodist Missionary Society has become the Overseas Division of the Church. The old London Missionary Society has become a part of the Council for World Mission. The Paris Missionary Society has merged into a new international organization.

This important development has considerable significance for the Churches in these countries and for the Churches with which they are related in Africa. It means that the missionary nature of the Church is more fully realized and its universal dimension is expressed in its basic structure. What was a temporary phenomenon becomes a permanent feature. At the same time the younger Churches overseas which have achieved experience and autonomy are no longer in the old dependent relationship to a special body of people, but are able to establish church-to-church relationships in a partnership of mission to the world. It means a great deal to younger Churches that they come into an equal fellowship and are no longer in an apparently subservient relationship.

'The relationship must be one of independence but not isolation. We want to be independent but also want links with other Churches and countries in a variety of ways. The Churches so linked need to be interested in and to trust each other. This is no longer a missionary situation, so there are no more missionaries, only exchange church workers.' The quotation clearly expresses the feeling of a younger Church. The document[11] from which it is taken spells out in great detail what this means in practical administration.

The significance of this development towards more mature relationships must be seen in relation to the world mission of the Church. The relationship between Churches in mission is altogether different from the old relationship between a western-based society and a branch of its mission overseas. As the report goes on to point out, it develops the identity of the Church in its own community and culture, and sets it free to make its own decisions; it develops a new degree of responsibility in the local church and enables a genuine localization to take place. In some Churches in Africa this has already happened; in many it is still a long way in the future.

The process of development and maturity and the present impending challenges of world mission suggest that the existence of missionary societies *per se* is no longer tenable. If the Churches of the world have indeed a new understanding of their essential missionary nature, and if we are living in a new age of world mission in which there is mutual responsibility and interdependence, then the era of missionary societies is at an end. Their period of service is drawing to a close; the Churches of the world can together increasingly take up the combined responsibility of working together in the fullness of Christian witness and service to the whole world. Missionary societies inevitably perpetuate the old thought-forms, attitudes, and relationships. A multiplication of missionary societies everywhere, as it is sometimes suggested today, would revert to the past, which belongs to an experience which was vital, fruitful, and historically right but which has been left behind in the growth of the world Church. The Kingdom of God can best be served by strengthening and invigorating the Churches in the totality of their mission, rather than by seeking to recapture the old forms and attitudes.

A resolute working towards the ending of missionary societies, and the acceptance of overseas departments of the Churches, can help Christians to break out of their imprisonment within the complex of traditional attitudes which have become such an integral part of western missionary thinking. Definite and drastic structural changes, however difficult to envisage and accomplish, are a valuable means of re-education towards a greater and not a diminished involvement. We are not at the end of world mission but, more accurately, at the beginning. The world resources of the Church are infinitely greater than they ever have been in personnel, in experience, in understanding, and in material strength. The needs and challenges of a perilous global society are apparent for everyone to see. The Good News of God's redeeming love in Jesus Christ, the very ground of our being, and the proven experience of his Spirit in human life seem more real and effective than at any time in history. The gospel is the only hope that we can ever see and grasp. The mission of the Church is before us and not behind us in history. It is infinitely greater than an oversimplified concentration on personal evangelism. Division and faithlessness have been the perennial weaknesses in the past and can only cause ineffectiveness in the future.

Canon Douglas Webster expressed the issue well:

There must be concrete deliverance from whatever bondage defaces
and dehumanizes mankind today. . . . Evangelism in these terms
means agitation. He who brings the Good News joins the struggle
against bad conditions and injustice everywhere. The full-blooded
salvation of the Bible does not bypass economic and political
realities. The transformation of the dark side of these realities is part
of what salvation means. Salvation brings with it joy and drives away
everything that cancels joy. Salvation is deliverance from all forms of
human bondage . . . no human condition is outside its reach because
it is always the action of the God who cares through the people he
sends![12]

One of the grounds sometimes given for the continuation of a
missionary society is that it can become, in a new role, a point of
interchange for the movement of church workers from one part of the
world to another. This is not an essential role which belongs to the
nature of a society and it has the appearance of a temporary expedient.
It is a function which can most logically be performed by a department
of a Church in mature relationship with other Churches in different
countries. The Church is the essential unit, rather than special
institutions; Churches in expanding and deepening relationship with
other Churches.

If we set before our minds the conception of each Church with a
structural element of external or overseas responsibility, we can begin to
see every Christian community in each place involved in a universal
dimension as part of its essential life and witness. History has
determined that missionary societies have limited relationships with
particular areas overseas. It is beyond the resources of a society to be
knowledgeable about and in intimate relationship with more than a few
isolated places on a world map. The supporters or members of a society
tend to know about and be concerned for the particular places in the
world with which they have almost by accident developed a relationship.
It may be long-standing, real, and intimate, but it is restrictive and tends
to continue within its limitations. A department of a Church, staffed
by others as well as missionaries, has the chance of a new beginning, to
relate with a much wider range of Churches overseas and thus to
become a participant in the world mission of the Church in a more
realistic way. Christians can become better informed about their fellow
Christians, involved in a wider sphere of prayer for Churches in other
continents, and stimulated by new education and a wider change of

personnel. Thus the shell of the traditional missionary society can be broken and it can enter, with the Church more deeply involved, into a fuller sharing in world mission.

An example of this process can be taken from Christian literature. The old pattern was for a small part of a society's resources to be donated to assisting Christian literature activities in its related Churches overseas. Now, through a Church participating in Joint Action for Christian Literature Overseas or through the World Association for Christian Communication, Christians in every Church can become partners in helping this work among many Churches in all the continents.

One of our basic needs is to produce a real shift in the thinking of Christians in the West which has necessarily been tied by its association with missionary societies to giving to people in a distant place. The giving is traditional and it is associated with sending funds and people. Mission in which people are thus involved is in an activity which takes place in an area far removed from where they are. Missionary societies are essentially identified with giving rather than receiving. It is a church which can receive rather than a missionary society. Yet our involvement in world mission is out of balance if it is fundamentally a giving to what other people do in an area about which we are only dimly conscious. Mission is not really giving or receiving, but sharing in God's work everywhere in the world. It is far easier to achieve this understanding if we are involved as Churches with other Churches, because they are so clearly equally dependent upon God and manifestly are endeavouring to fulfil his purposes. Churches are essentially part of God's mission, using their common resources and equally sharing a servant role in the Body of Christ. Autonomous Churches are not subservient one to another. They have the opportunity of developing a more mature relationship than that of giving and receiving which naturally tends to characterize the relationship of a missionary society with the Churches overseas with which they are connected. However much one may struggle against it, there is inevitably a possessive or paternalistic element in a missionary society relationship, which can more readily be overcome and eliminated as Churches are forced to work out more virile relationships between one another. How often one hears the revealing phrase 'our work' in this country or that which is reminiscent of old dependent relationships. A more rigorous relationship between Churches is perhaps the best means of breaking old attitudes of giving to dependent work, and of establishing in people's minds that we share in a common task of participation in God's mission which is equally demanding everywhere.

As has already been indicated, there is strong resistance to change in missionary societies and an unwillingness to contemplate fundamental readjustments. There is usually present a strong commitment to the institution and a weak commitment to ecumenical development and to new forms of joint action for mission.

This state of affairs has been particularly manifest in recent developments in the old and prestigious Conference of British Missionary Societies which came into being soon after the famous ecumenical conference at Edinburgh in 1910. The world of missionary societies was then the seed-bed for church reunion and church co-operation. It is a sign of the times for old missionary structures that it is going out of existence and has become a division of the British Council of Churches. The significance of this development and the steps leading to it is twofold: a tendency in difficult and challenging days to revert to traditional concepts of the missionary society; and a clear limitation on the extent to which old institutions will co-operate and engage in joint endeavour.

Africans rightly resent the filtering of knowledge about their countries through the minds and voices of missionaries, so that the Churches of Europe have a particular image conditioned by a particular interpretation. With all the means of communication – television, newspapers, and speeches – the image of an African country in the mind of a typical Englishman often bears only a limited resemblance to the actual situation. There is a profound responsibility upon the Churches in this country to help the people of Britain to understand more accurately and deeply the lives of others overseas and to be able to listen to what they are saying.

A certain visitor from overseas came into a group of very kind and well-intentioned people, who were interested in his visit and entertained a desire to make it a happy one. His English was inadequate, so that he often needed helping with words, and sometimes a small sentence had to be repeated several times before he grasped what was meant. In point of fact the meeting never took place, except in a formal sense, because there was no real communication and little mutual knowledge. The group had not the attitude or the technique for starting and maintaining communication with such a person; embarrassment and difficulty won the day and there was no interchange of ideas.

The relationship of many people in Britain to Third World countries with which we have been directly connected for several centuries is like that experience, but it is generally much worse, because the average citizen has no strong desire to project himself into another culture or any compelling motive to help it develop. If the missionary movement has been one of the main channels of communication for the last two centuries between people in this country and the peoples who were coming into view at the end of the eighteenth century, how is it that there is such a gap in our understanding? People of the Caribbean islands and the ex-colonies of Africa probably understand and know about us far better than we do about them. When we are considering racial questions, or world economic matters, or liberation movements, how out of touch we are is starkly revealed. Part of the Church's task is to help the members of the human family to find one another in terms of reconciliation, understanding, peace, and justice. Again, this role cannot be fulfilled in the missionary society context; all the associations are contrary to the exercise of this responsibility. It needs much more than a missionary interpretation.

It may not be true of some of the missionary societies, but it is still unquestionably true of the majority, that they are related to, concerned for, and supportive of work overseas only if a missionary from the society is in the particular country. The bloodstream of a society is its network of missionaries. This relationship to world mission is now out-of-date and inadequate.

In the mission of the future, to which we are moving, away from the older missionary society complex of attitudes, we can visualize discipleship and church membership necessarily involving the Christian in a local and a universal participation. It belongs to the Church to be concerned with all the world, and to belong to the Church is essentially to share in its outreach to the world. The Church's business is the whole message and work of salvation, expressed in its fullness in the Old Testament and in the New, and manifested in the life, death, and resurrection of Jesus Christ. One or more of the sections of a Church's life need to be involved in, to a greater or lesser degree, all aspects of world mission. To select only a part is both to distort the image of the gospel presented to the world by the Church and to nurture the individual in a restricted form of expression.

Through the organization of the Church and through its educational material the wide range of mission to the world must be expressed. In some way the Church must be related to other Churches in the world, through exchange of personnel and through ecumenical institutions.

Ideally this needs to be beyond the limitations of a confessional grouping, for they tend to be self-defeating in the attempt to achieve a universal dimension and foster too much introversion and domestication.

Through participating in the life of a Church, a Christian should necessarily be involved in world mission; in sharing in support for evangelism outside one's national frontiers as well as within; in aid for human development; in health care; in assistance for Christian groups suffering oppression; in service for people in areas of emergency or deprivation; in forms of struggle to defend human rights at home and overseas; in opposition to injustice; in various types of education; and in trying to wrestle as Christians with the global problems of universal economic and political systems which enslave and dehumanize rather than liberate. The individual Christian cannot comprehend and be directly involved in all these aspects of mission, but by membership of a Church he identifies himself with a community of people which is thus engaged. For a Christian to be involved in world mission is therefore something much greater than giving support to a missionary society. That may have sufficed in the past, but participation in world mission must in the future signify a further sharing in all that one understands by God's transforming work in the world through Jesus Christ and his Church. Nothing less than this is really being faithful to the Scriptures or the accumulated experience of the Christian Church. A great deal of our missionary work in Britain is but a fragmentary sharing in the salvation of the Christian gospel.

Christian mission to Africa, starting in the ways which we have noted, included from its beginning the whole range of application of the gospel to the human life in the continent. The history of the Church in Africa, and its present involvement, is testimony to this fact. The pattern of our relationship as western Churches must change radically from the past. It does not now mean sending large numbers of recruited personnel. It does mean that there is a new era before us in which, by the providence of God, the Churches of Africa called into being by His action can joyfully join with a wider fellowship of Churches in witness and service.

In conclusion we may take particular note of two exceptional and significant attempts to deal with the twin problems of western missionary societies conditioned by centuries of missionary involvement and young Churches in Africa and elsewhere not having the opportunity of engaging in the world mission of the Church. The first concerns the Paris Missionary Society and the second the old London Missionary

Society which was such a vital part of the scene in the earliest days. These examples of experiment and pioneering are instructive for the older missionary societies.

In 1964 the Churches associated with the PMS set up a committee to prepare plans to end the sole involvement of the missionary society and to engage the associated Churches. Three years later a 'joint apostolic action' was started in Dahomey. Later a similar international team was established in France, 'to signify that the mission of the Churches is from everywhere to everywhere. The mission field is no longer solely Africa, but the contemporary world in its entirety.'[13]

From this joint action emerged the Communauté Evangélique d'Action Apostolique (CEVAA). Funds and personnel were now pooled from all the Churches and allocations were decided by the Council of the CEVAA. It was composed of thirteen Churches with the original Churches which had supported the PMS. Thus the representatives from all the Churches, both overseas and in France, decide on the total use of resources. The administrative body consists of officials appointed from any of the Churches, and Christians from different nations debate and decide policies and programmes. The missionary society has died and the Churches are together engaged in the wide range of Christian mission in different countries.

Unity of witness and action remains the fundamental objective of the Community in order to give concrete expression to Unity in Christ and respect for human dignity. We are conscious of the fact that contemporary man is grappling with the problems of hunger, oppression, war, and also with the ideological and political conflicts which weigh heavily in the life of our societies. Such situations remind us, once again, that we must re-read together the Holy Scriptures, the gospel, in the context of our varied cultures and particular situations in order to understand better what our Lord wishes to say to the world today.

The use of the term 'missionary' presents a problem not only for young people who offer their services to the churches but also for the Christians with whom they have to collaborate. This stems from the fact that in the past missionaries were sent by societies and not by churches which felt directly responsible for mission. On the other hand, in the welcoming church the term 'missionary' was always considered a title of superiority over other workers in the local church.[14]

A road needs to be opened up which will lead Christians in Britain to discover themselves responding to the larger world. The old European outreach will only disappear if the structures are altered. The objective to be achieved is for Christians and Churches to find themselves as partners with others around the world, not just in selected places 'where we have our missionaries' but with others engaged in global mission. This is unlikely to happen while the old societies and orders remain. Similarly Christians in countless congregations in the six continents need to become aware of a variety of fellow workers in their midst, not of a western style only, but of sufficient diversity to express the universality of Christianity. Only thus can the Christian family speak to a world divided by inequality and racialism.

Two events in Britain illustrate the contemporary importance of this issue for the Churches. They indicate an awareness of the underlying problems, but in the larger context of the whole missionary scene they indicate a limited response to the challenge before the Church.

In July 1977 the old London Missionary Society, formed in 1795, and its successor the Congregational Council for World Mission, finally disappeared. A new Council for World Mission was born, which received all the resources of the old bodies and placed them at the disposal of a Council created from twenty different national Churches in Africa, Asia, Europe, and the Caribbean. The missionary societies have disappeared. By an act of faith the Churches have agreed to share their gifts and resources, with overall direction from a representative international body which gives equal weight to the young and the old.

This development is not unlike that of the CEVAA, with a shared responsibility at the centre and a pooling of available resources. Its appeal may not be so romantic for the European mind, and there will be a decrease in the sense of self-importance as decisions will be made elsewhere. The mood of presiding over the destiny of others will finally disappear and a new spirit of true partnership will undoubtedly develop. The courage of this decision must be admired, for it has meant in both cases mentioned, the end of the missionary society and the beginning of a new chapter of working humbly with others on their terms.

The second illustration is the report of a working party on relations between the Church of England, the General Synod, and the Missionary Societies of the Church of England, published in 1977. The working party looked at the situation of eight major missionary societies and a number of similar organizations, all voluntary bodies, determining relations between the Church and the rest of the world: 'How can the Church of England enter into this sort of church-to-church relationship when a major part of its relations with the Church overseas is in the hands of voluntary missionary societies?'

The answer of the working party is a proposal which will go before the General Synod, to establish a small secretariat with authority to speak to the General Synod (through the Board of Mission and Unity) and to the whole Church, and with a consultative body formed from all the agencies involved. 'It is designed to be a co-ordinating body of those agencies within the Church of England which see their work as integrally determined by and related to Partnership in Mission in the Anglican Communion.'

The missionary agencies will remain in being and will continue both their fund-raising and recruitment at home and their relationship with particular areas overseas. A new dimension of administration is inserted which may form a channel to the Church at home, but relations with the world will perhaps retain their established pattern.

Some attempts are therefore being made to bring to an end the traditional form of the missionary movement from Europe and involve Christians across the world in a task which has just begun. A chapter in church history, which in many ways was glorious, has come to an end. Men and women of different nationalities, at a particular period of history, responding to the call of Christ, displayed astounding originality and set in motion a movement which has had astonishing results. Their actions will continue to be instructive for many succeeding generations. A similar vision, inspiration, and originality are called for in our own age.

The task before us is to see the Christian and the Church in relation to all mankind, without the temporary facility of a missionary society. The associations linked with those institutions need consciously to be set on one side. Against the background of the last 200 years can we formulate, in the light of that experience, the manner in which the Christian relates to the world? Relationships are more important than money or the inclinations of individuals. The Christian takes all world relationships and obligations seriously, conscious of a profound commitment to witness and service, seeking the good of all in righteousness and freedom, aware of the power and love of God as shown in Jesus Christ, and ready to receive or to send witnesses of His truth. As so often, a poet from the past expresses an idea more adequately than contemporary attempts:

Freely to all ourselves we give,
Constrained by Jesu's love to live
The servants of mankind.

If Christians and the Churches approach the modern world in that spirit and work out the necessary apparatus, there is much to engage them.

Notes

CHAPTER 1

[1] One of the most thorough reappraisals of the missionary enterprise is in the work of the International Documentation and Communications Centre which was founded in Rome in 1962 and has issued a number of reports under the heading *The Future of the Missionary Enterprise*: they represent a view of the Church's mission which is different from that held by most missionary supporters in the West. The Centre, with headquarters in Via S. Maria dell'Anima, Rome, is trying to create new attitudes among Christians to the world. Report no. 9, issued in 1974, deals with the nature of the missionary movement. It is significant that this work is well known in America and in Europe but receives almost no attention in Britain.

[2] In *A History of Christian Missions*, Pelican History of the Church series, vol. 6 (1964), Bishop Stephen Neill records the expansion of Christian missions largely in terms of numerical growth of Christians and churches. The attitude that Christian mission issues in more dioceses and more numerous adherents is much less acceptable now than in the past. Religious growth by itself is less impressive. When little attention is given to the nature of the transformation which occurs, the extension of the ecclesiastical and liturgical seems less convincing. Bishop Neill has written elsewhere of 'the dreadful superficiality of much of the work' in Africa.

[3] *Drumbeats from Kampala*, the report of the First Assembly of the All Africa Conference of Churches (1963).

[4] The Great Commission, 'Go therefore and make disciples . . .' (Matt. 28.19–20) is very frequently quoted now as a basis for authority, but it has played only a small part in the motivation of the modern missionary movement. The obligation to obey a command has not of itself seemed adequate for a foundation on which to build the missionary vocation. With William Carey it apparently took a dominant position in his mind, but subsequently it was only one ingredient among others in the motivation of Christians for missionary service. J. van den Berg writes: 'A feeling of obligation was always present, but it never functioned as a separate stimulus; it was always connected up with other motives' (*Constrained by Jesus' Love*: 'An Inquiry into the Motives of the Missionary Awakening in Great Britain in the Period between 1698 and 1815' pp. 164–5).

[5] *Black Theology – the South African Voice*, edited by Basil Moore, was published in Britain because it could not be published in South Africa; subsequently it has been banned. It contains an impressive essay by Steve Biko, who died in 1977 after a week in prison.

[6] Ibid. Preface, p. viii.

[7] Ibid. Nyameko Pityana, p. 59.

[8] Ibid. Sabelo Ntwasa, pp. 107ff.

[9] Ibid. Sabelo Ntwasa, p. 146.

CHAPTER 2

[1] C. P. Groves, *The Planting of Christianity in Africa*, vol. 1, p. 163. The four volumes of this monumental study in the Lutterworth Library are the main source in the English language for the history of the missionary movement in Africa.

[2] Peter Hinchliff, *The Church in South Africa*, p. 3.

[3] Groves, op. cit., vol. 1, p. 169.

[4] Geoffrey Moorhouse, *The Missionaries*, p. 35. This book, with a journalistic style, is one of the first attempts to look back and assess the whole missionary involvement with the expanding world of the nineteenth century. It tends to be selective and out-of-balance, as it relies too heavily on the records of the Church Missionary Society; it is, however, a lively and colourful introduction to the subject.

[5] Groves, op. cit., vol. 1, p. 132.

[6] Groves, op. cit., vol. 1, p. 130.

[7] Groves, op. cit., vol. 1, p. 131.

[8] Groves, op. cit., vol. 1, p. 137.

[9] See, for example, J. du Plessis, *History of Christian Missions in South Africa*. A good bibliography is given in Hinchliff, op. cit.

[10] Adrian Hastings, *Church and Mission in Modern Africa*, p. 55.

[11] Ibid., p. 59.

CHAPTER 3

[1] There is a fascinating similarity between the Industrial Revolution and the modern missionary movement. Both had their complex of roots in Britain, both aroused enormous ingenuity and energy, and both changed the face of the earth. Both were in debt to the Evangelical Revival of the eighteenth century. The Quaker movement had a hand in both; the Darby family, for example, played a major role in the decisive development of using coke for smelting ironstone at Coalbrookdale in the Severn valley. The great cast-iron bridge across the river (1776) was completed at the time when the modern missionary movement was beginning. Railways were built at the same place and time and had similar international implications; iron rails were apparently first cast at Coalbrookdale around 1767. See, for example, T. S. Ashton, *The Industrial Revolution 1760–1830*. Oxford University Press, Open University edn 1973; and M. J. T. Lewis, *Early Wooden Railways*. London, Routledge & Kegan Paul, 1970.

[2] 'The Slave Ship', painted by J. M. W. Turner sometime before 1840, powerfully depicts the horror and the revulsion of sensitive people at the common practice of throwing slaves overboard to lighten the ship in times of emergency. Further information on this practice is given by James Walvin in *Black and White. The Negro and English Society 1555–1945* (London, Allen Lane, Penguin, 1973), pp. 92–3.

[3] C. M. MacInnes, *Bristol and the Slave Trade* (Bristol Branch of the Historical Association, University of Bristol, 1968), p. 6.

[4] At the Treaty of Tordesillas in 1494 a boundary was agreed, 370 leagues west of the Cape Verde Islands; Spain secured a monopoly to the West and Portugal to the East.

[5] The record of the struggle against slavery in Britain and against the slave trade is given by Thomas Clarkson in *The History of the Rise, Progress, and Accomplishment of the Abolition of the African Slave Trade by the British Parliament*. Lord Mansfield's judgement is set down in full in Stiv Jakobsson's *Am I not a Man and a Brother?*, p. 47. It reads as follows:

> Immemorial usuage preserves a positive law, after the occasion or accident which gave rise to it has been forgotten; and, tracing the subject to natural principles, the

claim of slavery can never be supported. The power claimed never was in use here, or acknowledged by the law. Upon the whole, we cannot say the cause returned is sufficient by the law; and therefore the man must be discharged.

There is, however, controversy over the significance of Lord Mansfield's judgement. James Walvin, op. cit., ch. 7, gives a detailed and fascinating account of the great legal case of 1772. He maintains convincingly that the judgement merely prevented an owner from taking a slave out of England, but did not in law or in fact end slavery in England. There was, however, a sudden increase in the number of destitute slaves in London.

6 An example of Thomas Clarkson at work in local research is given in Peter Marshall's *The Anti-slave Trade Movement in Bristol*. Bristol Branch of the Historical Association, University of Bristol, 1968. One of the unique contributions of Clarkson was careful investigation at English ports.

7 The history, size and treatment of the black community in Britain are recorded in absorbing detail in James Walvin's study of the period 1555–1945. (See note 2.) Richard West says: 'There are no good statistics on the Negro community in England, but by 1785 it almost certainly numbered between twenty and thirty thousand. Although some of these blacks were in Bristol, Liverpool, and the other west-coast ports, the majority had assembled in London, especially in Paddington and around the Mile End Road. Their colour and their inclination to congregate made blacks conspicuous and gave an inflated idea of their number' (*Back to Africa*, p. 15).

8 Moorhouse, op. cit., p. 49.

9 Moorhouse, op. cit., p. 45.

10 In his study of the various churches and missionary groups J. van den Berg shows clearly that in the earlier period, before 1790, the response of Christians to the non-Christian world was largely in respect of the Atlantic area, associated with the blacks of Africa and those transported to the West, and with the Indians of North America.

11 Early Moravian missionary work in St Thomas and Greenland, and elsewhere, is vividly described in J. Taylor Hamilton's *A History of the Missions of the Moravian Church during the Eighteenth and Nineteenth Centuries*.

12 In the first two chapters of his study (see note 10) J. van den Berg examines the overseas missionary element in European Christianity before the eighteenth century. Chapter 3 lays the foundation for the missionary movement clearly in the Evangelical Revival of the eighteenth century: 'In the middle part of the eighteenth century . . . the forces were resolved that only a short time afterwards were to change the face of the world' (p. 66).

13 J. van den Berg, op. cit., pp. 93–105.

14 In the *Collection of Hymns* of John Wesley published in 1779, these words occur in hymn 526. Some of the verses read as follows:

> v. 2 Lord, if thou didst thyself inspire
> Our souls with this intense desire
> Thy goodness to proclaim,
> Thy glory is we now intend,
> O let our deed begin and end
> Complete in Jesu's name!

> v. 3 In Jesu's name behold we meet,
> Far from an evil world retreat,
> And all its frantic ways;
> One only thing resolved to know,
> And square our useful lives below,
> By reason and by grace.

      v. 4 Not in the tombs we pine to dwell,
             Not in the dark monastic cell,
             By vows and grates confined;
             Freely to all ourselves we give,
             Constrained by Jesu's love to live
             The servants of mankind.

      v. 5 Now, Jesus, now thy love impart,
             To govern each devoted heart,
             And fit us for thy will:
             Deep founded in the truth of grace,
             Build up thy rising church, and place
             The city on the hill.

[15] British Council of Churches report, 'Violence in Southern Africa. A Christian Assessment', p. 5.

CHAPTER 4

[1] *The Cambridge History of Africa*, ed. J. E. Flint, vol. 5 (1790–1870), pp. 215ff; N. Allen Birthwhistle, *Thomas Birch Freeman*.

[2] Groves, op. cit., vol. 1, p. 253.

[3] *Black Theology*, Preface, p. viii.

[4] Hinchliff, op. cit., p. 66.

[5] *Black Theology*, p. ix.

[6] Bishop Abel Muzorewa, quoted in *World Parish*, journal of the World Methodist Council. 1975.

[7] Edwin W. Smith, *Robert Moffat*, p. 101. Moffat was unaware that African religion existed: a missionary 'seeks in vain to find a temple, an altar, or a single emblem of heathen worship. No fragments remain of former days, as mementoes to the present generation, that their ancestors ever loved, served, or reverenced a being greater than man.' Also *Cambridge History of Africa*, chs. 12–13.

[8] One of the small but highly significant publications which indicates the shift in attitude to other religions is Carl F. Hallencreutz's *New Approaches to Men of Other Faiths*. WCC Research Pamphlet no. 18. 1969. It traces the development of thinking on this issue during this century. The subject of relations with other religions is also dealt with in chapter 8 (see note 11).

[9] Hymn 339 in the *Methodist Hymn Book*.

[10] The important part played by Africans from South Africa in the evangelization of northern Malawi is described by W. A. Elmslie in *Among the Wild Ngoni*, first published in 1899.

    'Accompanying Laws on this journey was William Koyi, who was destined to play a vital role in the subsequent work of the Mission amongst Mombera's Ngoni. Koyi, a Gaika from South Africa, had been educated at the Lovedale Missionary Institute by Dr James Stewart. When the Livingstonia Mission appealed to Stewart for African volunteers for work in Malawi, four Lovedale trainees, including Koyi, responded. Laws was quick to appreciate that the ability of Koyi to speak Zulu would be of particular value to the Mission in dealing with the Ngoni amongst whom Zulu was still the language of the aristocracy. Therefore, in 1882, when Laws was finally able to implement his earlier promise to Mombera to send a representative to live in his area, he chose Koyi, who settled near the chief's headquarters.

    Koyi's courage and Christian devotion so far from any form of support or assistance from the Mission or from a central government was remarkable. For his first three years in Ngoniland he was able to do little more than bear witness to his faith, but his mere presence in the hostile and often perilously dangerous region permitted Laws to send Elmslie there in 1885 to take charge. The fact that Koyi and Elmslie survived at all was, it seems, largely due to the understanding achieved between Mombera and Laws at their first meeting' (3rd edn), Introductory Note, p. x). See also Richard Gray, 'Christianity and Religious Change in Africa', in *African Affairs*, vol. 77, no. 306, January 1978, pp. 89ff.

[11] W. H. During was a minister of the United Methodist Free Churches in Sierra Leone in 1875. He was transferred by the UMFC to Mombasa in East Africa in 1880. After serving for some years at the first UMFC mission station in East Africa, at Ribe, he was moved to the Tana River area and remained there until 1886. He is mentioned in some of the early records as accomplishing a very valuable ministry. See Oliver A. Beckerlegge, *United Methodist Ministers and their Circuits*. London, Epworth Press, 1968.

[12] James Walvin, op. cit., shows that before 1600 the African was highly regarded in Britain. 'Somewhere between 1600 and 1700 the English view of the African had changed'; the African was now a commodity. Walvin gives an interesting study of Shakespeare's contribution to the race question (pp. 23–8).

[13] The relationship between the birth of the missionary movement and the campaign against the slave trade and slavery is explored in Jakobsson, op. cit. My indebtedness to this author is expressed in the Introduction to this book. Earlier studies had either exaggerated or played down the work of Wilberforce, Clarkson, and the other famous characters. Later the emphasis had been placed on the economic factors which brought slavery to an end (cf. Eric Williams, *Capitalism and Slavery*). In the General Conclusions Jakobsson says: 'The missionary societies which were interested in missions to West Africa also turned their attention to the West Indies. There were more or less strong connections between the missionary agencies and the movements for the abolition of the slave trade between Africa and the West Indies and for the emancipation of the slaves in the British colonies in the West Indies and in Africa. . . . It is obvious that the societies wanted to support the anti-slave trade movement and to recompense the Áfricans who had suffered on account of the European slave trade' (p. 581). The book contains a very fine bibliography.

[14] See *Journals of Isenberg and Krapf*, 1843; new edn, 1968.

[15] Groves, op. cit., vol. 11, p. 17.

[16] Edward Shillito, *François Coillard. A Wayfaring Man*, p. 58.

[17] Hugh J. Schonfield, ed., *Travels and Researches in South Africa: David Livingstone*, p. 47.

[18] Owen Chadwick, *Mackenzie's Grave*.

[19] A brief record of the work of the Universities Mission to Central Africa, up to the middle years of this century, is given in Gerald W. Broomfield's *Towards Freedom*.

CHAPTER 5

[1] The provision of atlases for the great missionary conferences was a sign of the expansive mood in which they met. The pattern was established at the important conference in Edinburgh in 1910 (*Statistical Atlas of Christian Missions*).

[2] *International Review of Missions*, October 1924, p. 493.

[3] Ibid., p. 493.

[4] Ibid., p. 499.

[5] Le Zouté Conference Report, 1926, p. 163.

[6] J. H. Oldham, *Relation of the International Missionary Council to Africa*. Unpublished memorandum, 20.12.27.

[7] No other book anticipated the rise of the race question in the world to anything like the degree of J. H. Oldham's *Christianity and Race*. Not only did he foresee the

emerging problem and the relevance of the gospel to it, but he understood the slow shift in understanding of Christian mission which was taking place.

[8] Willingen Report, 'The Missionary Obligation of the Church', p. v.

[9] Ibid., pp. 8–9.

[10] Ibid., p. 14.

[11] Ibid., p. 19.

[12] Published in Stuttgart in 1966.

[13] The statistics in this table are taken from *Christianity Today*, November 1971.

[14] See P. W. Brierley, *UK Protestant Missions Handbook*.

[15] See J. D. Douglas, ed., *Let the Earth Hear His Voice*. USA, World Wide Publications, 1974. This 'comprehensive volume on world evangelization' (1,472 pages) was published after the Lausanne Congress on World Evangelization and contains the addresses and group reports.

CHAPTER 6

[1] This example of a first, limited step towards a moratorium was reported in the WCC monthly magazine *One World*, June 1975, p. 12.

[2] Minutes and report of the Bangkok Assembly 1973, p. 22.

[3] The Fifth Assembly of the World Council of Churches met in November 1975 at the Kenyatta Centre in Nairobi. The moratorium idea associated with Africa was in many people's minds and received mention, but was not apparently dealt with in any significant way. It did not come as an issue before the plenary sessions. Kenneth Slack in *Nairobi Narrative* (London, SCM Press, 1976), p. 54, describes one of the memorable speeches to the Assembly made by Canon Burgess Carr. Having spoken about the old shackles which kept Africa in bondage, he then moved the Assembly with the honesty and poignancy of his reference to the new shackles which men newly delivered could fix around their own wrists.

[4] Taken from the report of a Task Force for Ecumenical Sharing of Personnel, Division of Ministries, NCCC 1975.

[5] Dr Colin Morris was preaching the annual Church Missionary Society sermon in January 1975.

[6] Taken from Document 5 of the Consultation on Moratorium at Le Cénacle, Geneva, called by the Ecumenical Sharing of Personnel, WCC in December 1974.

[7] Canon Burgess Carr was speaking in New York in January 1975 at the headquarters of the NCCC. The speech was entitled 'The Mission of the Moratorium'.

CHAPTER 7

[1] J. T. Hamilton, *Moravian Missions*, p. 15.

[2] The remarkable story of the Jesuit involvement in China is given in Columba Cary-Elwes' *China and the Cross*.

[3] The Reith Lectures are published annually in *The Listener*. This quotation is taken from the 26 November 1970 issue.

[4] *International Review of Missions*, January 1975, pp. 58ff.

CHAPTER 8

[1] Johannes Blauw, *The Missionary Nature of the Church*.

[2] J. A. Dachs, ed., *Christianity South of the Zambezi*.

[3] A comprehensive understanding of Christian mission, including the personal, social, and universal, naturally figured largely in the debate at the Fifth Assembly of the

World Council of Churches. Kenneth Slack (op. cit., p. 41) describes the speech of Bishop Arias from Bolivia: 'Then Bishop Arias enunciated his definition of evangelism in the light of this more than down-to-earth life-experience. "To evangelize is to help men to discover the Christ hidden in them and revealed in the gospel. To whom must we say 'Man does not live by bread alone', and with whom must we pray 'Give us this day our daily bread'? Can we continue to treat men as 'souls with ears'? Or as stomachs without souls? Can we announce the gospel in the same way to the oppressor and the oppressed, to the torturer and the tortured? In other words, how can the gospel be authenticated unless it is faithful both to the Scriptures and to real people in real contexts?"'

[4] Dachs, ed., op. cit., p. 199.
[5] The full text of the bishops' statement is given in *Violence in Southern Africa*, Appendix 1. Bishop Donal Lamont's notable witness is given in *Speech from the Dock*. CIIR 1977.
[6] Professor Brian Johanson, as chairman of the Justice and Peace Department of the South African Council of Churches, has constantly laid stress on political and social action arising from fundamental belief in the love of God. The quotation is from p. 30 of *Human Rights in South Africa* published in 1974 by the South African Council of Churches. Brian Johanson is now minister of the City Temple, London.
[7] Acceptance of the concept that the gospel must be applied in the political arena has not been general until comparatively recent days. It is an attitude which has come strongly out of the Africa experience. It was out of the experience of Sophiatown near Johannesburg that Bishop Trevor Huddleston began to understand this truth with real conviction (cf. *Naught for your Comfort*, p. 171). Many have entered into this experience through missionary service. Another notable example was the courageous involvement of the present Bishop of Lichfield, the Right Revd Kenneth Skelton, when he was Bishop of Matabeleland.
[8] Stephen H. Travis, *Epworth Review*, September 1974, p. 10.
[9] *The Church and Human Rights in Africa*, published by the All Africa Council of Churches, p. 19.
[10] Ibid., p. 31.
[11] J. V. Taylor, *The Primal Vision*, Introduction. Contact and relationship with other faiths has been a major concern in the missionary world for decades. It is interesting to see it now becoming a burning issue in the Ecumenical Movement and in the deliberations of local churches. Not surprisingly it attracted serious attention at the Fifth Assembly of the WCC at Nairobi. Representatives of other faiths were present. A programme of study and action for local churches was given in the report (Slack, op. cit., pp. 66–7).

CHAPTER 9

[1] John Mbiti, 'The Crisis of Mission in Africa', in *African Journal of Theology*, no. 5, December 1972.
[2] Adrian Hastings, *African Christianity*. London, Geoffrey Chapman, 1977.
[3] Douglas Webster, CMS sermon 'For Us Men and for Our Salvation', 1972.
[4] AACC *Newsletter*, vol. 1, no. 5, June 1975.
[5] Douglas, op. cit., p. 99.
[6] Ibid., p. 94.
[7] Ibid., p. 97.
[8] *Breaking Barriers*, ed. David Paton, p. 44.
[9] Slack, op. cit., pp. 62, 86.
[10] David B. Barrett, *Schism and Renewal in Africa*.

[11] Report of the Consultation of the United Church of Papua and New Guinea and the Solomon Islands with the Co-operating Churches 1974.

[12] Webster, CMS sermon 1972. (See note 3 above.)

[13] The story of the beginning of the CEVAA and the preparation for it in the old Paris Missionary Society is told in *International Review of Missions*, October 1973, p. 408.

[14] Ibid., p. 411.

Bibliography

A selection of books which have been useful, and some of which have been fascinating.

Ajayi, J. F. A., *Christian Missions in Nigeria, 1841–1891*. Longmans 1965.

Albrecht, Paul, *The Churches and Rapid Social Change*. SCM Press 1961.

All Africa Conference of Churches, *Drumbeats from Kampala*. Lutterworth Press 1963.

Allen, W. O. B. and McClure, E., *Two Hundred Years: The History of the Society for Promoting Christian Knowledge 1698–1898*. SPCK 1898.

Anderson, E., *Churches at the Grass Roots*. Lutterworth Press 1967.

Anderson-Morshead, A. E. M., *History of the Universities' Mission to Central Africa*. UMCA 1909.

Angola, A Symposium: Views of a Revolt. IRR and OUP 1962.

Ayandele, E. A., *The Missionary Impact on Modern Nigeria*. Longmans 1966.

Baëta, C. G., ed., *Christianity in Tropical Africa*. International African Institute and OUP 1968.

Bangkok Assembly 1973. Minutes and Report. Geneva, WCC, 1973.

Baptist Missionary Society, *Annual Reports and Magazines*. London.

Barber, James, *Rhodesia. The Road to Rebellion*. OUP 1967.

Barrett, D. B., *Schism and Renewal in Africa*. OUP 1968.

Beetham, T. A., *Christianity and the New Africa*. Pall Mall Press 1967.

Berg, J. van den, *Constrained by Jesus' Love*. Kampen, J. H. Kok N.V., 1956.

Birmingham, David, *The Portuguese Conquest of Angola*. IRR and OUP 1965.

Birtwhistle, N. Allen, *Thomas Birch Freeman*. Cargate Press 1950.
—— *William Threlfall*. Cargate Press 1966.

Blauw, Johannes, *The Missionary Nature of the Church*. Lutterworth Press 1962.

Brierley, P. W., *UK Protestant Missions Handbook.* Evangelical Missionary Alliance 1977.

British Council of Churches, *Violence in South Africa: A Christian Assessment.* SCM Press 1970.

Broomfield, G. W., *Towards Freedom.* UMCA 1957.

Cary-Elwes, Columba, *China and the Cross: Studies in Missionary History.* Longmans Green 1957.

Chadwick, Owen, *Mackenzie's Grave.* Hodder & Stoughton 1959.

Churches' Commission on International Affairs (with AACC), *The Churches and Human Rights in Africa. Khartoum Consultation.* Geneva, CCIA, 1975.

The Churches in International Affairs: Reports. Geneva, WCC and CCIA, 1970–73.

Clarkson, Thomas, *The History of the Rise, Progress and Accomplishment of the Abolition of the African Slave Trade by the British Parliament.* 2 vols. Longmans Green 1808.

Connexional Overseas Consultation. Methodist Missionary Society 1961.

Coupland, R., *Kirk on the Zambezi.* OUP 1928.

—— *The Exploitation of East Africa, 1856–1890.* Faber 1968.

Cuming, G. J., *The Mission of the Church and the Propagation of the Faith.* (Studies in Church History.) CUP 1970.

Dachs, J. A., ed., *Christianity South of the Zambezi.* Salisbury, Rhodesia, Mambo Press, 1973.

Davis, Charles, *Christ and the World Religions.* Hodder & Stoughton 1970.

Debrunner, H., *A Church Between Colonial Powers.* Lutterworth Press 1965.

Ellenberger, V., *A Century of Mission Work in Basutoland.* Lesotho, Morija Press, 1938.

Elmslie, W. A., *Among the Wild Ngoni.* Missionary Researches and Travels, No. 12 (3rd edn). Cass 1970.

Findlay, W. G. and Holdsworth, W. W., *The History of the Wesleyan Methodist Missionary Society.* Epworth Press 1921.

First, Ruth, *South West Africa.* (Penguin African Library.) Penguin 1963.

Flint, J. E., ed., *The Cambridge History of Africa,* vol. 5 (1790–1870). CUP 1976.

Fraser, Ian M., *The Fire Runs.* SCM Press 1975.

Fyfe, Christopher, *A History of Sierra Leone.* OUP 1962.

Gray, Sir John, *Early Portuguese Missionaries in East Africa*. Nairobi, East African Literature Bureau, 1958.

Groves, C. P., *The Planting of Christianity in Africa*. 5 vols. Lutterworth Press 1948.

Hamilton, J. T., *Moravian Missions: A History of the Missions of the Moravian Church*. New York, Times Publishing Co., 1901.

Hastings, Adrian, *Church and Mission in Modern Africa*. Burns & Oates 1967.

—— *Mission and Ministry*. Sheed & Ward 1971.

—— *Wiriyamu*. Search Press 1974.

Hinchliff, P., *The Church in South Africa*. SPCK 1968.

Hole, Charles, *The Early History of the Church Missionary Society for Africa and the East to the end of 1814*. CMS 1896.

Huddleston, Trevor, *Naught for Your Comfort*. Collins Fontana 1957.

Human Rights and Christian Responsibility. St Pölten Report. Geneva, WCC and CCIA, 1974.

IDOC: Documentation Participation Project, *The Future of the Missionary Enterprise*. Report No. 9. Geneva, WCC, 1974.

International Review of Missions. London 1912.

Isenberg, C. W. and Krapf, J. L., *Journals*. First published 1843; new impression, Cass 1968.

Jakobsson, Stiv, *Am I not a Man and a Brother?* Uppsala, Gleerup, 1972.

Journal of African History, The, Oliver, Roland and Fage, J. D., eds. CUP.

Justice and Peace Commission, Rhodesia, *The Man in the Middle*. CIIR 1975.

Kittler, G. D., *The White Fathers*. A. H. Allen 1957.

Krapf, J., *Travels, Researches and Missionary Labours during an Eighteen Years' Residence in Eastern Africa*. Truber 1860.

Langworthy, H. W., *Zambia Before 1890*. Longmans 1972.

Latourette, K. S., *A History of the Expansion of Christianity*, vol. 5. Eyre & Spottiswoode 1944.

Lewis, Cecil and Edwards, G. E., *Historical Records of the Church of the Province of South Africa*. SPCK 1934.

Livingstone, David, *Travels and Researches in South Africa*. Michael Joseph 1937.

Lovett, Richard, *The History of the London Missionary Society, 1795–1895*. 2 vols. London 1899.

MacInnes, C. M., *Bristol and the Slave Trade*. Bristol Branch of the Historical Association, University of Bristol, 1968.

Macpherson, Robert, *The Presbyterian Church in Kenya*. Nairobi, Presbyterian Church in East Africa, 1970.

Manual of Portuguese East Africa. HMSO 1920.

March, Z. A. and Kingsnorth, G. W., *An Introduction to the History of East Africa*. CUP 1965.

Martin, B. and Spurrell, M., eds., *The Journal of a Slave Trader, John Newton*, Epworth Press 1962.

Missionary Obligation of the Church: The Report of the Methodist Conference Commission. Methodist Church and Epworth Press 1955.

Missionary Obligation of the Church: Willingen Report. IMC 1952.

Moore, Basil, ed., *Black Theology*. C. Hurst 1973.

Moorhouse, Geoffrey, *The Missionaries*. Eyre Methuen 1973.

Moreira, E., *Portuguese East Africa: A Study of Religious Needs*. World Dominion Press 1936.

Morris, Colin, *Church and Challenge in a New Africa*. Epworth Press 1964.

Mungeam, G. H., *British Rule in Kenya, 1895–1912*. Clarendon Press 1966.

Nash, Margaret, ed., *Out of the Dust: The Moratorium Debate*. Johannesburg, South African Council of Churches, 1977.

Naudé, Beyers, *The Trial of Beyers Naudé*. Search Press 1975.

Neill, Stephen, *The Unfinished Task*. Lutterworth Press 1957.

—— *Colonialism and Christian Missions*. Lutterworth Press 1966.

—— *A History of Christian Missions*. Pelican 1964.

Oldham, J. H., *Christianity and Race*. SCM Press 1924.

Oliver, Roland, ed., *The Middle Age of African History*. OUP 1967.

—— *The Missionary Factor in East Africa*. Longmans Green 1952.

Parrinder, Geoffrey, *Africa's Three Religions*, 2nd edn. Sheldon Press 1976.

—— *African Traditional Religion*, 3rd edn. Sheldon Press 1974.

Partnership for World Mission. Report of the Working Party on Relations between the Church of England, the General Synod, and the Missionary Societies. Church Information Office 1977.

Paton, David, ed., *Breaking Barriers: Nairobi 1975*. The Official Report of the Fifth Assembly of the World Council of Churches. SPCK 1976.

Paul, John, *Mozambique*. (Penguin African Library.) Penguin 1975.

Perham, M., *The Colonial Reckoning*. (The Reith Lectures.) Collins 1961.

—— and Curtis, L., *The Protectorates of South Africa*. OUP 1935.

—— and Simmons, J., *African Discovery*. Faber 1942.

Plessis, J. du, *A History of Christian Missions in South Africa*. Longmans 1911.

Randolph, R. H., S.J., *Church and State in Rhodesia*. Salisbury, Rhodesia, Mambo Press, 1971.

Ranger, T. O., *Revolt in Southern Rhodesia*. Heinemann 1967.

Richards, C., *Some Historic Journeys in East Africa*. OUP 1961.

Setiloane, Gabriel M., *The Image of God among the Sotho-Tswana*. Leiden, Brill, 1973.

Shillito, Edward, *François Coillard*. SCM Press 1923.

Sicard, S. von, *The Lutheran Church on the Coast of Tanzania, 1887–1914*. Uppsala, Gleerup, 1972.

Simons, H. J. and R. E., *Class and Colour in South Africa, 1850–1950*. (Penguin African Library.) Penguin 1969.

Smith, Edwin W., *The Blessed Missionaries*. OUP 1950.

—— *Robert Moffat*. SCM Press 1925.

Statistical Atlas of Christian Missions. Edinburgh World Missionary Conference 1910.

Stonelake, Alfred R., *Congo: Past and Present*. World Dominion Press 1937.

Sundkler, B. G. M., *Bantu Prophets in South Africa*. Lutterworth Press 1948.

—— *The Christian Ministry in Africa*. SCM Press 1960.

—— *The Church Crossing Frontiers*. Uppsala, Gleerup, 1969.

—— *The World of Mission*. Lutterworth Press 1965.

—— *Essays on the Nature of Mission. In Honour of Bengt Sundkler*, ed. Beyerhaus, P. and Hallencreutz, C. F. 1969.

Taylor, J. V., *The Primal Vision*. SCM Press 1963.

—— *The Growth of the Church in Buganda*. (World Mission Studies.) SCM Press 1958.

Thompson, E. W., *The Methodist Missionary Society: Its Origin and Name*. Epworth Press 1955.

Todd, J. H., *Africa Mission*. Burns & Oates 1961.

Vere-Hodge, E. R. and Collister, P., *Pioneers of East Africa*. Nairobi, Eagle Press, 1956.

Waddell, Hope Masterton, *Twenty-nine Years in the West Indies and Central Africa*. Cass 1970.

Ward, W. E. F., *A History of Ghana*. Allen & Unwin 1948.

Webb, P. M., *Salvation Today*. SCM Press 1974.

Welbourn, F. B., *East African Rebels*. (World Mission Studies.) SCM Press 1961.

Wellington, J. H., *South West Africa and Its Human Issues*. OUP 1967.

West, Richard, *Back to Africa*. Jonathan Cape 1970.

Westermann, D., *Africa and Christianity*. OUP 1937.

Wheeler, D. L., and Pelissièr, René, *Angola*. Pall Mall Press 1971.

Willoughby, W. C., *The Soul of the Bantu*. SCM Press 1928.

Wilson, F. and Perrot, D., *Outlook on a Century*. Cape Province, S.A., Lovedale & Sprocas, 1973.

Wilson, M., *Religion and the Transformation of Society*. CUP 1971.

—— and Thompson, L., *The Oxford History of South Africa*, 2 vols. OUP 1971.

Wright, Marcia, *German Missions in Tanganyika, 1891–1941*. OUP 1971.

Index

African art, destruction of 55–7
African Christianity
in general 128–9, 145; and the
Ecumenical Movement 137
African culture, destruction of 55–7
African religion, not understood by the
early missionaries 55, 96
All Africa Conference of Churches
(AACC)
in general 76, 93, 137; Kampala
Assembly 8; Lusaka (1974) 16, 93;
Moratorium debate 16, 93, 98; on
David Livingstone 66; General
Secretary 93–4, 102, 106, 150; and
human rights 144
American missionary societies
in general 69, 77–8, 92, 158; Board of
Commissioners for Foreign Missions
37, 68, 161; in South Africa 47
Anglican Church
in South Africa 47; in the Caribbean
48; in Sierra Leone 62; see also Church
Missionary Society, Society for
Promoting Christian Knowledge,
Society for the Propagation of the
Gospel, Universities Mission to Central
Africa

Bangkok Conference
on 'Salvation Today' 91–2;
Moratorium debate 102; see also
World Council of Churches
Baptist Church
in general 36; Missionary Society 36;
William Carey's proposal 36, 121; in
India 48
Barotseland
work of François and Christina
Coillard 64–5; David Livingstone
65–6

Basle Mission
recruitment of missionaries 37; in
Ghana 44–5; on West Coast of Africa
62
Berg, Johannes van den, author of
Constrained by Jesus' Love 2; on
missionary motives 40
Bible Societies 146
Black Theology (statements by black
writers in South Africa) 14, 53
Blauw, Johannes, author of The
Missionary Nature of the Church 129
Botswana 63, 65

Call see Missionary vocation
Castle and Falcon, the (meeting place
for the early missionary societies) and
the London Missionary Society 36;
and the Church Missionary Society 37,
121
Chaplains, at coastal trading ports 32, 37,
44, 47, 53
China, missionaries in 21, 48, 110–11
Christian Aid 112–13, 118
Christian Love
and Evangelical Revival 56; as basis of
mission 67, 185
Christian mission
and slave trade 49; nature of 49ff, 74,
85, 134–5, 139; and education 50–51,
68; and agriculture 51; and medicine
51–2; and leprosy 52; and human
rights 52, 139–40, 144–5; and
colonialism 53; local responsibility
101, 117–18; and African Christians
128; in Old and New Testaments
130–32; universality of 132–3; as task
of Church 133; future of 133; in word
and deed 138–9; see also Missionary
work

Stewart, Revd Dr James
 and Malawi 58; and South Africa 63
Sudan
 Roman Catholic missions 67; United
 Presbyterian Church 77; civil war 89
Sundkler, Bengt, bp
 and biblical understanding of Christian
 mission 130; *see also* Bibliography

Theological training 14, 91, 146
Thompson, Thomas, on Gold Coast 44
Transkei, early missionary work in 47
Turner, J. M. W.
 his painting, 'The Slave Ship' 27

Uganda
 Roman Catholic missions to 12, 67;
 Mill Hill Fathers 67
United Methodist Free Churches 58, 61
United Presbyterian Church statistics 77
Universities Mission to Central Africa 64,
 66

Victoria Falls 65
Voyages of discovery
 stimulation of missionary activity
 38–40; James Bruce 39; Captain
 James Cook 39, 48

Wesley, Charles 38, 41
Wesley, John 38–9
Willingen Conference 75–6
Wiriyamu, Portuguese atrocities at 93
World Council of Churches
 Nairobi Fifth Assembly 75–6; CWME
 91, 102, 159; consultations 93; Dr
 Philip Potter 99, 143; on Moratorium
 102; Faith and Order, Ghana 116;
 Bangkok 134–5
World Missionary Conference
 London (1888) 64, 69; Edinburgh
 (1910) 71, 100

Xavier, Francis
 his journeys around Africa 110–11

Zaire 12, 128
Zambezi
 pioneers in Z. valley 63; Coillard's
 crossing of Z. river 65; churches south
 of 135
Zambia, Synod of United Church in
 105–6
Zanzibar
 as base for entering East Africa 61, 63;
 centre of slave trade 67